science
short course

CW01664534

ny

S180 Life in the oceans: exploring our blue planet

Written by Angela Colling

Contributors

The structure and content of the S180 course were devised by Angela Colling, Julian Priddle, Philippa Priddle and John Wright:

Angela Colling	(*Author and Course Team Chair*)
Julian Priddle	(*Science Training and Education Partnership*)
Philippa Priddle	(*Science Training and Education Partnership*)
John Wright	(*Consultant*)

Other people involved in the production of this book:

Isla McTaggart	(*Course Manager*)
Elizabeth Whitelegg	(*Science Short Course Programme Director*)
Gerry Bearman	(*Editor*)
Janice Gilbert	(*Graphic Artist*)
Jenny Nockles	(*Graphic Designer*)

Martin Angel (the course assessor) and Vicki Billings are thanked for their valuable advice and comments.

The Open University acknowledges the co-operation of the BBC in providing access to the Blue Planet TV series, without which this course would not be possible.

The Frontispiece shows a group of planktonic organisms, all of which are zooplankton (animal plankton), with the exception of the 'hairy' chains of diatom cells on the far left and very top, which are phytoplankton (plants). The diatom chain on the far left is a few tenths of a millimetre long. In the centre-left of the image is a group of radiolarians. To the left of these is a larval crustacean, and a female copepod with two egg sacs. The two round objects at the top are fish eggs.

The Open University, Walton Hall, Milton Keynes, MK7 6AA, United Kingdom

First published 2002

Edited, designed and typeset by The Open University

Printed in the United Kingdom by the Alden Group, Oxford.

ISBN 0 7492 5224 3

This publication forms part of an Open University course S180 *Life in the oceans: exploring our blue planet*. Details of this and other Open University courses can be obtained from the Call Centre, PO Box 724, The Open University, Milton Keynes MK7 6ZS, United Kingdom: tel. +44 (0)1908 653231, e-mail ces-gen@open.ac.uk

Alternatively, you may visit the Open University website at http://www.open.ac.uk where you can learn more about the wide range of courses and packs offered at all levels by the Open University.

To purchase this publication or other components of Open University courses, contact Open University Worldwide Ltd, Walton Hall, Milton Keynes MK7 6AA, United Kingdom: tel. +44 (0)1908 858785; fax +44 (0)1908 858787; e-mail ouwenq@open.ac.uk; website http://www.ouw.co.uk

S180i1.1

Contents

Introduction to the course

This course is based around the Blue Planet BBC TV series, but whereas that series was very much about animal life in the oceans, this course is about the oceanic environment as a whole, the challenges this environment provides for marine life, and the responses of individual organisms and populations. It is *not* intended to be a comprehensive course in marine biology, and its content is to a large extent determined by that of the Blue Planet videos. In addition to a compilation of videos, and this book, you will also be using a CD entitled *Life in the Oceans*, another Open University course text entitled *Discovering the Deep Oceans*, and some other supplementary material.

Chapters 1 to 9 of this book are specifically designed to help you get the most out of the Blue Planet videos. We begin with a discussion of the diversity of life in the oceans, for which you will be using the 'Biological Diversity' module of your *Life in the Oceans* CD. This is followed by a description of the main features of the marine environment itself – the shape of the ocean basins and the nature of seawater. Chapter 3, on tides, should be read with the 'Tidal Seas' video, while Chapter 4 sets up the theoretical background for the enormous biological productivity shown in the 'Seasonal Seas' video. Chapter 5 explains why much of the open ocean is, by contrast, an 'oceanic desert', although certain regions are very rich in nutrients and have abundant life.

The second CD module, on 'Living in the Oceans', is best studied at the start of Chapter 2, while the third, on 'Ecosystems and Food Webs', follows Chapter 5. The principles introduced there will be used again in the context of fishing, in the final part of the course.

In the 'Open Ocean' video, you will see powerful hunters like marlin and tuna ranging across the oceans in search of food, and in Chapter 6 we will look at *how* fish swim, and why tuna are particularly efficient swimmers. Accompanying this chapter are two Open University videos, which revise the material in Chapter 6 and also look at why dolphins are such good swimmers, and why sperm whales are champion divers. In Chapters 7 and 8 – 'Coral reefs' and 'Polar seas' – we investigate two contrasting marine environments, again largely concentrating on topics that come up in the accompanying videos.

The next part of the course involves more detailed study of a particular region of the oceans – the deep sea. Here you will be studying Chapter 10 of this book along with the video on 'The Deep' and *Discovering the Deep Oceans*, which looks at how scientific ideas develop, and also builds on many of the scientific concepts introduced in this book.

In the final part of the course, you are asked to consider one of the most serious problems facing humanity at the present time – the global fishing crisis. Again, you will be using separate printed material (not included in this book). The Blue Planet video for this part of the course is entitled 'Deep Trouble'.

This course draws on material from a wide range of scientific disciplines. In order that you can study it effectively whatever your background, we have provided a course *Glossary*. Terms given in **bold** in the text are important ones which will be used later.

Each of the three parts of the course involves using a different suite of study techniques, and by the end you should be well on your way to developing a range of useful skills. One of the most important skills you will have started to develop is that of bringing together material from a range of different scientific disciplines – physics, chemistry, biology and geology – i.e. areas of science that have traditionally been studied in isolation from one other. Increasingly, scientists are finding that to make further progress in their chosen field they need to combine knowledge and understanding from related disciplines. Nowhere is this more true than in the study of the oceans.

What lives in the oceans?

1

This course is mainly about life in the oceans at the present time, but to understand why there is such a great diversity of marine life, you need to know a little about life in the distant past. We do not know for sure where life began – most scientists believe that it began in the oceans, others believe that it began in warm pools on land; yet others think that life was brought to Earth from space in the form of organic molecules in comets and meteorites. But wherever it began, life first flourished in the oceans, and it was here that life forms first diversified. Only about 450 million years ago – very late in the Earth's history – did living organisms begin to colonize the land.

▶▶ *We suggest that you now study 'Biological Diversity', the first module of your* Life in the Oceans *CD. This module has three parts, or activities: (1) an overview of the main events in the evolution of life in the oceans over geological time; (2) an introduction to the classification of marine organisms; and (3) a summary of the main groups of marine animals, which you will be able to consult later by 'clicking' with your mouse on the appropriate group of branches (how this works will become clear when you are actually studying the CD). To get the most out of the module, you might find it helpful to begin by reading through the following notes about the geological time-scale. You can look at them again when you have finished the module, if you wish.* ◀◀

Notes on the geological time-scale

The 'Biological Diversity' module begins by showing the geological time-scale. The names up the right-hand side (which you do not need to remember) are the geological eras, which are major intervals in the Earth's history, identified on the basis of fossils (if present), ages of rock formations (measured using natural radioactivity) and other features of the geological record, as follows:

Hadean ('like Hades', 'hellish'): the time between the origin of the Earth about 4600 million years ago, and the time of formation of the earliest known rocks. The Earth was very hot, with extensive volcanism, and there was no life.

Archean ('ancient', 'beginning'): between about 3800 and 2500 million years ago. The time of the first life forms – single-celled bacteria, then simple photosynthetic organisms. Atmospheric oxygen levels began to rise during this time.

Proterozoic ('former life'): between about 2500 and 540 million years ago. Primitive multicellular organisms began to evolve, the earliest of which were simple seaweed-like plants. There were two major glaciations during this time.

Paleozoic ('ancient life'): between about 540 and 245 million years ago. Shelled animals evolved, then the first vertebrates (including fish). During this era, life moved onto the land, amphibians evolved, then reptiles. The first forests brought about a major increase in atmospheric oxygen levels. The era was characterized by major climatic changes (including glaciations), and ended with a mass extinction.

Mesozoic ('middle life'): between about 245 and 65 million years ago. Dinosaurs evolved, and then mammals, followed by the first flowering plants. This era ended abruptly with mass extinctions of marine animals and dinosaurs, probably in a catastrophe related to a meteorite impact.

Cenozoic ('recent life'): from 65 million years ago up until the present. This is the era when mammals have prospered and diversified, with the earliest hominids appearing about 5.3 million years ago.

In the 'Biological Diversity' module, the time-scale is expanded for the late Proterozoic onwards, and for the Mesozoic it is divided into *periods*, which, like the longer eras, have been identified as different from one another on the basis of fossils and other features of the geological record. In this module, the names of periods are shown in *italic*, to distinguish them from the names of eras, which are shown in roman, or upright, type.

1.1 Beginnings

The oldest recognizable fossils of living organisms are of stromatolites, mats of simple algae (marine plants) which built up in shallow marine waters. Stromatolites were very widespread throughout the Archean and much of the Proterozoic, until they began to decline about 850 million years ago. Organisms that we would recognize as animals had probably developed by 1000 million years ago, and the first for which we have any physical remains were flourishing by 600 million years ago. It seems from the fossil remains that the animals were living in a wide range of marine environments, from the deep sea to tidal flats.

These earliest animal fossils are only flattened impressions made in what was once sandy or silty sediment, but they are surprisingly well preserved, perhaps because at that time there were no large predators or scavengers to destroy and scatter remains, and few burrowing animals to churn up the sediment. The animals seem to have been quite large – some were perhaps a metre across – but they did not have any supporting skeletal hard parts. Most of them were disk-shaped or pancake-like, with a simple sac-like body directly surrounding a digestive cavity reached by a single orifice (i.e. with no separate gut), rather like present-day sea-anemones or jellyfish. Disk-like or tubular organisms are circular in cross-section and so are described as having *radial symmetry*.

This early stage in the evolution of animals is represented by the lowermost branches of the 'tree' in the third activity of the 'Biological Diversity' module. All later animals have *bilateral symmetry*, with matching left-hand and right-hand sides. The early evolution of radially symmetric animals and the later arrival of bilaterally symmetric animals can be seen in Figure 1.1, which provides a summary of information available from the tree in 'Biological Diversity'.

The radially symmetric faunas seem to have gone into a decline around 540 million years ago, but as mentioned in the first part of the 'Biological Diversity' module, at about that time there was a great increase in the diversity of other groups of more complex animals. With the 'Cambrian Explosion' of diversity there appeared animals with identifiable body parts – heads, legs, muscular guts with two openings (mouth and anus) – as well as fluid-filled body cavities. Many animals now had skeletal hard parts, or shells.

- What does the appearance of shells suggest?
- It suggests that animals were now developing protection against *predation* by other animals.

Figure 1.1 Simplified evolutionary tree, showing how diversification has led to the phyla of animals we know today (listed down the right-hand side in capitals). In this diagram, time goes from left to right (Ma means millions of years). Apart from the fact that this tree is laid on its side, its layout is very similar to the tree used in 'Biological Diversity'. The numbered groups of phyla (1 to 7) correspond to the same groups as those on that tree, although there, for reasons of space, the positions of groups 5 and 6 are swapped round (i.e. on the tree, branches 1–7 are in numerical order, from left to right). Phyla are introduced in 'Biological Diversity'; see also Section 1.4. All phyla have marine members, but in this course we will not deal with any animals in group 5. For each phylum, we have given some typical members and (in bold) an estimate of the total number of species (terrestrial + marine) in that phylum.

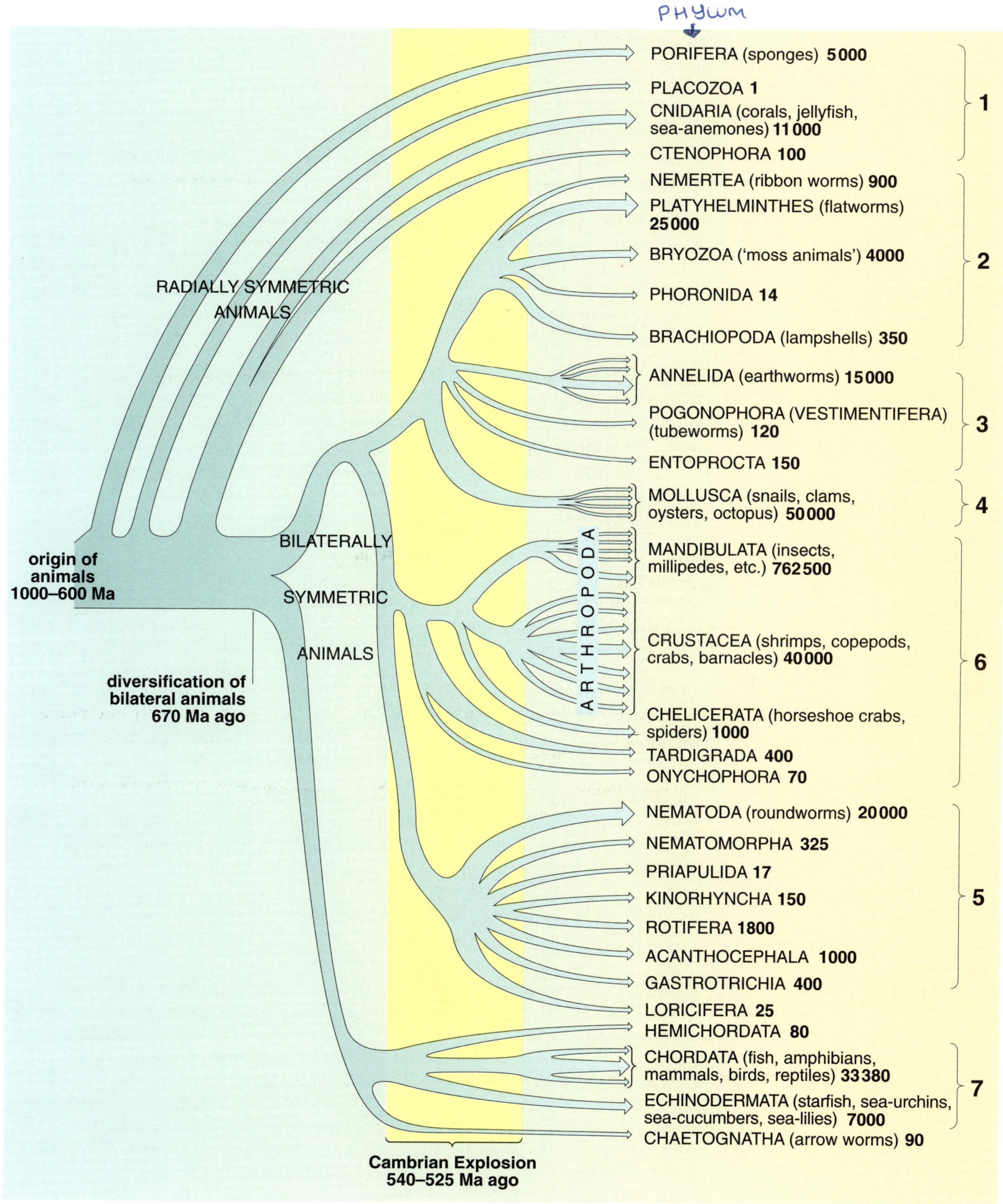
PHYLUM
PORIFERA (sponges) 5000
PLACOZOA 1
CNIDARIA (corals, jellyfish, sea-anemones) 11 000
CTENOPHORA 100
1
NEMERTEA (ribbon worms) 900
PLATYHELMINTHES (flatworms) 25 000
BRYOZOA ('moss animals') 4000
PHORONIDA 14
BRACHIOPODA (lampshells) 350
2
ANNELIDA (earthworms) 15 000
POGONOPHORA (VESTIMENTIFERA) (tubeworms) 120
ENTOPROCTA 150
3
MOLLUSCA (snails, clams, oysters, octopus) 50 000
4
MANDIBULATA (insects, millipedes, etc.) 762 500
CRUSTACEA (shrimps, copepods, crabs, barnacles) 40 000
CHELICERATA (horseshoe crabs, spiders) 1000
TARDIGRADA 400
ONYCHOPHORA 70
6
ARTHROPODA
NEMATODA (roundworms) 20 000
NEMATOMORPHA 325
PRIAPULIDA 17
KINORHYNCHA 150
ROTIFERA 1800
ACANTHOCEPHALA 1000
GASTROTRICHIA 400
5
LORICIFERA 25
HEMICHORDATA 80
CHORDATA (fish, amphibians, mammals, birds, reptiles) 33 380
ECHINODERMATA (starfish, sea-urchins, sea-cucumbers, sea-lilies) 7000
CHAETOGNATHA (arrow worms) 90
7
RADIALLY SYMMETRIC ANIMALS
BILATERALLY SYMMETRIC ANIMALS
origin of animals 1000–600 Ma
diversification of bilateral animals 670 Ma ago
Cambrian Explosion 540–525 Ma ago

Animals were generally much more active – there was more burrowing (many different types of burrow have been preserved), and the body plans of many animals suggest that they could scuttle or 'swim' over the sea-floor. The most abundant group of animals were the arthropods (Arthropoda), characterized by an external skeleton, and paired jointed limbs (group 6 on the 'tree'). As you can see from Figure 1.1, in terms of diversity, the arthropods are still the most successful group today, and include crustaceans, insects and spiders.

At the beginning of the second part of the 'Biological Diversity' module, we stressed how the diversity of life at the present day is a snapshot in time of the continuing process of biological evolution and change. Organisms now living on the Earth are members of different groups which began to flourish at different times. Although many organisms have disappeared from the Earth, sometimes in large-scale extinctions, there has generally been a continual increase in the number of species.

Figure 1.2 shows how the number of families (i.e. groups of closely related genera, cf. Figure 1.3) with hard parts – skeletons and shells – has changed over time, as a result of evolution and extinctions. The first group of families, shown in the topmost graph, are those that evolved in the Cambrian Period, and then declined over the next 200 million years. The next group became dominant near the beginning of the Paleozoic and declined markedly at the end of it. The final group are those animals which have become increasingly successful, particularly over the last 250 million years. These are sometimes referred to as the Modern Fauna (fauna = animals, flora = plants).

Present-day animals with hard parts comprise the Modern Fauna (bottom graph) plus some of the animals which first flourished in the Paleozoic (middle graph), plus a tiny number of surviving Cambrian animals (top graph). (Of those animals shown in Figure 1.2, only the Trilobita, the Hyolitha, the Eocrinoidea and the Graptolithina are extinct.)

Roughly how many families with hard parts are there altogether, at the present time?

According to Figure 1.2, at the present time (0 on the horizontal axis) there are about 700 Modern families (bottom graph) plus about 100 of the families which dominated in the Paleozoic (middle graph) (plus a negligible number of Cambrian families, top graph), i.e. about 800 families in all.

Figure 1.2 The change in diversity, in terms of numbers of families, of (*top*) animals (fauna) which first flourished in the Cambrian (see text), (*middle*) those which dominated during most of the Paleozoic (from the Ordovician to Permian), and (*bottom*) the animals which have been increasingly successful, particularly since the Triassic (i.e. in the Mesozoic and Cenozoic). Note that this diagram includes only families with hard parts (shells and skeletons), which are well preserved in the fossil record, and that nearly all of them have only marine representatives. The abbreviations along the time axis correspond to periods (as given in 'Biological Diversity'): Ca = Cambrian, O = Ordovician, S = Silurian, D = Devonian, Crb = Carboniferous, P = Permian, Tr = Triassic, Jur = Jurassic, Cret = Cretaceous; T + Qt are the periods of the Cenozoic, the Tertiary and Quaternary. *Note:* On the horizontal axis, geological time goes from left to right, and the scale is in millions of years (Ma) before the present day.

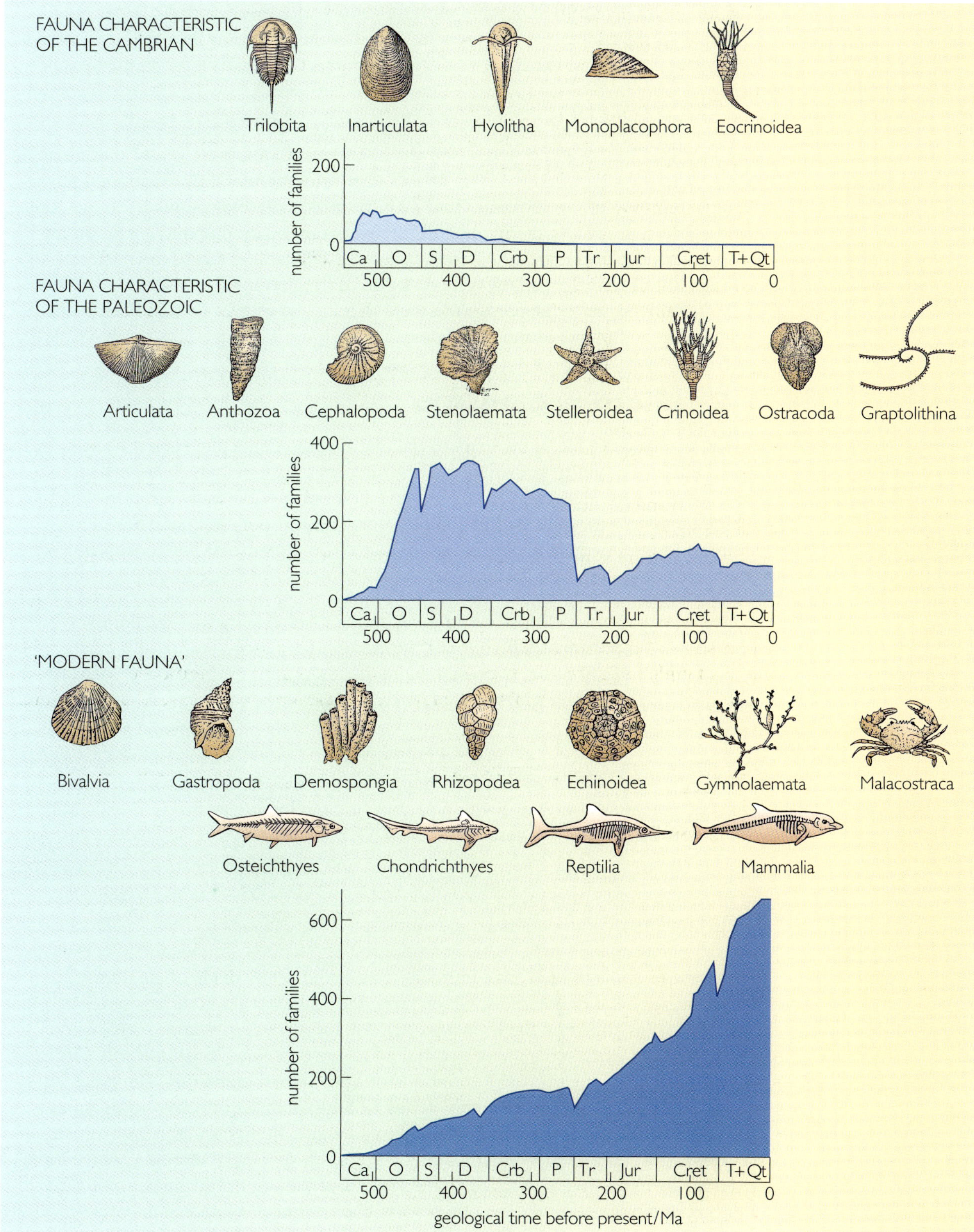
FAUNA CHARACTERISTIC OF THE CAMBRIAN
Trilobita
Inarticulata
Hyolitha
Monoplacophora
Eocrinoidea
number of families
200
0
Ca
O
S
D
Crb
P
Tr
Jur
Cret
T+Qt
500
400
300
200
100
0
FAUNA CHARACTERISTIC OF THE PALEOZOIC
Articulata
Anthozoa
Cephalopoda
Stenolaemata
Stelleroidea
Crinoidea
Ostracoda
Graptolithina
number of families
400
200
0
'MODERN FAUNA'
Bivalvia
Gastropoda
Demospongia
Rhizopodea
Echinoidea
Gymnolaemata
Malacostraca
Osteichthyes
Chondrichthyes
Reptilia
Mammalia
number of families
600
400
200
0
geological time before present/Ma

You do not have to remember any of these details. However, do look at the small drawings of representative members of the different faunas, as they will help you appreciate the relative antiquity of different groups of animals alive in the oceans today.

All known phyla, living and extinct, originated in the sea, although some later migrated into freshwater or terrestrial environments. In all, there are 44 marine phyla (a new one was identified in 2001) and 28 terrestrial phyla. Of the 33 animal phyla, 32 have representatives in the sea and 12 have representatives on land. On the other hand, there appear to be many more different *species* on land than there are in the sea, perhaps because there is a greater variety of habitats on land. However, this assessment could reflect a lack of knowledge of the ocean – for example, we have only recently begun to appreciate the great richness of species of small organisms living in the sediments of the deep ocean.

1.2 Micro-organisms

So far, we have not mentioned any of the marine organisms that cannot be seen by the naked eye, colloquially known as micro-organisms. Viruses, which are little more than some genetic material surrounded by a layer of protein, and cannot grow or reproduce unless they are within another organism (i.e. they are parasites), are the simplest living things, and almost do not qualify as organisms. The most primitive true micro-organisms are bacteria and cyanobacteria (which are more plant-like and are also known as blue–green algae). Present-day bacteria and cyanobacteria are very similar to the first life forms mentioned near the beginning of the 'Biological Diversity' module, and are the most primitive organisms alive on Earth today. Bacteria and cyanobacteria have cell walls (unlike viruses) but do not have their genetic material packed into a nucleus. Organisms which have cells with nuclei are known as *eukaryotes* (pronounced 'you-carry-oats' – the name means 'true nucleus') to distinguish them from the more primitive *prokaryotes* ('before nucleus'). As mentioned in the first activity of 'Biological Diversity', it was the evolution of eukaryotes that allowed the development of multicelled organisms (corresponding to the far left-hand side of Figure 1.1).

Single-celled organisms (with nuclei) are known as **protists**. The term covers a range of different types of organism, including single-celled plants, single-celled animals (or **protozoans**, *zoon* = animal), and single-celled organisms that have characteristics of both plants and animals. Notable amongst single-celled animals in the oceans are the foraminiferans (which have intricate chambered shells made of calcium carbonate) and the radiolarians, which have delicate external skeletons of silica, often with spines (as shown in the Frontispiece). All species of radiolarians and many foraminiferans drift in the upper ocean, and so are described as **planktonic** (drifting); in particular they are known as **zooplankton** (i.e. animal plankton). The great majority of marine plants are single-celled floating plants, collectively known as **phytoplankton** (*phyton* = plant) or planktonic algae. In high-latitude and temperate seas, the most conspicuous phytoplankton are often species of diatoms, which have external skeletons made of silica; some species of diatom have spines, some have a pill-box or elongate shape, and others form chains. You may spot some or all of these types of diatom in the Blue Planet videos (note that, like all phytoplankton, they are very small, ranging from two-thousandths of a millimetre to one millimetre across). After diatoms, the second most conspicuous phytoplankton are often the dinoflagellates, some species of which feed on small zooplankton and other phytoplankton, and so resemble animals more than plants. In terms of numbers of individuals, the most abundant phytoplankton are usually extremely small species, collectively known as 'picoplankton'.

The term **algae** (singular: alga) was originally used to mean any simple plant-like organism (found in the sea, in ponds, or on damp tree trunks, paths and walls). As far as marine life is concerned, the term algae is now used somewhat loosely to include not only phytoplankton and some simple bottom-living plants, but also the plants we call seaweeds – sometimes referred to as macro-algae (i.e. 'big algae'). Like phytoplankton, seaweeds are surrounded by their 'growing medium' – water plus nutrients. Because they take in nutrients from the surrounding water, seaweeds do not need a system to transport water up into the plant. They also do not need roots as such, although they do have structures known as *holdfasts* so that they can remain fixed in one place. Furthermore, as they are supported by the surrounding water (and sometimes also by gas bladders), they do not need the strengthening woody structures found in land plants.

1.3 Plants and bacteria: making organic material and breaking it down

As you will have realized while working through the 'Biological Diversity' module, plants have been largely responsible for the evolution of our atmosphere. Before plants became abundant, concentrations of oxygen in the atmosphere were very low, which in turn had implications for the types of animals that could evolve. With increasingly abundant plant life, more and more oxygen was released into the atmosphere.

This 'new' oxygen was produced as a by-product of **photosynthesis**, the process whereby plants build their own organic material by harnessing the energy of sunlight to combine atmospheric carbon dioxide (CO_2) with water (H_2O) to produce a range of carbohydrate compounds (e.g. starches, sugars, cellulose). Expressed in words, the process of photosynthesis can be written as follows:

$$\underset{\text{(from the atmosphere)}}{\text{carbon dioxide}} + \text{water} + \text{light energy} \longrightarrow \text{carbohydrate} + \text{oxygen} \qquad (1.1\text{a})$$

Animals cannot build their own organic material and so have to rely on plants, either directly (if they are herbivores) or indirectly (if they are carnivores). In order for plants and animals to make use of organic material such as carbohydrate, it has to be broken down (metabolized) into all the different substances an organism needs to carry on living. The energy needed for all these processes is released from carbohydrate (and other organic molecules) by a process known as **respiration**. Respiration can be expressed in a 'word equation' as follows:

$$\text{carbohydrate} + \text{oxygen} \longrightarrow \text{energy} + \text{carbon dioxide} + \text{water} \qquad (1.1\text{b})$$

- Do you notice anything interesting about this equation?

- The equation for respiration (1.1b) is the *reverse* of the equation for photosynthesis (1.1a). Note also that while photosynthesis captures or *fixes* energy, respiration releases it.

All living organisms need to respire. In the case of air-breathing marine animals (mammals and reptiles), oxygen is taken in with air into the lungs, and carbon dioxide is breathed out. In the case of planktonic organisms and most marine animals, the oxygen for respiration is taken up from oxygen dissolved in seawater, and the waste carbon dioxide is returned to solution in seawater. During photosynthesis, phytoplankton take up carbon dioxide from solution in seawater and release oxygen into solution in seawater.

Eventually, all organisms die. In the oceans, as on land, dead organic material is broken down by bacteria. In environments where oxygen is present, bacteria break down dead tissue in a process resembling respiration (cf. Equation 1.1b), and so release the components of the organism back into the seawater. These components are not only the elements present in carbohydrates (carbon, hydrogen and oxygen) but also other constituents essential for life, which are sometimes in short supply. We will come back to this topic in Chapter 4.

In this course, we will be concentrating mainly on animals. However, it's important not to forget the fundamental role of plants in making organic material that is then available to support other organisms, and of bacteria in breaking it down so that its 'raw materials' can be re-used.

1.4 Taxonomic classifications

Taxonomy is the science of describing and classifying organisms. In this course, we do not expect you to become taxonomic experts, but during your study you should find that you are becoming clearer about how different marine animals relate to one another.

In the second activity of the 'Biological Diversity' module, you looked at the relationship of the common starfish, *Asteria rubens*, first to other starfish (in the genus *Asteria*), then to other animals in the Class Asteroidea. Figure 1.3 uses the example of two species of whale to demonstrate the classifications used in taxonomy in slightly more detail. To help clarify the sometimes confusing relationships between the different types of whales, we have included order, sub-order and family subdivisions, which are not dealt with in 'Biological Diversity'.

One of the confusing aspects of taxonomic classification is that features used to classify animals are sometimes present only at an early stage of the life cycle (e.g. embryo or larval stage). For example, the Phylum Chordata – the chordates – includes all animals which at some stage have a skeletal rod (known as a 'notochord'), a hollow nerve cord down the back, and gill slits. As you will have seen in the third activity of 'Biological Diversity', animals of the Phylum Chordata include the Cephalochordata ('head-chords'), the Urochordata ('tail-chords') and the Craniata (craniates, which have brains within skulls), also known as the Vertebrata (vertebrates). This means that vertebrates, including whales and ourselves, are closely related to small and apparently simple marine animals, including sea-squirts, salps and tunicates (in the case of the Urochordata), and lancelets (in the case of the Cephalochordata). Tunicates have notochords as larvae, and in vertebrates the notochord is present in the embryo but is then replaced by vertebrae (i.e. a backbone). Human foetuses briefly have gills. You do not need to remember these details which are included to explain why taxonomic classifications can be less than obvious! We will return to the whale family, and study them in more detail, in Chapter 8.

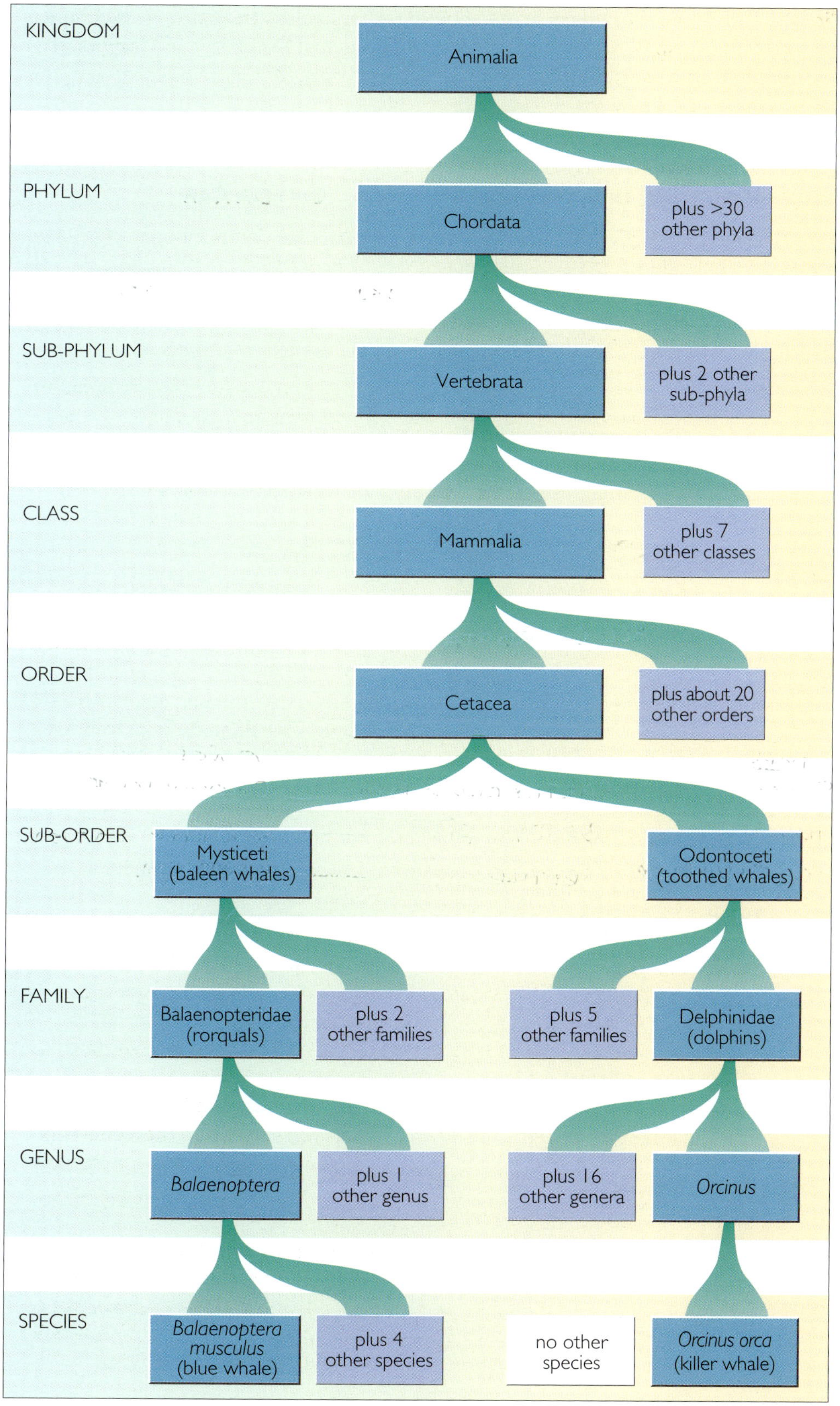

Figure 1.3 Taxonomic hierarchy showing the classification of two related animals that have a high profile in the Blue Planet videos: the blue whale, *Balaenoptera musculus*, which is a baleen whale (i.e. a plankton-feeder), and the killer whale, *Orcinus orca*, which is the only species in the genus *Orcinus*. (Note that the 'Biological Diversity' module does not deal with the subdivisions order, sub-order and family.)

To consolidate what you have learnt about taxonomic classifications, we recommend that you now go back to the third activity of 'Biological Diversity' and use the tree to answer the following questions.

Question 1.1

(a) To what phylum do corals belong? (Remember that corals are primitive animals, so will be one of the early 'branches' of the tree.) CNIDARIA

(b) To which of the following three types of animals are corals thought to be (1) most closely related, and (2) least closely related: sponges (2), jellyfish, sea-anemones (1)? ◀

Question 1.2 Remembering that crustaceans are arthropods, work out whether peracarid crustaceans (Peracarida) are more closely related to lobsters ✓ or barnacles. ◀

Question 1.3 At the end of the second activity of 'Biological Diversity' (frame 2.4.1), you were shown four animals which, although not very closely related, have very similar body plans. The animals were shark, tuna, ichthyosaur (extinct) and dolphin.

(a) Why does such 'convergent evolution' come about? - ADAPTATION TO SIMILAR ENVIRONMENT + LIFESTYLES

(b) How are these animals related to one another, and to which taxonomic class does each belong? ◀ ALL CHORDATA

ALL SIMILAR SHAPE

You should feel free to go back to the 'Biological Diversity' module at any time to check or investigate relationships between different marine animals.

	TYPE	CLASS
SHARK	CARTILAGINOUS FISH	CHONDRICHTHYES
TUNA	BONEY FISH	OSTEICHTHYES
ICHTHYOSAUR	REPTILE	REPTILIA
DOLPHIN	MAMMAL	MAMMALIA

Introduction to the marine environment

2

This chapter does not relate specifically to any particular Blue Planet video, but in a sense it 'sets the scene' for all of them. Here we introduce terms, topics and concepts that will be useful in later chapters and in *Discovering the Deep Oceans*.

It is frequently said that 'the oceans cover about 70 per cent of the planet', but this phrase does not really convey very much about the size and nature of the 'living space' available to marine organisms. For one thing, organisms may live on the sea-bed, or in the body of the ocean (sometimes referred to as 'the water column'). The first group of organisms are described as **benthic** or the '**benthos**' (Greek for 'depth'), and the second group are described as **pelagic** (after *pelagos*, Greek for 'ocean'). Planktonic organisms (or, as a group, '**plankton**') are those that live in the water column and cannot make their way against a current; pelagic animals capable of swimming against a current (e.g. fish, adult squid) are described as **nektonic** (or, as a group, '**nekton**'). Living conditions for both benthic and pelagic organisms are greatly affected by where they live in relation to the sunlit surface layers. Of course, the most distinctive aspect of living in and around the oceans is that it involves being continually (or, in the case of some organisms, periodically) submerged in salty water.

▶▶ *If you wish, you can now study the short 'Living in the Oceans' module on your* Life in the Oceans *CD (alternatively, you could save it until the end of Chapter 3). This takes an introductory look at what it is like living in the ocean, from the point of view of a selection of organisms. The organisms considered are a baleen whale (i.e. a whale that feeds on plankton), a planktonic alga, a copepod (small crustacean), a squid, and an angler fish. You will come across all of these organisms again later, either in the text or in one or more of the videos.* ◀◀

2.1 What is seawater?

The oceans contain 97 per cent (%) of the water on Earth. Most of the rest is locked up in ice-caps and glaciers, and the remainder is in lakes, rivers, streams and groundwater (in rocks and soil), and in the atmosphere as water vapour and clouds. While the water in the ice-caps and glaciers may remain there for thousands of years, rivers continually flow into the sea, and water is continually evaporating from the surface of lakes and the ocean (particularly at low latitudes), forming clouds, and releasing precipitation (rain, snow, hail) over land and sea. Groundwater, too, is continually seeping into the sea, while being recharged by rainwater from above. This continual cycling of water through different natural 'reservoirs' is known as the **hydrological cycle** (or 'water cycle').

Rivers flowing into the sea carry with them not only solid particles of mud, silt and organic material, but also substances that have been leached from the minerals in rocks by rainwater – these are in *dissolved* form, i.e. they are no longer solid (you couldn't get them back, even with the finest sieve) and their constituents are separated from one another by large numbers of water molecules. Here is a simple analogy: imagine that you took a chunk of rock salt, put it in a bowl and continued to pour water over it until it had apparently vanished – it would no longer exist in its solid form, but its constituents would now be *in solution* in the water in the bowl.

Rock salt is made up of crystals of sodium chloride, which has the chemical formula NaCl (Na for sodium, Cl for chlorine); sodium chloride crystals are made up of **ions** of sodium, written Na^+ (these are sodium atoms that have each lost an electron, and so have become positively charged) and chloride ions, written Cl^- (chlorine atoms that have each gained an electron, are so are negatively charged). In solid rock salt, the ions are bound together, and the positive and negative charges cancel out. When rock salt dissolves, water molecules, which are themselves weakly charged, effectively pull the ions apart and come between them, so that the ions become independent from one another. If you warmed your solution of sodium and chloride ions (or left it to stand for some time), the water would gradually evaporate away, and eventually solid rock salt would recrystallize.

Dissolved constituents such as sodium and chloride are sometimes referred to as 'dissolved salts', even though they are separate ions and not salts at all. Sodium and chloride are the most abundant ions in seawater, but greater or lesser amounts of nearly all the naturally occurring elements have been found dissolved in seawater. It is the presence of these dissolved ions that causes the sea to be 'salty'.

Rivers have been flowing into the sea for billions of years, and you would be forgiven for thinking that the oceans must therefore be continually getting saltier and saltier. However, this is not the case, because an equilibrium situation has been reached, whereby the rate at which each constituent is being removed (e.g. by chemical reactions with sea-floor rocks) is balanced by the rate at which it is being supplied in rivers. The concentration of dissolved constituents in seawater – its **salinity** – is, on average, about 35 grams of dissolved ions ('salt') in every litre of seawater. By convention, this is often simply written as 35, with no units.

Because seawater contains dissolved constituents, its **density** is greater than that of freshwater: a cubic metre of seawater weighs about 1030 kilograms (kg), while a cubic metre (1000 litres) of freshwater weighs almost exactly 1000 kg.

- How does this affect the buoyancy of organisms in seawater?

- As you will know if you have swum in both freshwater and seawater, it is much easier to float in seawater, i.e. seawater provides greater buoyancy than freshwater.

Buoyancy in marine organisms will be discussed in Chapter 6.

Seawater also contains dissolved gases; these are by and large the same gases that are found in the atmosphere. As in the atmosphere, the most abundant gases in seawater are nitrogen (N_2), oxygen (O_2), argon (Ar) and carbon dioxide (CO_2). However, their relative proportions in seawater differ from those in the atmosphere because they dissolve in seawater to different extents, and (with the exception of argon, which is inert) their distribution within the ocean is affected by their participation in biological and chemical reactions.

- Can you suggest which gas is actually *added* to surface waters as a result of biological activity?

- Oxygen. As you read in Section 1.3, photosynthesis by marine plants produces this gas as a by-product.

As a result of photosynthesis, and the fact that oxygen is forced into solution in seawater when air bubbles formed at the crests of waves are churned down into the water column, surface waters are generally supersaturated with oxygen, i.e. contain more dissolved oxygen than would normally be dissolved in seawater at that temperature. However, as oxygen is used by *all* organisms in respiration, and particularly by bacteria in decomposition of dead material, its concentration generally declines in the top 500–1000 metres (m) of the ocean.

The atmospheric gas that dissolves most readily in seawater is carbon dioxide – it is in fact a special case, because dissolved CO_2 reacts with water and so exists in seawater in a number of different forms. So while nitrogen is the most abundant gas in the atmosphere, carbon dioxide is the most abundant gas in the ocean. For all gases, the colder the seawater is, the more dissolved gas it can hold.

Seawater contains a huge range of particles in suspension, some living (viruses, bacteria and phytoplankton), some of organic origin (faecal pellets, debris from dead organisms), and some inorganic (e.g. clay brought down by rivers, dust carried out to sea on the wind).

2.1.1 Seawater: a most unusual liquid

Water is an unusual liquid in many ways, and seawater is stranger still. It is not possible to go into all its properties here, but we should look briefly at some of the most important, from the point of view of life on Earth.

Water has a very high specific heat – that is, it takes more heat energy to raise the temperature of a given volume of water by 1 °C than it takes to raise the temperature of any other liquid (with the exception of liquid ammonia) by the same amount. An important consequence of this is that the ocean heats up more slowly than the continents in the summer, and cools down more slowly than the continents in the winter. As a result, temperatures in the ocean fluctuate within a much smaller range than those in most terrestrial habitats. Throughout the ocean as whole, temperature ranges from −1.9 °C (the freezing temperature of seawater) in some polar regions, to about 30 °C in the tropics, i.e. a range of about 32 °C in all (or about 42 °C if we include shallow and restricted seas). The global range on land is about three times greater – to give an extreme example, the highest recorded air temperature is about 58 °C and the lowest is about −68 °C.

The latent heat of vaporization of water is probably the highest of *all* substances. In other words, more heat energy is needed to convert a given mass of liquid water to a gas (i.e. to water vapour) than would be needed to convert the same mass of any other liquid to its gaseous form. This means that enormous amounts of heat are taken up from the surface of the ocean when water is converted into water vapour (i.e. evaporates) and is carried away by the atmosphere, to be released when the water vapour condenses to form cloud in a cooler environment. This, along with the high specific heat of water, means that the oceans play a huge role both in controlling the global climate and in influencing climate locally (the role of the Gulf Stream in transporting heat from lower latitudes towards north-western Europe is well-known).

Another unusual property of water relates to the way in which its density changes with heating and cooling. Most liquids simply expand and become less dense when they get warmer, and contract and become more dense when they get colder, becoming denser with continued cooling even after they have become sufficiently cold to solidify (i.e. to freeze). Water, on the other hand, becomes least dense when it is coldest – ice floats on water. Imagine how different the world would be if ice sank! As suggested above, seawater (unlike freshwater) cools all the way down to −1.9 °C before freezing. The consequences of this strange behaviour provide one of the themes in *Discovering the Deep Oceans*, which you will be reading in the second part of the course, alongside Chapter 10.

● What other properties of water can you think of?

A property of water that may immediately have come to mind is that it is transparent; more specifically, it is transparent to visible light, with the result that you can see through it. However, water is *not* completely transparent to visible light – if it were, you would be able to see the sea-floor from a boat even in very deep water, and the deep ocean would be as well illuminated as the land! Furthermore, it is much less transparent to thermal (infrared) radiation, and hardly transparent at all to ultraviolet radiation. We will have a closer look at these topics in Chapter 4.

In fact, sound can travel through seawater much further than light (or any other form of **electromagnetic radiation**), and is used by a variety of different marine organisms for long-distance communication (while light is often used for 'close-up' communication). Over much of the depth range in the oceans, the actual *speed* at which sound travels is determined largely by the pressure exerted by the overlying water, which increases with increasing depth. We will be having a closer look at sound in Chapters 4 and 6, and at the effects of pressure in the oceans in Chapter 6, and again in Chapter 10 and *Discovering the Deep Oceans*.

Finally, as we have seen, water is very good at dissolving substances. In fact, it can dissolve more substances and in greater quantities than any other liquid. It is because of this great dissolving power that the sea is so salty.

2.1.2 Living in seawater

There are two important aspects of living in the oceans that we should focus on first, because they affect all marine organisms – the temperature of the surrounding water and its salinity.

The geographical distributions of all species, both terrestrial and marine, are limited by the temperature ranges within which they can function. In the ocean, the temperature of surface waters generally decreases with increasing latitude, i.e. with increasing distance from the Equator. As you will see in Chapter 5, this simple pattern is somewhat distorted by surface currents, but generally speaking marine species are found in bands which are approximately parallel to lines of latitude. Furthermore, the limits of the distributions of many species coincide with major 'jumps' in temperature – one such jump occurs off Cape Hatteras on the east coast of the USA, where the warm Gulf Stream leaves the continental shelf and turns eastward, moving out into deeper water (cf. Figure 5.9).

As mentioned in Section 2.1.1, water in the oceans very rarely gets warmer than about 30 °C, and although shallow pools on the seashore can get much warmer, even near-surface waters in the tropics are generally no warmer than 32 °C. Below the warm surface layers, much of the body of ocean water is at about 3–4 °C, and at high latitudes in winter and in parts of the deep sea, temperatures may be 0 °C or below. All chemical reactions, including those in living organisms (i.e. biochemical reactions), proceed faster at higher temperatures and slower at lower temperatures, so animals need physiological 'strategies' to ensure that they function as efficiently as possible. There are two basic ways in which they can do this.

Marine mammals and birds regulate their body temperature to keep it at a constant and relatively high level, so as to enable biochemical reactions within their body to function in a relatively stable environment at a relatively high rate. Most marine mammals keep their temperature at about 38 °C. To generate sufficient heat to maintain such temperatures, they generally have a higher metabolic rate than land mammals of similar size.

- How do you think being surrounded by ocean water will affect a marine mammal whose body temperature is about 38 °C?

- As discussed earlier, ocean water is rarely warmer than 30 °C, and is usually much colder. Marine mammals are therefore nearly always warmer than their surroundings, and so will continually lose heat to the environment.

To minimize this heat loss, marine mammals tend to be well insulated – whales and seals have a thick layer of blubber (subcutaneous fat), while sea-otters and polar bears spend a lot of time keeping their fur fluffed up and well cared for. Marine mammals also have a special kind of 'heat exchanger' blood circulatory system, which reduces heat loss. We will come back to this topic in Chapter 8.

By contrast, the body temperatures of most fish and all subtidal marine invertebrates (i.e. those that are permanently submerged) are determined by the temperature of the surrounding environment, i.e. by the ambient temperature. Thus if their surroundings warm up, so do they; if their surroundings become cooler, they cool down too. An increase in ambient temperature causes the metabolic rate to rise, along with the rate at which physiological processes occur. This increased activity could result (for example) in a faster rate of feeding, but could also lead to inefficient use of energy and of reserves that would otherwise be used for growth and reproduction. However, most fish and marine invertebrates inhabit waters whose temperatures fluctuate relatively little throughout the year, and they are able to regulate their metabolic rates so as to optimize the use of energy resources to allow a balance between 'fuelling' of activity on the one hand, and allowing growth and reproduction on the other.

Living in the oceans means being surrounded by salty water (i.e. water containing a high concentration of dissolved ions). Perhaps because living organisms first flourished in the oceans, the total salt content of the blood and body fluids of most marine invertebrates is about the same as that of seawater of average salinity (although the proportions of individual ions may not match that in seawater). However, in most fish, the salt content of the blood is only about 30–50% of the surrounding seawater. The reason for this is not known, although it may be because fish evolved in fresher coastal waters or estuaries (or because the early oceans generally had a much lower salinity than present-day oceans), and fish enzymes therefore evolved to function best in low-salinity waters.

There are important physiological consequences for such fish. Many living membranes are 'semipermeable', allowing the passage of pure water but not of the materials dissolved in it. During osmosis, as this process is called, water tends to diffuse across the membrane so as to even out the concentrations of ions in the fluids on either side. In the absence of any compensating mechanisms, this results in a continual loss of freshwater from the fish to the surrounding sea (ancient Egyptians used this principle in mummification, drying out bodies by immersing them in natural salt). Primitive fish – sharks and rays – maintain a high concentration of urea (a waste product) to keep their osmotic balance. Other fish (known as 'bony fish', as explained in Chapter 6) drink substantial amounts of seawater, but excrete very small quantities of urine and actively pass dissolved salts out across their gills. Sea turtles, seabirds and marine mammals also have various means of preserving osmotic balance with their environment.

2.2 The shape of the ocean basins

Clearly, the shape of the ocean basins and the topography of the sea-floor are the main factors determining how much of the different types of marine habitat are available as living space. Figure 2.1 shows the topography of the sea-floor represented in three dimensions, with the highest (i.e. shallowest) areas highlighted in yellow (as if lit from the right).

If you have not had much experience in interpreting maps, you should bear in mind that this type of map projection, in which the surface of the spherical Earth is projected onto a flat plane, greatly exaggerates areas of the Earth at high latitudes, and makes high-latitude features that are in reality quite close together look as if they are far apart. For this reason, areas of the map poleward of latitudes 70° N and 70° S have been omitted. Lines of longitude are vertical in this projection and, as on all maps, are determined with respect to 0° (the Greenwich meridian); 180° W, which is labelled, is the same as 180° E.

- Take a moment to study Figure 2.1. What features can you make out?

- The most obvious feature is probably the enormous mountain chain that snakes down through the Atlantic Ocean. This links up with less well-defined mountain chains in the Indian and Pacific Oceans. Also striking are numbers of arc-shaped depressions, mainly around the northern and western Pacific.

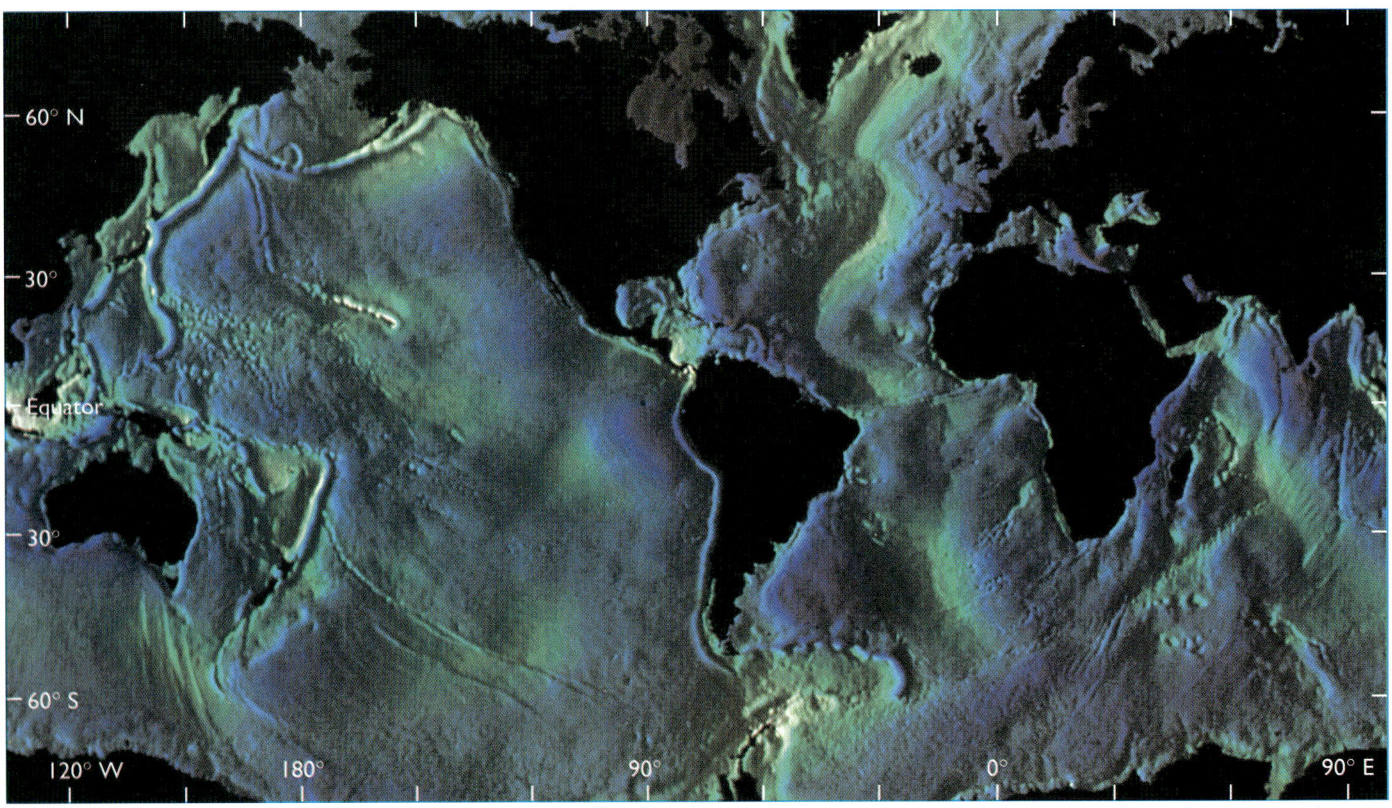

Figure 2.1 Representation of the topography of the sea-floor, shown as if lit from the right. The shallowest areas are highlighted in yellow, and the deepest areas are blue. (This map was made using satellite measurements of the shape of the sea-surface; you need not worry about how this technique works.)

The mountain chain that snakes down through the Atlantic is the Mid-Atlantic Ridge. Hidden in the dark depths of the ocean, it rises over 2 kilometres (km) above the sea-bed, and is part of the longest mountain range on Earth. It is no accident that it seems to follow the shape of the coastlines on either side, and that these coastlines look as if they would fit together like a jigsaw. That is because until about 200 million years ago, there was no Atlantic Ocean. Then, starting first in the north, the continental landmasses began to split apart, roughly along the line of the present ridge, and a new ocean basin began to open. New ocean floor was formed as molten basalt erupted and solidified, and over millions of years the newly formed ocean floor moved away from the central ridge, causing the continents on either side to move apart at a few centimetres a year – about the speed at which fingernails grow. So-called 'spreading ridges' (or 'spreading axes') like the Mid-Atlantic Ridge are also known as **constructive margins**, because they are the places where new sea-floor is 'constructed' (cf. Figure 2.3 overleaf).

The arc-shaped depressions (around the northern and western boundaries of the Pacific, and in the Atlantic off northern and southern South America) are **ocean trenches**, which are sites where ocean floor is destroyed. If you study Figure 2.1 carefully, you can see that there is also an ocean trench running down the western side of South America. For obvious reasons, trenches are also known as **destructive margins**.

So, new sea-floor is continually being formed at mid-ocean ridges, and is continually being destroyed at trenches. The continual formation and destruction of the Earth's outer layer, or **lithosphere** (*lithos* is Greek for rock), and the resulting motion of the lithospheric plates over the Earth's surface, is known as **plate tectonics**. As you can see from Figure 2.2 (overleaf), there are six or seven large lithospheric plates and many smaller ones. Some of these moving plates (e.g. the Pacific Plate) consist entirely of oceanic lithosphere, which is relatively dense; others (e.g. the African Plate) consist partly of oceanic lithosphere and partly of less dense (more buoyant) continental lithosphere. (The term 'crust' is often used instead of lithosphere, especially if the overlying sediments are being included.) Over hundreds of millions of years, the continents move relative to one another. In other words, plate tectonics is the mechanism driving the phenomenon known as **continental drift**.

Figure 2.3 shows sea-floor being created at a spreading ridge, moving away from the ridge, and being destroyed at trenches. The right-hand side of the diagram shows ocean crust sinking below a continent and being destroyed by melting. This process is known as **subduction**, so trenches are often called 'subduction zones'. The volcanoes that erupt in the overlying crust are known as 'subduction zone volcanoes'.

The left-hand side of Figure 2.3 shows the result of oceanic lithosphere being subducted below crust that is *also* oceanic. Here, the subduction zone volcanoes form on oceanic crust, and the trenches and the volcanic island chains have the characteristic arc shapes seen in Figures 2.1 and 2.2. Island arcs are common in the western Pacific; indeed, you can imagine the hypothetical cross-section in Figure 2.3 as being a simplified slantwise (north-west–south-east) section across the Pacific, from the Philippines to the coast of South America and the Andes.

Figures 2.1 and 2.2 show that the western Pacific is also the setting for many of the ocean's volcanic islands and **seamounts** (completely submerged volcanoes) which, like the islands of the volcanic arcs, rise up quite steeply from the deep sea-bed. Many of these islands and seamounts formed when the ocean crust passed over

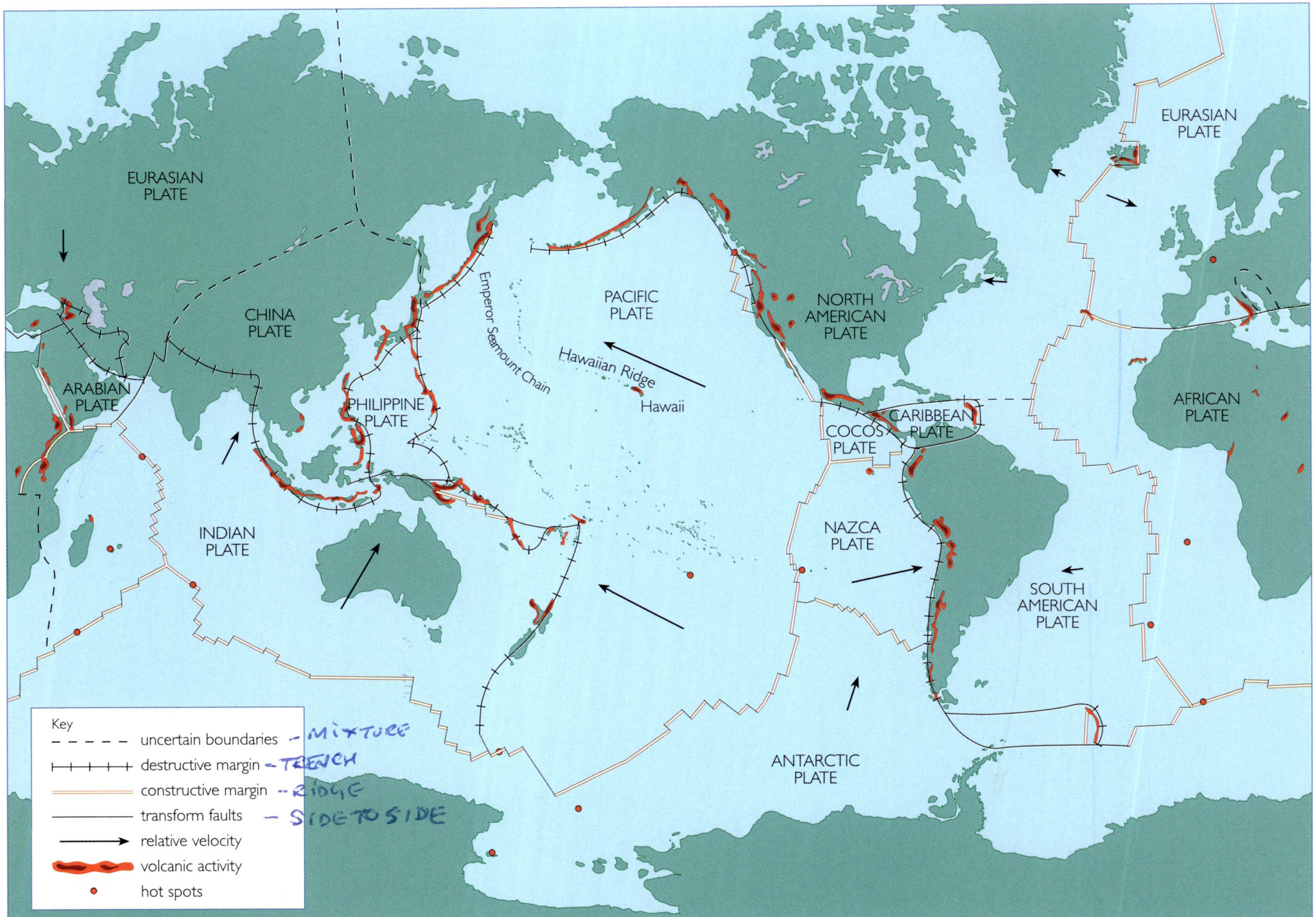

Figure 2.2 The Earth's lithospheric plates, and the boundaries between them. Transform faults are offsets in the mid-ocean spreading ridges; the other types of plate boundaries (see key) are discussed further in the text. Arrows indicate the relative motions of the plates, assuming that the African Plate is stationary; the arrow in the key corresponds to a relative velocity of 5 centimetres per year (cm yr^{-1}). Red areas indicate locations of active (or recently active) volcanism (other than that which occurs along spreading ridges – see Figure 2.3).

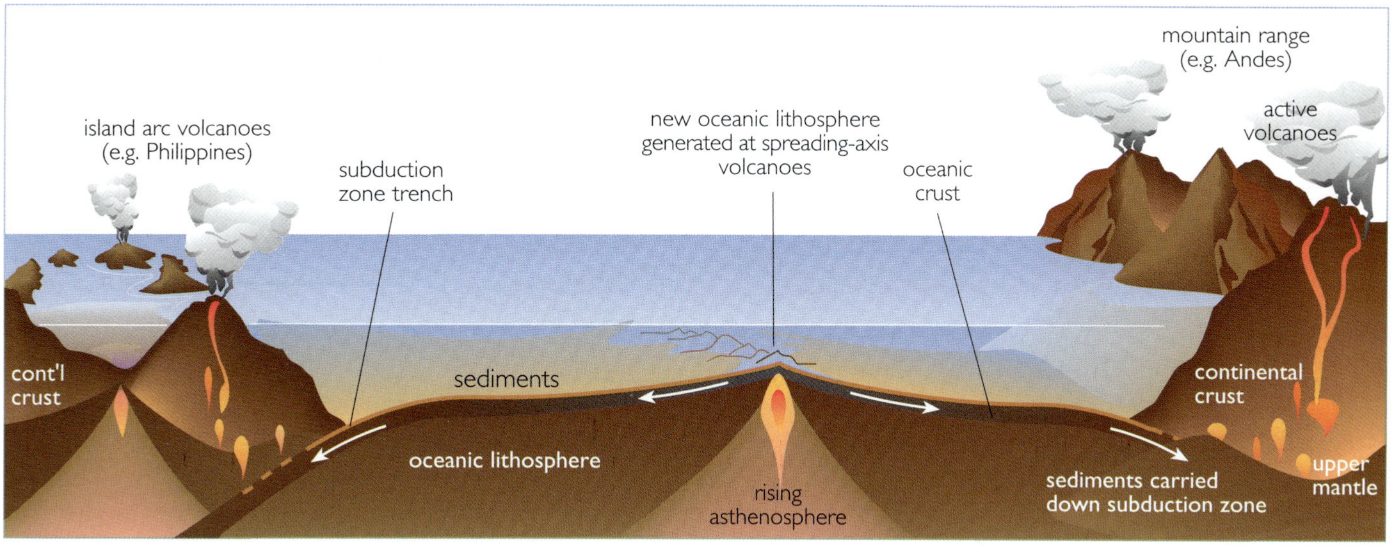

Figure 2.3 Three-dimensional diagram showing the processes associated with the creation and destruction of oceanic lithosphere. New oceanic lithosphere is created by magma (molten rock) rising from below (this underlying layer is known as the asthenosphere). The ridge itself is uplifted because it is warmer, and therefore less dense and more buoyant, than the rocks on either side. However, as the lithosphere moves away from the ridge, it cools, contracts and sinks, eventually becoming covered by a few kilometres of sediment; the arrows show the direction of sea-floor spreading. Note that the vertical scale is greatly exaggerated.

isolated 'hot spots' of volcanism, which from time to time punch through the ocean floor. As you will see, the islands and seamounts produced by volcanism in the oceans (and in some unusual circumstances, the volcanism itself) play a significant role in providing environments that are highly conducive to abundant marine life.

Figure 2.4 (overleaf) brings together information about the general shape of ocean basins and the penetration of sunlight down into the oceans. In a schematic way, it illustrates the distribution and extent of the different marine environments: the coastal environment, shelf seas and the broad extent of the open ocean, with both pelagic and benthic communities. In terms of area, continental margins (shelf, slope and rise) occupy about 20% of the total sea-bed, mid-ocean spreading ridges occupy about 33%, other ridges and seamounts occupy about 3%, trenches less than 2%, and abyssal plains 42%. No light at all penetrates below about 1000 m depth (i.e. below 1 km), so more than 60% of the sea-bed habitat is completely and permanently dark, as is 70–75% of the *volume* of living space in the water column.

- Compare Figure 2.2 with Figure 2.4. Which coastlines have narrow continental shelves and which generally have wide continental shelves?

- Coastlines like those around the Pacific, which have trenches (i.e. subduction zones) where oceanic lithosphere of one plate sinks below continental lithosphere of another plate, have narrow continental shelves (cf. right-hand side of Figure 2.4). Coastlines which do not involve a change of plate (e.g. those bordering the Atlantic) mostly (but not always) have wide continental shelves.

Continental shelves have a very gentle topography because during the last glacial period, when sea-level was lower, they were eroded more or less flat by wave action. Areas of ocean that overlie regions of continental shelf (particularly extensive areas,

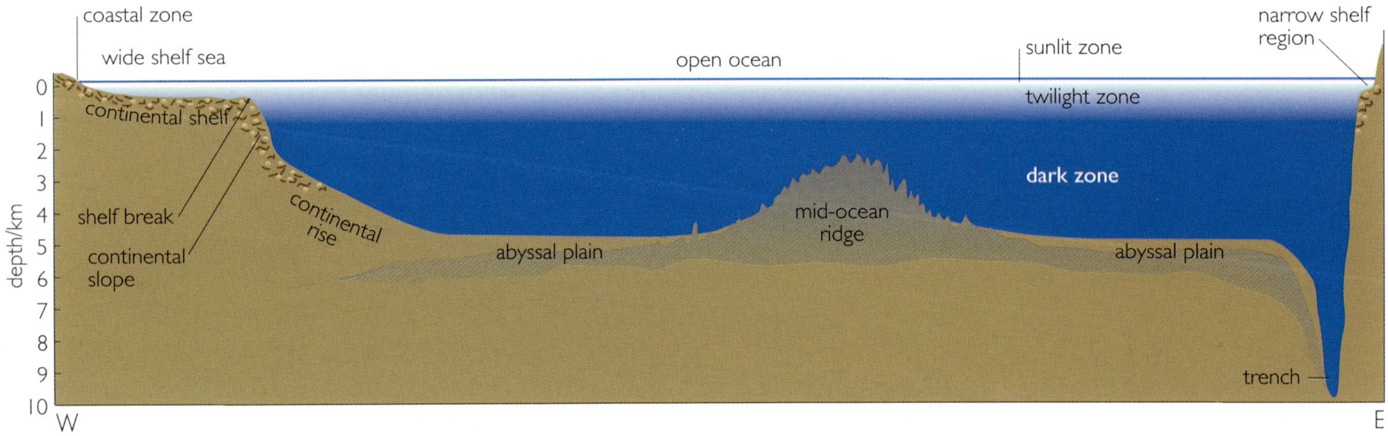

Figure 2.4 Schematic west–east cross-sectional diagram of an ocean basin (i.e. a vertical slice through an ocean basin) showing the main topographic features. The shelf break is the edge of the continental shelf. The speckles on the continental shelf, slope and rise indicate relatively coarse sediments (sand, etc.), which contrast with the fine sediments of the abyssal plains. The depth zones are those referred to in the Blue Planet videos. *Important:* The vertical scale is greatly exaggerated compared with the horizontal scale, which means that slopes look much steeper than they are in reality.

such as over the Grand Banks off Newfoundland), or semi-enclosed shallow seas overlying continental crust (such as the North Sea), are known as **shelf seas** (these are the subject of the Blue Planet video on 'Seasonal Seas').

In the Blue Planet videos, the terms 'seas' and 'oceans' are used interchangeably. We will try to use these terms more specifically, using seas to mean 'shelf seas'. (Confusingly, certain enclosed areas, including the Red Sea and the Mediterranean, are referred to as 'seas', even though they do not overlie continental crust.)

The Blue Planet videos sometimes use the term 'shallows' to mean near-surface, sunlit water in the open ocean, but it is more commonly used to mean simply shallow water near the coast. Either way, 'shallows' refers to water which is better illuminated and (often, but not always) warmer than deeper water.

Question 2.1 Look again at Figures 2.1 and 2.2. Of which ocean, if any, could Figure 2.4 be a cross-section? ◀ NONE

The proportion of ocean area that is shallow sea has fluctuated significantly over geological time. For example, a climatic change that resulted in growth or decline of large ice-sheets, like those that now cover Antarctica and Greenland, would be accompanied by either a fall in sea-level as water was added to the ice-sheet, or a rise in sea-level as the ice melted. This would mean that the area of continental shelf that was submerged would either decrease or grow.

- Why would this have important implications for marine organisms?

- A growth in the area of continental shelf would mean an increase in the area of relatively shallow water that could be colonized by organisms that prefer shallow, sunlit water – including benthic plants, corals and shellfish beds.

2.3 Shorelines, sediments and the sea-bed

We should now look briefly at the various types of shoreline and sea-bed that are available for colonization by marine organisms. The characteristics of such **substrates** determine which organisms will be able to flourish in a given area. Seaweeds need rocks for their holdfasts to attach firmly to. Much less conspicuous are the single-celled algae that live on sand grains, and those that form mats on muddy sediments.

Animals that live attached to the sea-bed or move over it – e.g. mussels, corals, sponges and starfish – are known as **epifauna**. Epifauna are particularly abundant on rocky or hard substrates, but are also found on sandy or muddy substrates. Such soft substrates also support animals that burrow. Animals that live partly or wholly within the sediment – e.g. many bristleworms (polychaetes), bivalve molluscs (e.g. cockles), and other invertebrates – are known as **infauna**.

In some unusual circumstances, beaches are made up of debris from living organisms – the best known example is the coral sand of some tropical islands, but beaches are also sometimes accumulations of shells. Mostly, however, beaches and continental shelves are covered to various extents by sediments derived from the land – that is to say, rocks and boulders of various sizes, sand, silt and mud. These are the products of erosion of the land, including nearby cliffs – not necessarily the ones at the back of the beach in question, but certainly cliffs not so very far away. This is why regions with volcanic rocks have black beaches, and places with limestone or chalk cliffs have pale-coloured beaches. The most common beach material is quartz sand, because the mineral quartz is a major component of the granitic rocks which largely make up the continents.

Under the influence of the elements, rocks erode away – how fast this occurs depends on the type of rock, as you can see from a visit to a churchyard: granite headstones survive much better than headstones carved from softer rocks like limestone. Some of the constituents of eroded rock are carried away in solution, and will contribute to the saltiness of seawater; the solid fragments will be of various sizes – boulders and pebbles, sand of different grain-sizes and – finest of all – silt and mud. If the environment in which they are initially deposited is subjected to fast-flowing water and/or vigorous wave action, the smaller fragments will be carried away, leaving the larger, heavier ones behind. If the environment is quiet, with only slow currents and/or gentle waves, the smallest particles will not be carried away, and silt and mud carried from elsewhere may have a chance to settle out. Thus, 'high energy' beaches tend to be characterized by lots of exposed rock, with boulders and pebbles, and often sand as well, while 'low energy' beaches tend to have a lot of beach sediment that is silty or even muddy.

Question 2.2 Thinking about the British Isles, can you suggest some good examples of (1) low energy and (2) high energy shorelines? ◀

So, beaches may be rocky and/or sandy; and if there is a sheltered river mouth nearby, or an enclosed lagoonal area, they may also be muddy. The continental shelf may similarly be rocky, sandy or muddy. If it is sandy or muddy, there will be ripples of various sizes on the sea-bed, as well as sand- and mud-banks, and other features, all caused by waves and currents. Several Blue Planet video sequences clearly show the sandy nature of much of the continental shelf.

Some continental shelf regions, including parts of the North Sea and the English Channel, have gravelly sediments, which were deposited by glaciers. During the last glacial period, which ended about 11 000 years ago, sea-level fell as much as 100 m below that of the present day. At high latitudes, glaciers extended much further towards the open ocean (as did rivers at low latitudes) and sediments carried by glaciers (and rivers) were deposited on coastal plains that are now submerged continental shelf. Then the ice melted, and the sea once more inundated the shelves, covering the recently deposited sediments of gravel, sand and mud. Eventually, the action of the waves and currents winnowed away the finer sediments – the mud and the sand – leaving behind the gravel.

Continental shelves slope down away from the coast very gently indeed – they have an average slope of only 1 in 1000, or, as an angle, ~ 0.1° (the symbol ~ means 'about'). The edge of the continental shelf (known as the 'shelf break') has been 'softened' by layers of sediment, and is usually between 20 and 150 m depth (on average, about 130 m depth), although that off the UK is at about 200 m depth. The **continental slope** (cf. Figure 2.4) is much steeper than the continental shelf, on average about 1 in 20 (~ 4°) but sometimes more, as off the south-western British Isles (the South-West Approaches). Part-way down the continental slope, the gradient becomes less steep; this is the start of the **continental rise**, formed from sediment that has been carried down from the continental shelf, often in dramatic flows of water, sediment and rocks known as turbidity currents. Turbidity currents can carve out submarine canyons – gullies in the continental slope and rise – the size of the Grand Canyon. The gradient of the continental rise is about 1 in 100 (~1°).

Note how, in Figure 2.4 (and Figure 2.3), we have had to exaggerate the vertical scale greatly relative to the horizontal scale, in order to show the sea-bed topography clearly. In reality, the oceans are so much wider than they are deep, that their width–depth relationship corresponds roughly to that of the width of a piece of paper compared to its thickness!

In the deep ocean, the continental rise merges imperceptibly into the **abyssal plain**. Abyssal plains are the flattest and most extensive environments on Earth. Beneath them is the rocky oceanic lithosphere which formed at the spreading ridge millions of years before, covered by the sediment that has been raining down ever since (cf. Figure 2.3). The sediments of the deep sea are fine clay and dust particles carried to the sea by rivers and by the wind, along with organic remains sinking from the sunlit surface layer. The fine-grained nature of the clay and biogenic (i.e. biologically produced) sediment on the deep sea-bed, compared with the coarser sediments of beaches and the continental shelf, can be seen in the middle section of 'The Deep' video. The deep ocean floor generally supports a very sparse fauna, but relatively recently it was discovered that there is an unexpectedly rich diversity of species.

The flat expanses of the abyssal plains are occasionally interrupted by a volcanic island or seamount, whose flanks may support luxuriant communities of animals (as you will see in the 'Open Ocean' video). In general, however, rocky areas in the deep ocean are rare, although there are areas of exposed rock on the steep sides of the deep ocean trenches. In shallower water, there are of course rocky intertidal zones, as well as those parts of the continental shelf and slope that are scoured by strong currents. In addition, the hard structure that has built up over thousands of years to form coral reefs also acts like a rocky environment (see Chapter 7). And finally, at the spreading ridges themselves, there is the rocky landscape of newly formed ocean floor, yet to be covered with sediment (Figure 2.4). This region mostly has a rather sparse fauna, but at various locations along the ridge, everything changes in the vicinity of hydrothermal vents, where water at 350–400 °C gushes out of the ocean floor. We will be devoting time to these extraordinary environments later in the course.

Of course, from the point of view of a benthic marine organism, the physical environment it experiences in its day-to-day existence is not only determined by the substrate it lives on and/or in, but on the temperature and other properties of the water in which it lives, by the flow of currents, and the turbulence caused by currents, wind and waves. In the case of organisms that live around the coast, these factors may be continually changing with the ebb and flow of the tides.

▶▶ *This is a good time to watch the introductory video, on VC1. To get the most out of the video, you might find it helpful to begin by reading through the notes below. You can read them again after watching, if you wish. The notes for later videos will refer to the time codes, which are provided in the top right-hand corner of the screen.* ◀◀

Notes on the introductory video

In Chapters 6 and 8, we will look more closely at how fish and marine mammals swim, so you might like to note down any striking aspects of the swimming styles of the marine mammals shown in this video (the blue whale and the sealions).

As you may already know, the blue whale feeds mainly on krill which it filters from seawater using baleen ('whalebone') plates. The expandable grooves in its throat, which allow it to engulf such huge volumes of water, mean that it is a type of baleen whale known as a **rorqual**.

Although we are not providing detailed notes on the various sequences in the introductory video, we will take this opportunity to say a little about marine reptiles (which feature prominently in this video) and seabirds, which appear in a number of videos. Although we will not be saying a great deal more about them, when they make an appearance you might like to watch out for their different feeding and swimming styles.

Marine reptiles

In this video, you will see three types of marine reptile – the marine iguana (found only on the islands of the Galápagos archipelago), marine turtles (of which there are eight species in all), and salt-water crocodiles, which live in coastal waters. All reptiles are cold-blooded and breathe air.

Marine turtles usually live in tropical waters, although they may be found at higher latitudes. Green turtles feed on seaweed and seagrasses in shallow water, but all other turtles are carnivorous. For example, leatherbacks (the biggest turtles) consume only gelatinous zooplankton living in the water column, hawksbills feed on sponges, and loggerhead turtles eat sponges, crabs and molluscs. Turtles have been killed for food for centuries, and all species are now considered to be endangered as a result of hunting and accidental trapping in fishing gear. We will be coming back to turtles again later, in the context of breeding (as in this video) and migration.

There is only one other type of marine reptile – the sea snake – of which there are 60 species. Sea snakes may come together in schools, and they live in estuaries, around coral reefs and in open tropical waters. They are extremely venomous, and feed on small fish and squid, which they kill with venom injected by their fangs. Many species lay their eggs on shore, but some give birth to live young at sea.

Shorebirds and seabirds

Like marine mammals and marine reptiles, marine birds (which like all birds, are warm-blooded) have evolved from terrestrial ancestors. In all, there are about 280 species of marine birds (the exact number depends on how the term is defined). There are two groups of marine birds: shorebirds, which often migrate between two terrestrial sites, winter feeding grounds and spring/summer nesting grounds; and seabirds, which are highly adapted to the marine environment and spend 50–90% of their time at sea.

Shorebirds – including the night herons seen in the video, and the more familiar sandpipers, plover and knot – cannot swim. They mostly feed on muddy, sandy or rocky intertidal zones (to be discussed in Chapter 3) and have a wide variety of beak types and methods of foraging. The length and shape of the beak are determined by where the bird feeds in the intertidal zone, and by what it eats.

Many species of seabird are as agile under water as above it. Some plunge into the water to seize zooplankton, fish or squid, some (e.g. pelicans) dive into surface layers, and others (e.g. gannets) plunge to much greater depths. Penguins, murres, puffins and shearwater pursue their prey underwater using their wings, while cormorants swim after their prey using their feet. The best underwater swimmers have short, flipper-like wings (as exemplified by penguins), while birds that fly long distances in search of food (e.g. albatross) tend to have long, relatively inflexible wings. There are a great variety of ways in which birds feed at the surface; these include skimming surface organisms from the topmost layer, pattering their feet, dipping, and grabbing food at the surface.

Many species of seabird nest in colonies of thousands (or even, in some cases, millions) in isolated locations away from predators, but within reach of rich feeding grounds. For reasons that will become clear, there are many more seabirds at high latitudes and temperate regions than there are in the tropics. You will be seeing some spectacular examples of large colonies in the videos.

Tides

3

The rise and fall of the tide are familiar to anyone who has been to the seaside, but it is not at all obvious that these changes in water level are the result of a kind of wave motion. We will explain what this means later, but first we should look at how the tides are generated.

3.1 What causes the tides?

Most people know that the tides are a result of the gravitational attraction of the Moon acting on the oceans, but the details of how and why tides are generated are not straightforward. The easiest way to begin is to imagine that the Earth is completely covered with water, and that the Moon is directly above the Equator. In these circumstances, the oceans would take on an ellipsoidal (oval) shape, as shown in Figure 3.1, with a bulge towards the Moon and (for reasons that we do not need to go into here) a bulge away from the Moon, and lower water levels in between.

- If the Moon and the ellipsoid of ocean remained stationary while the Earth turned on its axis within the ellipsoid of ocean, how many high tides (bulges) and how many low tides would an observer on the Earth (e.g. on an island near the Equator) experience over the course of 24 hours (i.e. during one complete rotation of the Earth)?

- Over the course of 24 hours, the observer would pass through two bulges, and two 'lows', i.e. they would experience two high tides and two low tides.

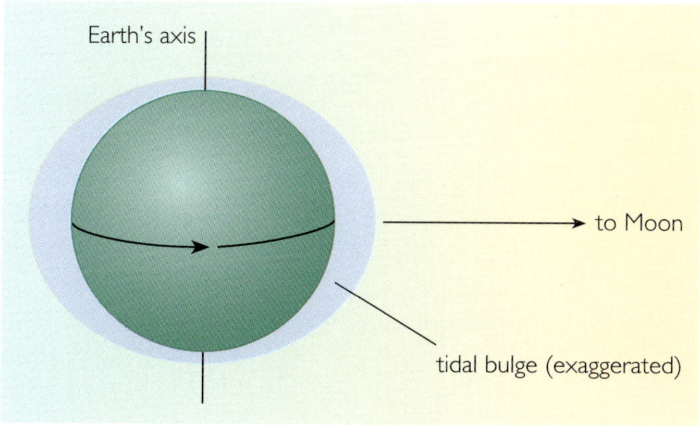

Figure 3.1 The Earth would rotate within an imaginary fixed tidal ellipsoid (shown greatly exaggerated) once every 24 hours. (In reality of course, the ocean cannot take on this ellipsoidal shape because the Earth is *not* completely covered in water.)

In the hypothetical situation just discussed, the Moon and the tidal ellipsoid remain stationary, but because the Earth is rotating, they both move in relation to the Earth. However, the Moon and the tidal ellipsoid do *not* remain stationary, and this affects the timing of high and low tides. While the Earth turns on its axis, the Moon is orbiting the Earth in the same direction that the Earth is turning, making a complete orbit every 27.3 days. As a result, the Moon gets back to the same position with respect to the Earth every 24 hours and 50 minutes (approximately). This is why you will see the Moon reach a particular height in the sky roughly 50 minutes later each successive night, and why the times of high and low tides at many locations are almost an hour later each successive day.

It is not generally appreciated that the Sun also has a significant effect on the tides, and acting on its own would give rise to one high tide and one low tide a day. It is the combination of the tides caused by the Sun with those caused by the Moon that gives rise to the monthly spring–neap tidal cycle, which is experienced along much of the world's coastlines. Figure 3.2 illustrates how this comes about. The tidal record at the bottom is for a location in the Tay estuary in Scotland, but from the point of view of Figure 3.2 you can consider it to represent the change in water level at any location where the tides show a spring–neap cycle, i.e. one in which tides with a relatively large tidal range alternate with tides with a relatively small tidal range.

Study Figure 3.2, and then check your understanding of what you have read so far in this section by trying Questions 3.1 and 3.2.

Question 3.1

(a) According to the changes in water level shown in Figure 3.2, which is the most dominant tide in the Tay estuary: the solar tide or the lunar tide?

(b) What is the tidal range at the location in the Tay estuary where the measurements were made: (1) at the peak of spring tides; (2) during the smallest neap tides? ◀

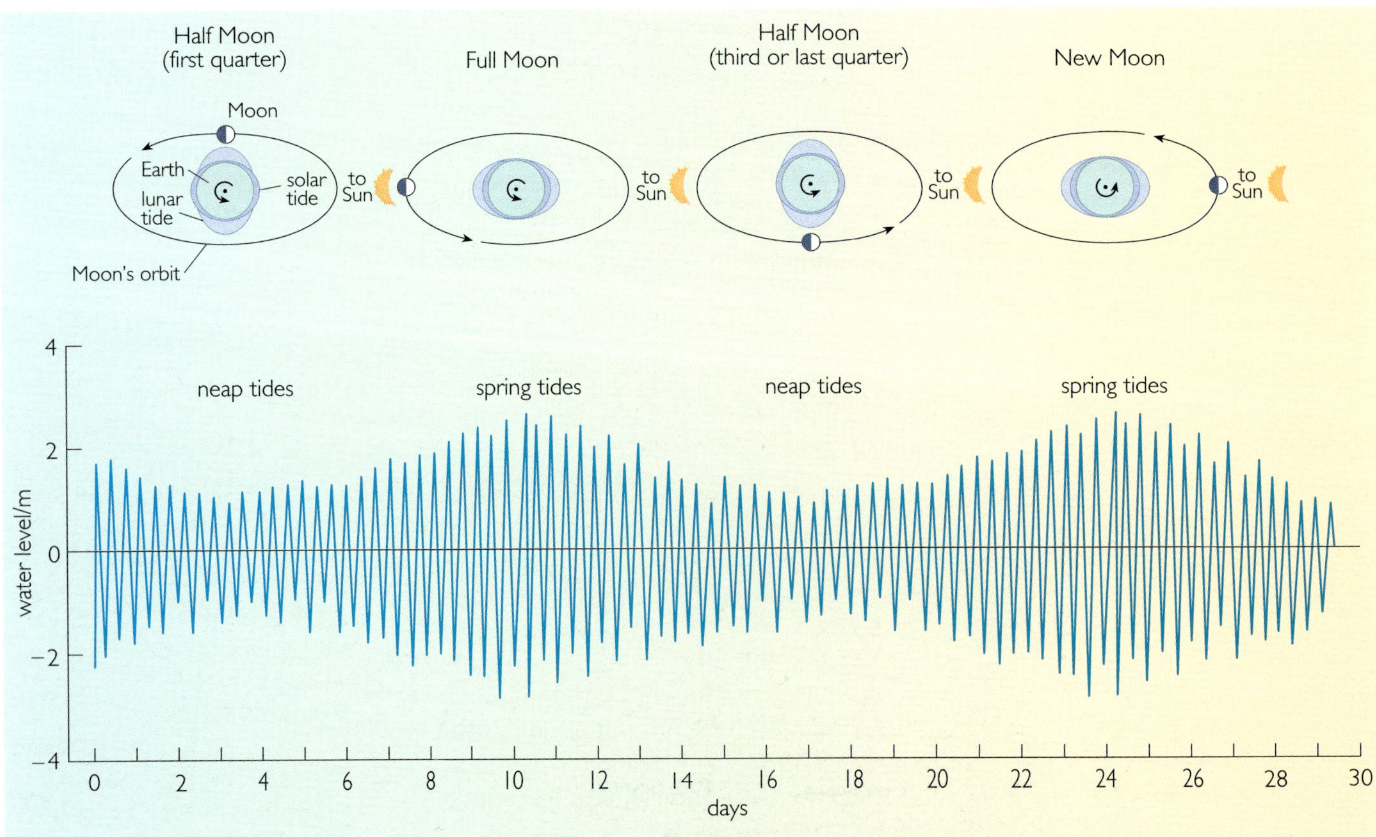

Figure 3.2 Together, the gravitational attractions of the Moon and Sun lead to the monthly spring–neap cycle. When the Moon, Earth (here viewed from above the North Pole) and Sun are aligned, the 'lunar ellipsoid' and the 'solar ellipsoid' combine and there are spring tides (here 'spring' has nothing to do with the seasons); when the Moon and Sun are positioned so that their ellipsoids are at right angles to one another, the result is neap tides. The plot along the bottom shows the resulting variation in water level, with periods of neap tides alternating with periods of spring tides, at a location in the Tay estuary. (The 0-line is mean sea-level.)

Question 3.2

(a) Explain whether the following statement is true or false:

'During the week following a Full Moon, when the Moon is waning, the tidal range will be decreasing.'

(b) When it is New Moon and spring tides for people in Britain, what phase of the Moon, and what part of the tidal cycle, are people in Australia experiencing? ◀

In fact, the situation is not quite as simple as we have been suggesting, because the Earth rotates on its axis much faster than the inertia of the vast mass of the ocean, and friction with the sea-bed, can be overcome. As a result, high tide commonly arrives some hours after the passage of the Moon overhead – a phenomenon known as **tidal lag**. The tidal lag is greatest at low latitudes (where it is about six hours) and has decreased to zero by latitude 65°; the precise lag is always constant at a given location. A further consequence is that, in reality, the biggest spring tides and the smallest neap tides occur a day or two *after* New Moon and Full Moon, and a day or two *after* first quarter and third quarter, respectively.

You may well have realized that tidal flows will be further complicated by the existence of landmasses, which prevent the tidal bulges from travelling directly round the Earth – in fact, the only place where a westward-moving bulge could travel unimpeded round the globe is the Southern Ocean around Antarctica. Instead of travelling around the globe as 'bulges', tides travel as very long waves: the crest of the wave is high tide and the trough is low tide.

Figure 3.3 shows schematically how a tidal wave might travel around a hypothetical ocean basin. The important thing to note is that although the highest and lowest tidal levels are experienced around the coast, the tidal wave also affects the centre of the ocean basin, except for the point around which the wave travels. For reasons which we do not need to go into here, tidal waves generally travel round ocean basins anticlockwise in the Northern Hemisphere and clockwise in the Southern Hemisphere.

Remember that it is only the *shape of the wave* which is travelling around the ocean basin. If you have not studied wave motions before, think of making a rope 'snake' by moving one end from side to side – this causes a wave motion to move along the

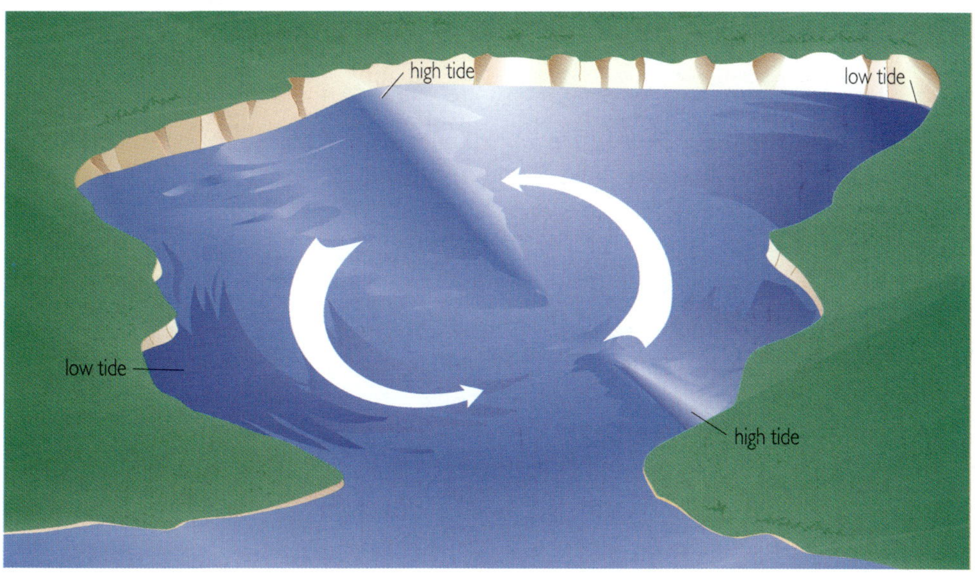

Figure 3.3 Schematic diagram to show how tides travel around an ocean basin as a very 'long' wave, with high tide being the crest of the wave and low tide the trough. This diagram shows a typical situation in the Northern Hemisphere (see text) applied to a hypothetical ocean. (*Note:* not to scale – heights of cliffs are greatly exaggerated; this ocean basin could be anything from a few hundred to a few thousand kilometres across.)

rope, but the rope as a whole remains where it is. The waves generated by wind blowing over the surface of the ocean are similar: although individual water particles describe circular or near-circular motions in the vertical plane, it is the *wave motion* which may travel for hundreds or even thousands of kilometres across the ocean, *not* individual water particles.

In the case of tides, high tides are caused by water flowing in such a way as to locally raise sea-level by 'piling up' water, and low tides result when sea-level is lowered by water flowing away again. This to-and-fro (or, in practice, often elliptical) movement of water is what we mean by tidal currents. The part of the tidal cycle when water is flowing to raise the local water level is known as the flood tide, and the part of the tidal cycle when water is flowing to lower the local water level is known as the ebb tide. At any one place, tidal currents change direction during the tidal cycle. When the tide is turning, tidal currents are in the process of reversing and are very weak; this is known as slack water. Tidal currents are usually strongest around mid-tide, i.e. in the middle of the flooding phase and in the middle of the ebbing phase.

It is important to note at this point that the giant waves often referred to as 'tidal waves' are usually generated by earthquakes and are nothing whatsoever to do with tides. The correct term for such a wave is *tsunami* – a Japanese word meaning 'harbour wave', referring to the fact that such waves only become visible when they enter shallow water. Once in shallow water, they can rear up to great heights and cause enormous destruction and loss of life.

For a number of reasons, predicting the actual tidal cycle at a given location is very complex. For one thing, in addition to the lunar and solar tidal cycles mentioned above, there are other smaller cycles; also, the actual tidal cycle experienced at any place is affected by the shape of coast and the topography of the sea-bed. Southampton Water, for example, has a 'double high water' (i.e. two high tides separated by a short period of lower sea-level which is still above mean sea-level), while nearby Portland has a 'double low water'. The Mediterranean experiences very small tides, partly because it is largely isolated from the tidal wave travelling around the Atlantic. Some locations, where the solar tidal cycle has much more effect than the lunar tidal cycle, have only one high tide and one low tide a day.

3.2 The influence of tides on marine life

Tides have a direct influence on marine life in two main ways:

1 Through the rise and fall of sea-level, which is most noticeable, and has most effect on marine life, around the coast (cf. Figure 3.3).

2 Through their effect on current speeds.

● Would you expect tidal currents to be faster at spring tides or at neap tides?

○ We would expect tidal currents to be faster during spring tides, when the differences in water level between high and low tide are at a maximum. At these points in the tidal cycle, the water in the tidal 'wave' has to be transported over greater distances in the course of the tidal cycle (i.e. over the course of about 24 hours 50 minutes), and larger volumes of water have to be moved to-and-fro.

3.2.1 Tidal currents

Tidal currents are an important component of the current pattern in shallow waters over continental shelves. Of course, there are also wind-driven currents which are strongest at the sea-surface, and become less strong with depth below the sea-surface.

- From what you know about how tides are generated, would you expect tidal currents also to be stronger nearer the surface? (Ignore the effect of friction with the sea-bed.)

- No. There is no reason why the motion of water in a tidal wave should be stronger at the surface than deeper in the water column.

At a given point on the Earth, all the water molecules, wherever they are in the water column, will be equally under the influence of the Moon's gravitational attraction. For this reason, there are tidal currents even in the deep ocean.

Locally, the speed of tidal currents is affected by the bottom topography, and especially by the constraining effects of islands, narrow straits or headlands. Water is almost completely incompressible, so the volume of water flowing *into* a given space over a given time has to be the same as the volume of seawater flowing *out* of the space over the same time. So, if a flow of water is forced to become narrower, it will speed up. You may have used this principle yourself to increase the strength of the jet of water coming out of a hosepipe – the smaller the nozzle of the hosepipe, the stronger the jet. In the 'Tidal Seas' video, you will see two spectacular examples of powerful tidal currents caused by large volumes of water being forced through narrow channels, in the first case between small islands, and in the second case, in the Nakwakto Rapids.

Waves generated by wind blowing over the sea-surface mix the uppermost layer of water, particularly in winter. Meanwhile, strong tidal currents flowing over the sea-bed generate turbulence in the bottom-most layer. In shallow shelf waters, these two mixed layers meet, so the whole water column is well-mixed. As will be explained in Chapter 4, mixing ensures that there is always a good supply of nutrients for phytoplankton, and this is the reason that relatively shallow water, with fast tidal currents, is often highly productive and able to support large populations of animals.

The extraordinary biological productivity of the waters of the Bay of Fundy between Nova Scotia and New Brunswick (which you will see in the video on 'Tidal Seas') are a result of vigorous mixing by strong tidal currents (particularly at mid-tide) in a region with an exceptionally high tidal range – 15 metres at the head of the bay. The large concentration of photosynthetic pigment in the waters of the Bay of Fundy may be seen towards the top right of Figure 5.9. Highly productive water is found over many continental shelves, including the North Sea and much of the continental shelf to the west of the British Isles (Figure 3.4 overleaf). We will be returning to the topic of high biological productivity in the next chapter, and the video on 'Seasonal Seas'.

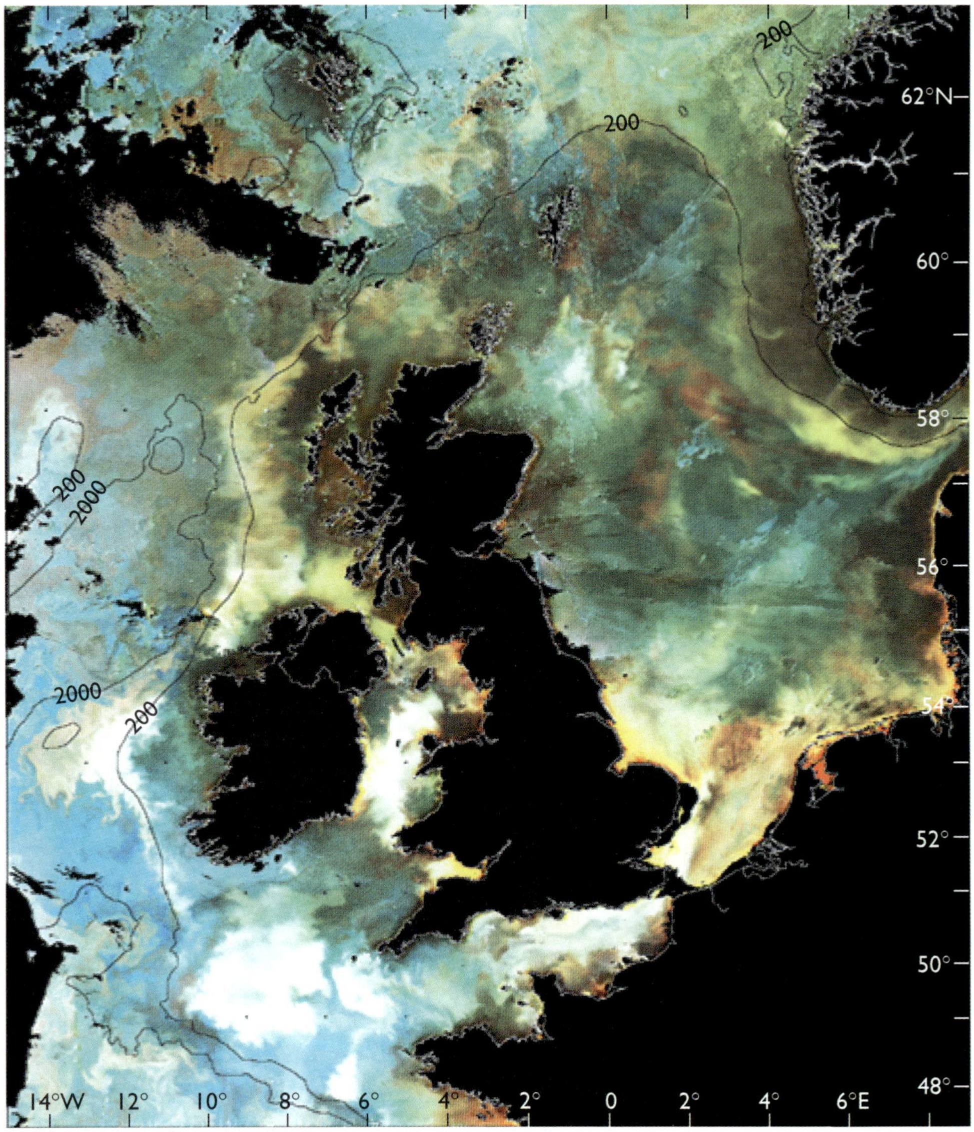

Figure 3.4 Satellite image showing the waters around the British Isles in close to real colour. The 200 m contour corresponds roughly to the edge of the continental shelf. In most of the area on the image, the water colour is dominated by the optical properties of phytoplankton. The pale coloration in the Channel, the southern, shallower part of the North Sea and the Irish Sea is due to particles (sediments, phytoplankton and organic particles) kept in suspension by turbulent mixing. Red coloration along coastlines (particularly those of mainland Europe and north-west England) is caused by high concentrations of sediment. White areas along the edge of the continental shelf, off south-west England, and in the northern North Sea, are probably blooms of coccolithophores (single-celled algae that have plates of calcium carbonate). Greenish coloration off Norway is the result of the outflow of water from the Baltic, with a large concentration of dissolved organic material.

3.2.2 Zonation

Along any coast affected by tides, the sea-level rises and falls twice every day (or in certain locations, where the solar tide is dominant, once a day). Below the lowest low-tide mark, the beach/sea-bed is always submerged. Above the highest high-tide mark, there is a zone which is never submerged, but is splashed by spray at high tide – this is sometimes called the splash zone. Between the high and low tide levels is a zone that is alternately underwater or exposed to the air: this is the **intertidal zone**.

- At any one location, does the intertidal zone always stay the same width?

- No, because the daily tidal range is bigger during spring tides and smaller during neap tides.

For this reason, 'tidal range' is often defined as the distance between the high tide level during spring tides and the low tide level during spring tides, both averaged over a long time. (You may see these written as mean high water springs and mean low water springs, or MHWS and MLWS, respectively.)

- Will two beaches with the same tidal range always have comparable areas of intertidal zone?

- No, because tidal range is distance measured vertically (cf. Question 3.1b). Therefore a gently sloping beach will have a much wider intertidal zone than a steeply sloping beach. (Think of those beaches where you have to walk for quite some time before being able to swim!)

The Blue Planet series does not look specifically at how organisms are distributed within the intertidal zone, but we can use this environment to look at some principles that apply throughout the oceans. The first of these is the concept of an **ecological niche**. An ecological niche is the combination of conditions – physical, chemical and biological – which characterize the environment occupied by a particular species.

Question 3.3 For a **sessile** organism – i.e. one that does not move around – living in the intertidal zone, what factors would be important aspects of its ecological niche? Jot down as many as factors as you can think of. ◀

Generally, in a given location, no more than one species occupies exactly the same ecological niche (although species can co-exist if plentiful space is available, perhaps because of predation). As a result, intertidal zones are characterized by vertical zonation – a banding of species occupying successively higher levels above low water mark.

Zonation is particularly noticeable on rocky shores, where it can be seen as horizontal bands of different colours and shades. Figure 3.5 (overleaf) shows examples of zonation on both a rocky shore and a sandy shore, off the coast of North America.

Relatively few animals are permanent residents of rocky shores.

- What phylum of animals is best represented in Figure 3.5a?

- The Mollusca: periwinkles are gastropod molluscs, and oysters and mussels are bivalve molluscs (perhaps surprisingly, barnacles are crustaceans; cf. Question 1.2).

Molluscs and crustaceans are the most abundant animals living on rocky shores. Around the British Isles, small periwinkles (*Littorina*) are found near the top of the intertidal zone, with barnacles just below. Then there may be a zone where barnacles

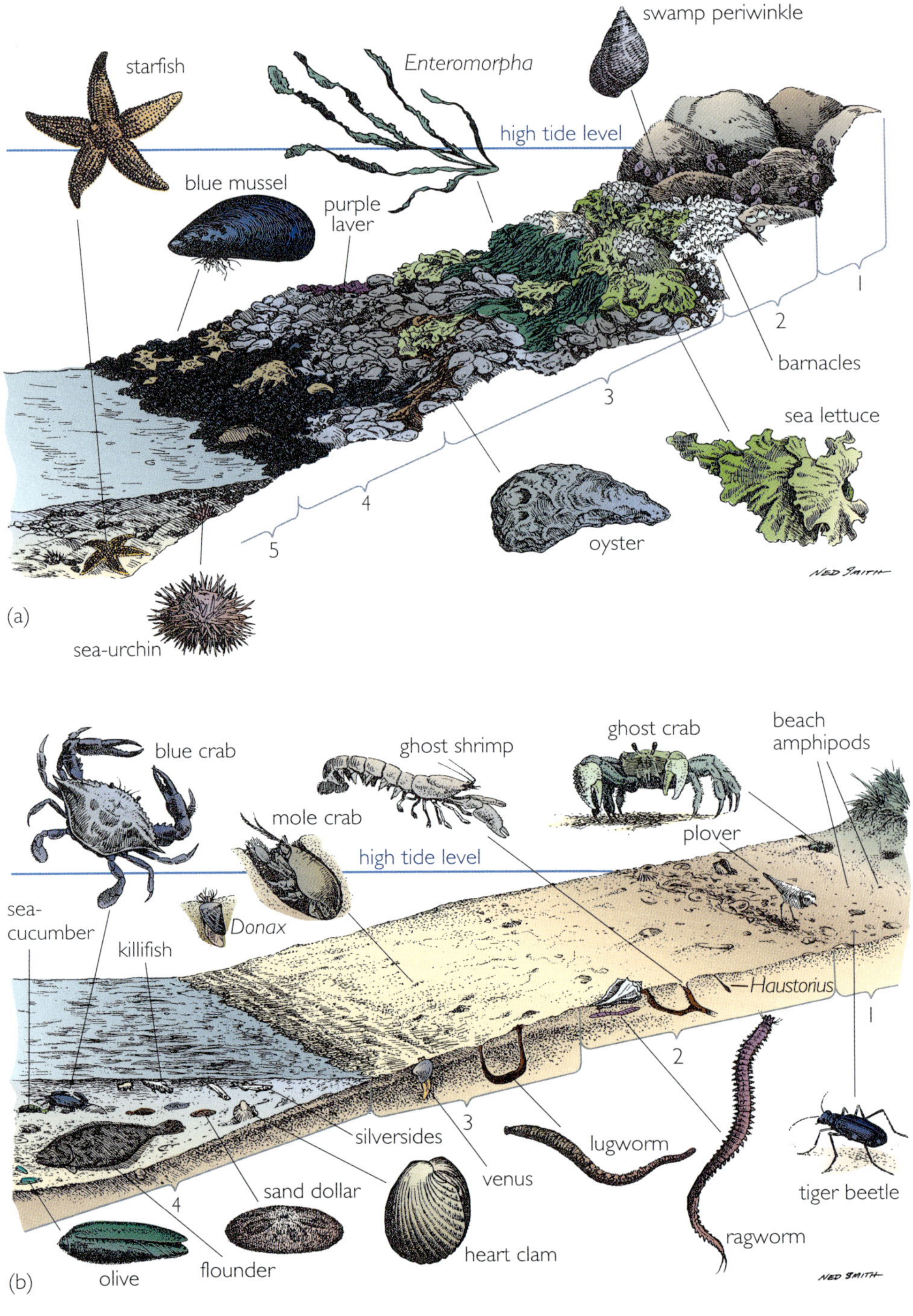

Figure 3.5 Cross-section to illustrate the intertidal zone (a) on a rocky shore (at low tide), (b) on a sandy shore (part-way through the tidal cycle). 1 is the splash zone, 2 the upper intertidal zone, 3 the mid-intertidal zone, 4 the lower intertidal zone, and 5 the subtidal zone (permanently submerged, not shown in (b)). (Note that the examples shown here are North American.)

are found along with mussels, common limpets (*Patella vulgata*), common periwinkles and dog whelks. In the lower part of the intertidal zone may be found blue-rayed limpets (*Patella aspera*), more barnacles, and sea-anemones. Limpets and periwinkles are grazing herbivores. When the tide is in, they move about, scraping diatoms and other small algae from the surfaces of rocks or of larger algae (see below). Apart from the dog whelk, which is a carnivore, all of the other animals mentioned above feed on plankton filtered from seawater. (We will return to the topic of feeding strategies in Section 3.3.) When the tide goes out, common limpets return to a home site, clamping down tight so that their shells fit into a groove they have worn in the rock. Other animals retreat to humid, sheltered sites under and amongst large seaweeds, in crevices, and under stones.

- In what important way, not so far referred to, does the zonation shown in Figure 3.5a differ from what we often see on rocky shorelines around the British Isles?

- Around the British Isles, seaweeds are usually abundant throughout the intertidal zone.

Light green seaweeds (algae) may be found at all levels, including the shallowest, in tide-pools and on all sorts of surfaces – e.g. stones and limpet shells. They are fairly small, but very fast-growing, and quickly become abundant if there is an influx of nutrients from (for example) sewage effluent. *Ulva* (sea lettuce) and *Enteromorpha* (both shown in Figure 3.5a) are particularly widespread, as is *Cladophora*, also known as blanketweed. Single-celled algae (particularly diatoms) are also found all over the rocky shore.

Unlike the green algae, brown and red seaweeds are generally perennial (i.e. they persist from year to year). On sheltered to moderately exposed rocky shores, the most noticeable organisms are the brown 'fucoid algae' whose main photosynthetic pigment is not chlorophyll but fucoxanthin. These have flexible stems (known as 'stipes') and a flattened leaf-like appearance. The brown seaweed that occurs highest up the intertidal zone is a tough species called *Pelvetia canaliculata*, whose partially rolled up fronds (forming channels), exceptionally thick cell walls, high content of mucilage (a mucus-like substance which reduces water loss, present in all seaweeds) and bushy growth all help it to resist long periods of exposure to the air. One of the best known of the brown seaweeds is *Fucus vesiculosus*, or bladder wrack. Another, *Ascophyllum nodosum* (knotted wrack or egg wrack), only grows in sheltered environments. In very sheltered conditions, it can live for 10 to 15 years, growing in thick masses which completely cover the rocks.

On rocky shores around the northern Atlantic, the commonest seaweed in the lower intertidal zone is another fucoid species, *Fucus serratus* (serrated wrack). Below the low tide mark grow the kelps (e.g. *Laminaria*), which sometimes form a kind of forest in shallow water. In many parts of the world, rocks below the low tide mark are covered by red encrusting algae, known as coralline algae, which have deposits of calcium carbonate in their cells. However, not all red algae live this deep – some (e.g. *Porphyra*, from which laver bread is made) may be found at the very top of the intertidal zone.

Seaweed cover produces a whole range of microhabitats which shelter other organisms, including small crustaceans. Larger seaweeds also sometimes have smaller ones living upon them, and these epiphytes (as they are called) are generally thin-walled and therefore attractive to plant-eaters (herbivores). The larger seaweeds may be a direct source of food themselves, and produce large amounts of organic debris, which also forms food for certain animals.

Generally speaking, within the intertidal zone the lower limit of a species' range is likely to be determined by biological factors, such as the presence of predators or competing species. The upper limit is often determined by physiological factors, such as the organism's tolerance to drying out when exposed to the atmosphere, or to extremes of temperature. Zonation and abundance of species may also be influenced by how easy it is for animal larvae or algal spores to settle. In areas exposed to large waves, the various zones are wider than in sheltered areas with a similar tidal range, as splashing extends the zones upwards.

Vertical zonation is also found on sandy beaches and sand and mud flats, but it is not as distinct or as immediately obvious (Figure 3.5b).

3.2.3 Coping with continual change

Because they are exposed for a larger proportion of each tidal cycle, intertidal organisms which live higher up the intertidal zone need to be better adapted to drying out (desiccation) and heating (or, at high latitudes, cooling) than those that live lower down. As far as plants are concerned, useful attributes include those of *Pelvetia canaliculata*, the brown seaweed which grows at the top of the intertidal zone (Section 3.2.2).

- More generally, from the point of view of resisting desiccation, do you think it would be better to be a large or small organism?

- To resist desiccation, it is better to keep surface area to a minimum. It is therefore better to be large, because the ratio of surface area to volume will be smaller (you may remember this from the 'Living in the Oceans' module).

However, the reverse is true when it comes to minimizing heat stress at low tide, as this is favoured by a larger surface area : volume ratio – small animals lose heat faster than large ones. A balance therefore has to be struck, so that the animal is not so small that it will dry up when exposed to the air, and not so large that it is unable to dissipate heat sufficiently fast through its body surface.

There are other techniques and aspects of body design that enable animals to avoid being overheated by the Sun at low tide. For example, some intertidal animals maintain their bodies at a temperature lower than their surroundings by making use of both evaporation and circulation of body fluids. Colour also plays a role in fitting organisms for their niche in the intertidal zone: lighter-coloured organisms reflect more solar radiation than darker-coloured ones, which can therefore absorb more. Mussels (*Mytilus edulis*), for example, have both light and dark forms, which are genetically determined. Along the Atlantic coast of North America, the dark-coloured form tends to predominate in northern areas, where freezing is a possibility, and the light-coloured form predominates further south where overheating is more likely.

Heat stress and desiccation are particularly problematic for intertidal animals (and plants) that live attached to rocky surfaces, but these difficulties also have to be dealt with by animals living on beaches, and on sand and mud flats. As the tide ebbs, tidal flats and beaches are exposed as water drains away, often leaving the sediment surface looking quite dry. However, below the apparently lifeless expanse are often large populations of animals, including bivalves and polychaete worms, as well as other invertebrates. Many intertidal animals have surprisingly deep burrows, extending perhaps 25 cm or more below the sediment surface. At high tide, the animals may emerge from their burrows, or extend siphons, tentacles or other feeding and respiratory organs to the surface of the sediment.

While burrowing animals may stay in the moist sand at low tide, others (e.g. mussels and barnacles) trap small volumes of water in their shells, and yet others are simply exposed to the air. These animals face the problem of being unable to take up dissolved oxygen from the water, or get rid of waste materials. A common means of combating a shortage of oxygen at low tide is to reduce the metabolic rate. Some burrowers (e.g. the lugworm, *Arenicola marina*) have oxygen-carrying blood pigments (e.g. haemoglobin) that only release oxygen for metabolic needs during low tide.

Some species have developed the capacity to breathe from the atmosphere. Mussels 'gape' at low tide, and can take oxygen from the air as long as their gills are moist. The tiny sand-bubbler crab, which you will see near the beginning of the video on 'Tidal Seas', lives in the upper part of the intertidal zone and spends quite long periods exposed to the air. On each leg, it has a membranous disk that allows it to take oxygen directly from the air, rather than from the water.

Organisms living in estuaries, where rivers enter the sea, are all to a greater or lesser extent affected by the tide. As the tide rises, seawater flows up the estuary, often flooding large areas of mud and sand flats. Because seawater is more dense than freshwater, it may form a kind of wedge which intrudes up the river below the outflowing freshwater, but if tidal currents and/or river flow are strong, the incoming seawater is mixed with the outflowing river water. Either way, estuarine organisms are alternately covered by seawater and exposed to the air, or alternately bathed in fresh river water and salty seawater (or a mixture of the two).

As mentioned in Section 2.1.2, the body fluids of most marine invertebrates are in osmotic balance with the water that surrounds them, but only relatively few of these can tolerate the extreme changes that living in an estuary would impose – the salinity at a given point in an estuary can fluctuate between 2 and 30 (undiluted seawater has a salinity of about 34–35). Most freshwater animals are able to regulate their body fluids to keep their internal salt concentration higher than that of the surrounding water, but relatively few could survive in salinities greater than 9. The species that are able to benefit from the sheltered and food-rich environments provided by estuaries are therefore those relatively select few – usually of marine origin – that are able to cope with the changing salinities.

Many crustaceans (e.g. some species of amphipods and the crab *Carcinus*), and the polychaete *Nereis diversicolor* (the ragworm) are, like freshwater animals, able to keep their internal salt concentration higher than that of the surrounding water. By contrast, most of the polychaete worms (e.g. *Arenicola*, the lugworm) and molluscs (e.g. the bivalve *Macoma*, and the snail *Hydrobia*) are able to tolerate considerable changes in the concentration of salts in their body fluids.

A number of marine species are capable of rapidly adjusting their osmotic balance to varying salinity. Many fish species can swim across strong salinity gradients – eels, striped bass and salmon are just a few examples that migrate from seawater to freshwater in a few weeks or even days. Many crab species also migrate over large salinity ranges.

At this point, we need to make a short diversion to look at a fundamental aspect of interactions between organisms in the ocean.

3.3 Feeding strategies and techniques

Although it is not specifically discussed in the 'Tidal Seas' video, at this stage it would be useful to think in a general way about *what* animals eat, and *how* they feed – a subject touched on in Section 3.2.2.

- What are the main categories of animal, in terms of what they eat?

- The two most obvious categories are **herbivore** (plant-eater) and **carnivore** (meat-eater). You may also have thought of **omnivore** (eater of everything – an animal that eats a wide range of food of various origins – humans and dogs are good terrestrial examples).

As on land, marine herbivores are sometimes divided into grazers, which remove plant material from a surface (e.g. as mentioned in Section 3.2.2, some species of gastropod mollusc scrape algae from rocks), and browsers, which bite off pieces of plant material.

Predators catch their own (animal) food and scavengers live on the food that other animals have not consumed. There is another very large group which also in a way consists of scavengers – the **detritus-feeders** (or detritivores). Detritus-feeders eat the remains of plants and animals (including the colonies of bacteria which are decomposing those remains), and the debris produced by other animals either during feeding, or as faecal pellets. Larger detritivores of necessity eat any microscopic flora and fauna living amongst the organic debris. Most detritus-feeders are benthic – i.e. they live on or in the sea-bed. There are five main ways in which they obtain their food.

1. Some, including several types of polychaete worm, have tentacles with cilia (small hairs), which they spread over or through the mud or sand. Particles of food are collected and brought to the mouth by beating of the cilia or movements of the tentacles.
2. Many bivalve molluscs (i.e. molluscs with two hinged shells, or 'valves' that can completely enclose the body) live buried in the sediment and extend long flexible siphons that they move over the sediment surface, sucking in particles like a vacuum cleaner. The food items are sorted from the sediment particles within the mantle. (The mantle of a mollusc is the part of the body which encloses the gills; it is the outer layer of the mantle which secretes the calcium carbonate shell.)
3. Some crustaceans, including some crabs and amphipods, sort particles mechanically with their appendages.
4. A number of detritus-feeders, including polychaetes such as *Arenicola* (the lugworm) and some echinoderms, swallow the sediment and digest any nutritious material (including small animals and algae) as it passes through the gut. They then expel the undigested material as a 'cast' on the sediment surface (you may well have seen such casts on recently exposed sand and mud). These detritus-feeding animals are therefore also known as **deposit-feeders**.
5. **Suspension-feeders**, as the name suggests, take food particles suspended in the water column. These particles may simply be sucked in, as in the case of cockles (*Cerastoderma*), which have short inflexible siphons and take in sediment and detritus when the sea-bed is disturbed by waves, or by the incoming tide. Particles may also be collected using feathery appendages which are extended out into the water column to trap particles. Like the other types of feeders described above, suspension-feeders cannot trap food selectively, so animals that consume plankton will also unavoidably take in other particles. For obvious reasons, suspension-feeders are often also called **filter-feeders**.

Some suspension-feeders, such as shallow-water species of sponges and tunicates, are *active*, using their own energy to push water through a filtering structure. This strategy is only worthwhile where concentrations of suspended particles are sufficiently high to repay the energy costs of pumping. Passive suspension-feeders, by contrast, extend tentacles or filtering 'arms' into the current, relying on it to bring food. This technique is only successful in environments where flow conditions are predictable, and the current is fast enough to bring a sufficient supply of food. Sea-lilies, feather stars and seafans are passive suspension-feeders, as are some species of polychaetes.

If you want to know more about the phyla to which polychaete worms, bivalve molluscs, crustaceans and echinoderms belong, you can click on the relevant groups of branches of the tree in the 'Biological Diversity' module on your CD. The appropriate branches are those for annelid worms (group 3), molluscs (group 4), arthropods (group 6) and chordates (group 7).

▶▶ *This is a good time to watch the 'Tidal Seas' video (VC1). For each animal shown, try to make a mental note of (or jot down) what category of feeder it is (when possible), and what its feeding technique is (remember that you can make use of the 'pause' button). For the sequence about land crabs towards the end, try to think about what the tidal range will be at the time in question, and how this will affect the speed of tidal currents.*

To get the most out of the video, you might find it helpful to first skim through the notes below: you can read them again afterwards, if you wish. ◀◀

Notes on the 'Tidal Seas' video

These notes are provided in the order in which the points come up in the video. The numbers are the time codes, shown in the top right-hand corner of the screen.

[0:19:47] The Amazon bore is analogous to a sonic boom. The shape and topography of the Amazon estuary are such that the speed of the tidal wave generated is greater than can be freely propagated up the river. As a result, the wave becomes compressed into a short, steep 'shock wave'. The Amazon bore – known also as the *pororoca* – reaches a height of about 5 m. There are many other less spectacular bores, for example in the Trent, Yangtze, Colorado and Elbe. The Severn bore reaches 1–2 m on spring tides.

[0:20:30] At this point, the narration states: 'The Moon *does* create strong tides out in the world's oceans …'. As you know, the rise and fall of the tide (or, looked at another way, the progress of the tidal wave; Figure 3.3) does indeed affect the whole ocean. Nevertheless, tidal ranges are greatest, and tidal currents therefore strongest, around the coast.

[0:23:03] 'The flowing tide may provide a feast … but before long it will turn.' Of course, tidal currents can cause mixing and high biological production, whichever direction they are flowing in. Here, the narration is referring specifically to the situation in the Bay of Fundy, where large areas of food-rich shallow water 'appear' at high tide.

[0:23:40] The small creatures living amongst the sand grains, pronounced 'myofauna', are spelt meiofauna; this means 'creatures of intermediate size', i.e. neither microfauna, which can only be seen properly under a microscope, nor larger 'megafauna' easily seen with the naked eye (e.g. crabs). (Translucent grains of the mineral quartz can be clearly seen here.)

[0:30:37] The small invertebrates disappearing into the mud include *Corophium* (an amphipod) plus several ragworms and a lugworm (all polychaetes).

[0:31:04–0:31:33] In this sequence, you can see beak shapes and feeding techniques of knot, redshank, oystercatcher and curlew.

[0:36:30] Surprisingly, barnacles are crustaceans (i.e. the same group as crabs, shrimps and copepods); the ones shown here are *stalked* barnacles, not the barnacles usually seen around the British Isles. Barnacle larvae are planktonic and recognizably crustacean, but the adults live attached to rocks, to coral skeletons, to shells of other animals, or even to whales. They feed [0:39:25] by sweeping phytoplankton from the water using six modified legs or *cirri* (plural of *cirrus*, meaning a tendril), hence the name of their taxonomic class, Cirripedia. When exposed at low tide, they withdraw into their shell (which is made up of a number of calcium carbonate plates) along with some seawater which prevents them drying out.

[0:41:59] Here, 'weak tides' means weak tidal *currents*.

[0:44:41] As you may realize from the text above, it is *not* generally true that the Moon's gravitational pull is weaker nearer the Earth's Equator.

[0:45:06] Jellyfish are classified as plankton even though they can swim, because they cannot make headway against more than a very weak current.

[0:45:49] '... the tide is sweeping the whole swarm towards the Bahamas ...' should strictly say '... tidal *currents* are sweeping ...'.

[0:46:25] Soft corals are corals without a hard skeleton of calcium carbonate. They do not form reefs (see Chapter 7).

[0:46:52–0:47:35] Seagrasses are flowering plants, not algae. They are found in shallow waters with a soft sea-bed, in temperate, subtropical and tropical regions. Most species grow in sheltered subtidal areas. The seagrass species *Zostera marina* (also known as eelgrass) is widespread in shallow waters around the Atlantic, eastern Pacific and Mediterranean. Other species of seagrass include turtlegrass (*Thalassia testudinum*), which dominates shallow soft areas in the Caribbean. Seagrasses probably evolved from land plants, and have simple reduced flowers. The pollen is dispersed by water.

[0:53:24–0:53:26] As seawater has a high concentration of dissolved ions, it is a good conductor of electricity.

[0:54:23] Why tides are large (extra high highs, extra low lows) at the equinox will become clear in Chapter 4.

[0:55:30] The statement 'the water starts losing what little oxygen it contained and quickly becomes stagnant' may be a bit puzzling. As discussed in Section 2.1, oxygen is added to surface water by being mixed down into it, and is also produced by photosynthesis. The water in the mangroves is unlikely to be oxygen-rich: it is sheltered and unlikely to have been recently churned up and thus oxygenated; it is shaded by the trees, and so does not support very much photosynthesis; *and* warm water can hold much less dissolved gas than cold water. Furthermore, the oxygen that *is* there will be being used up by respiration, and by the decomposition of leaves and other organic debris. As a result, the sheltered waters among the mangrove trees readily become low in oxygen (i.e. become 'flat').

[0:56:54] The influence of hurricanes on sea-level will be explained in Section 3.6.

Now try Questions 3.4 and 3.5, which relate to material in the 'Tidal Seas' video. (You may need to replay some sequences.)

Question 3.4 Towards the end of the 'Tidal Seas' video, there is a sequence about Christmas Island land crabs [1:00:33 to 1:02:19]. We are told that the crabs are breeding at a time of 'Half Moon in November'.

(a) At what stage of the tidal cycle (spring, neap, or in between) do the baby crabs return to the beach from the sea? What is the phase of the Moon at that time?

(b) Why do you think the baby crabs 'choose' this time to return to the land? ◀

Question 3.5

(a) How would you describe the feeding strategy of the surf-riding snails?

(b) Give at least *three* examples of suspension-feeders, shown in the 'Tidal Seas' video. For each, state whether they are active or passive suspension-feeders. ◀

3.4 Hitching a ride on the tide

The 'Tidal Seas' video contains some sequences of flounder 'hitching a ride on the tide' to travel in to shallow waters. Bottom-dwelling (i.e. **demersal**) fish populations living in shelf seas often use tidal currents to save energy on much longer journeys – the migrations that they make between their feeding areas and the spawning ground. Plaice living in the North Sea are a good example of this: when the tidal currents are flowing in the appropriate direction, they swim with the current a few metres above the bottom. At slack water, they descend to the sea-bed and remain there during the other half of the tidal cycle (while the tidal currents flow in the other direction). When the tide runs favourably once more, they then ascend into the water column and continue their journey.

Estuarine fish, and invertebrate larvae that need to develop in relatively fresh water, often stay on or near the bottom during the ebbing tide, and move up into the water column during the flood tide. This technique prevents them from being flushed out of the estuary, and in some cases is used to move upstream. Many other invertebrates and fish hatch in estuarine waters, but their larvae and juveniles need to be dispersed into coastal waters to develop. These animals may time their breeding so that the young can use the currents of the ebb tide to carry them out of the estuary.

3.5 Staying put, in spite of the tide

For many organisms living in the intertidal zone, staying put is simply a question of being as strongly attached to a rock as possible, or of being buried safe below the surface of the sand or mud. But what about those animals that do *not* live permanently attached to rocks or buried in the sediment? Many groups of organisms roam around in a particular part of the intertidal zone to which they are adapted – for example, sandhoppers and small crabs scavenging for scraps. How do these animals prevent themselves from being carried away from their home range, into a part of the intertidal zone to which they are not suited?

Sandhoppers are semi-terrestrial amphipod crustaceans which live by consuming algal debris along the strandline (they are the 'beach amphipods' in Figure 3.5b). You may well have seen them occasionally, but during the day they generally stay buried in the sand along a very narrow zone just above the high tide mark. At night, safe from birds, they are widely dispersed, foraging on moist sand in the intertidal zone. So how do they know when and where to burrow back into the sand? Sandhoppers are relatively easy to study in the laboratory and it turns out that they have an internal clock, which triggers emergence after dusk but is not dependent on how light or dark it is – which would not in any case be visible from under the sand! The sandhoppers' cycle, like most such internally generated daily ('circadian') rhythms, including that of humans, is slightly longer than 24 hours, but is 'reset' each day at dawn, when they return to the high tide line to burrow again. It seems that the sandhoppers are able to determine which direction to go as dawn approaches by heading for the light/dark boundary corresponding to the dune/sky horizon.

It might not seem strange that intertidal animals emerge from their burrows or rock crevices when covered by the flooding tide, but how do they avoid being carried downshore by the ebbing tide? For a number of crustaceans that have been studied (e.g. the isopod crustacean *Eurydice pulchra*, a close relation of the woodlouse), the answer seems to lie in the fact that they have an internal cycle which prompts them to emerge and become active only around times of high tide, being safely back in their shelters by the time the tide is ebbing. Another risk faced by intertidal animals is that of being stranded 'high and dry' during times of neap tides. Again, this may be combated by means of a 'modulation' of the tidal activity cycle mentioned above, whereby the periods of greatest activity occur just after New Moon and Full Moon. Possession of one or more internal clocks, whether simply ~ 24-hour or attuned to the local tidal cycle, combined with 'orientation cues' – e.g. the light/dark boundary corresponding to the horizon – may explain a lot of otherwise mysterious behaviour.

3.6 Tides and weather

In the 'Tidal Seas' video, there is a reference [0:56:54] to a hurricane leading to extra high tides. As this suggests, the heights of tides around the coast are significantly affected by the weather. When the atmospheric pressure is low (i.e. there is a depression), the weight of the atmosphere acting downwards on the ocean is less, and sea-level is correspondingly higher (this is sometimes called the 'inverse barometer' effect). In fact, a reduction of atmospheric pressure of 1 millibar results in a rise in sea-level of 1 centimetre.

A large rise in sea-level caused by very low atmospheric pressure is known as a **storm surge**. As low pressure centres are associated with storms and strong winds, the high sea-levels caused directly by the low pressure are very often made even higher by the effect of strong winds driving water onshore. This is why there are often flood warnings for coastal regions when exceptionally low atmospheric pressure is expected. Coastal areas around the southern North Sea are particularly vulnerable to flooding from storm surges.

Hurricanes – also known as typhoons and cyclones – are strong winds blowing around very low pressure centres (sometimes below 920 millibars). The combination of large volumes of water being driven onshore by strong winds, and the local rise in sea-level in response to the extreme low pressure, means that the resulting storm surges can be devastating, both for coastal wildlife and for local human populations, especially if the storm surge coincides with high tide.

▶▶ *This chapter has been focusing on the coast, but in the next two chapters we move out into the deeper waters over the continental shelf and the very deep waters of the open ocean. So if you have not already done so, you should now study the module 'Living in the Oceans' on your* Life in the Oceans *CD. As mentioned earlier, this module takes an introductory look at what it is like living in the ocean, from the point of view of a selection of organisms, all of which you will encounter later, either in the text or in one or more of the videos.* ◀◀

4 Light, life and nutrients

Phytoplankton are sometimes called the 'grass of the sea' because, directly or indirectly, they sustain almost all other marine life. As discussed in Section 1.3, because animals cannot build their own organic material, they have to depend on plants, either directly or indirectly. Building living material from non-living 'raw materials' is known as **primary production**.

- What are the raw materials used in photosynthesis?
- They are carbon dioxide (which in the case of phytoplankton photosynthesis is in dissolved form) and water.

For completeness, we should mention that some bacteria are primary producers, and they use other raw materials. The role of this type of bacteria in deep-sea ecosystems will be discussed later in the course.

In Section 1.3, we expressed photosynthesis in terms of the following 'word equation':

$$\underset{\text{(dissolved in seawater)}}{\text{carbon dioxide}} + \text{water} + \text{light energy} \longrightarrow \text{carbohydrate} + \text{oxygen} \qquad (1.1a)$$

(Note that we have now changed the label below 'carbon dioxide' to correspond to photosynthesis in the ocean.)

Carbohydrates are made up of carbon, hydrogen and oxygen, with one carbon atom and one oxygen atom for every two hydrogen atoms; the simplest carbohydrate is glucose, and its chemical formula is $C_6H_{12}O_6$. If we use this formula to represent organic matter in general, and adopt the convention of putting the energy used in the reaction over the arrow, we can write a chemical equation for photosynthesis as follows:

$$\underset{\text{(dissolved in seawater)}}{6CO_2\text{ (gas)}} + 6H_2O\text{ (liquid)} \xrightarrow{\text{light energy}} \underset{\text{carbohydrate}}{C_6H_{12}O_6} + \underset{\text{oxygen}}{6O_2\text{ (gas)}} \qquad (4.1)$$

Like any other equation, a chemical equation has to balance, i.e. for each type of atom involved in the reaction, there should be the same number on each side of the arrow. In this case, each side has 6 C's, 12 H's and 6 O's. (Don't worry if you are not comfortable with chemical equations – just concentrate on the 'word equation'.)

Figure 4.1 shows the distribution of primary production on Earth, based on data collected by satellite-borne sensors which measure concentrations of the plant pigment, chlorophyll. This map effectively shows how much plant material (i.e. plant **biomass**) is present *on average* throughout the year. It conveys nothing about the *rate* at which the plant material is produced (i.e. **productivity**), and cannot give any indication of seasonal variations at a given location.

Study Figure 4.1.

- Generally speaking, where are the most productive regions of the ocean? And would you say that marine production is limited by low temperatures?
- The most productive regions are along coasts (especially off river mouths), in shelf seas (cf. Figure 3.4) and in the open oceans north and south of about 35° of latitude. There is certainly no indication that marine production is limited by low temperatures – rather the opposite, in fact.

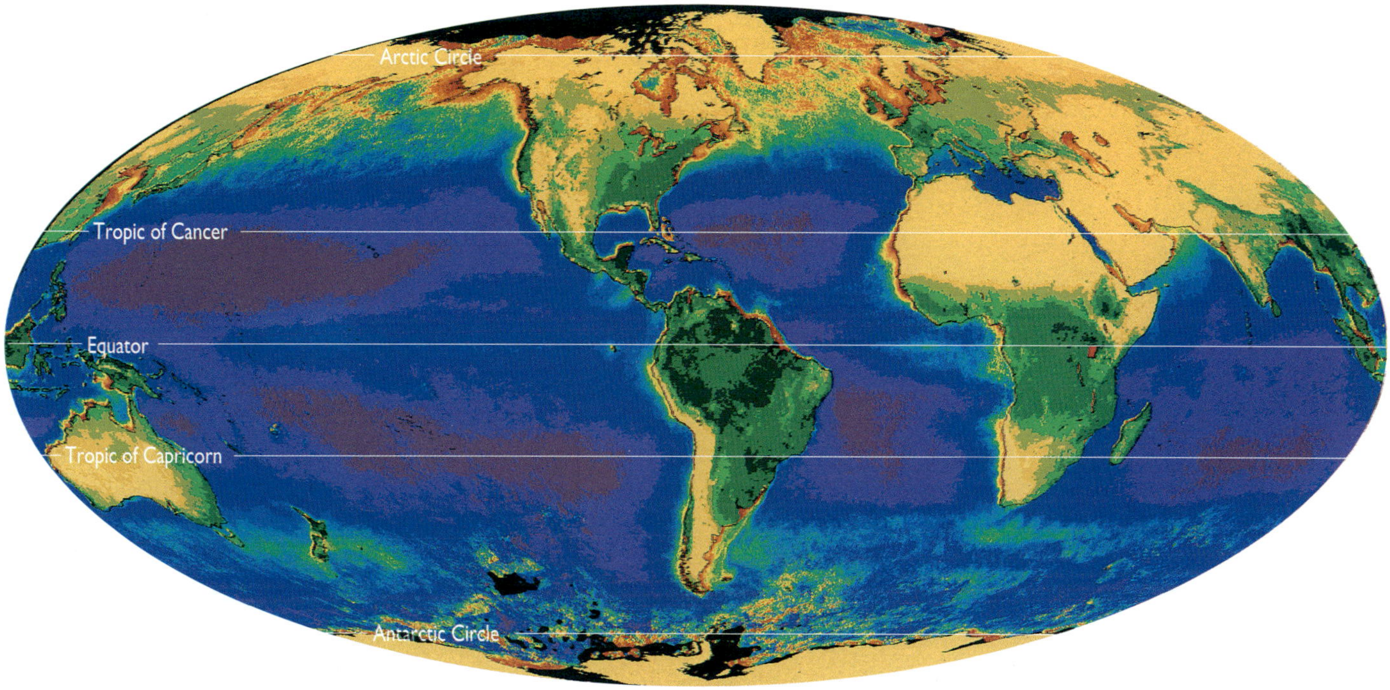

Figure 4.1 Terrestrial and marine plants together make up 99% of the living material on Earth. The map shows the average global distribution of primary production, i.e. plant growth, on land and in surface waters, as indicated by chlorophyll concentration (determined using satellite-borne sensors). In surface waters, regions of highest production are bright red, followed by yellow, green and blue. Least productive oceanic regions are shown purplish-red. (On land, the greatest production is in the tropical rainforests, shown in dark green. Differences between the roles of plants in oceanic and terrestrial ecosystems will be discussed in the 'Ecosystems and Food Web' module.) The Tropics of Cancer and Capricorn are at 23.4 °N and 23.4 °S, respectively.

The high production of plant material around coasts is partly a result of high concentrations of fertilizers and sewage entering the sea in rivers and in run-off from the land, and is perhaps not surprising. But why should marine production be greater in subpolar regions than it is in the tropics and subtropics? The answer to this will begin to become clear in the next section.

4.1 Why the Earth has seasons

Figure 4.1 strongly suggests that, in the oceans, primary productivity is *not* limited by low temperature. However, as noted above, this map does not tell us *anything* about the effects of seasonal changes in temperature or light levels. Before looking more closely at what these effects might be, let's see why the Earth has seasons at all.

Figure 4.2 (overleaf) shows the effect of a beam of sunlight falling upon the surface of the Earth at low latitudes (near the Equator) and at high latitudes (nearer to polar regions). The intensity of solar radiation at the Earth's surface (on the diagram, the number of rays per unit area) – and hence the surface temperature – depends on the angle of the rays with respect to the surface. The more oblique the rays, the larger the area over which the solar energy will be spread, and the lower its intensity at that location.

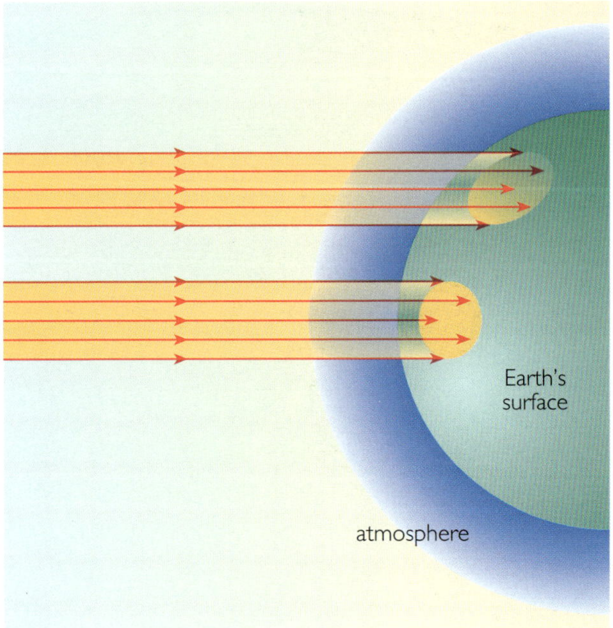

Figure 4.2 Schematic diagram showing why there is a difference in the intensity of solar radiation reaching the Earth's surface at different latitudes.

- Bearing in mind that the atmosphere absorbs a proportion of incoming solar energy, can you suggest *another* reason why the intensity of solar radiation at the Earth's surface, and hence the surface temperature, is generally lower at high latitudes than at low latitudes?

- The more oblique the rays, the greater the thickness of absorbing atmosphere they have to pass through before reaching the Earth's surface.

If the Earth's axis of rotation were at right angles to the plane of its orbit around the Sun, for any given latitude the angle at which the rays of the noonday Sun fell upon the Earth's surface would remain constant, with higher latitudes in both hemispheres always receiving less solar radiation than lower latitudes (Figure 4.3). The noonday Sun would be overhead at the Equator, and nowhere else. Everywhere on the globe, night and day would each be 12 hours long – there would be a permanent **equinox**.

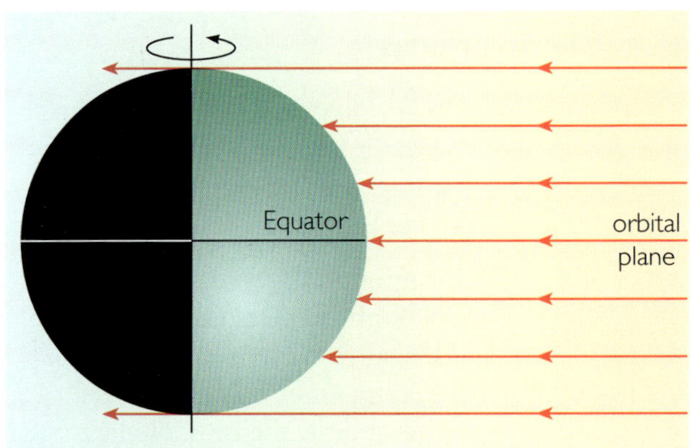

Figure 4.3 Hypothetical situation in which the Earth's axis of rotation is at right angles to the plane of its orbit around the Sun.

However, the Earth's axis of rotation is *tilted* with respect to the plane of its orbit, currently at an angle of 23.4°. As a result, the latitude at which the noonday Sun is overhead continually migrates between 23.4° N (the Tropic of Cancer) and 23.4° S (the Tropic of Capricorn) and back again. It is overhead at the Equator only twice a year, at the equinoxes, when the lengths of day and night are equal.

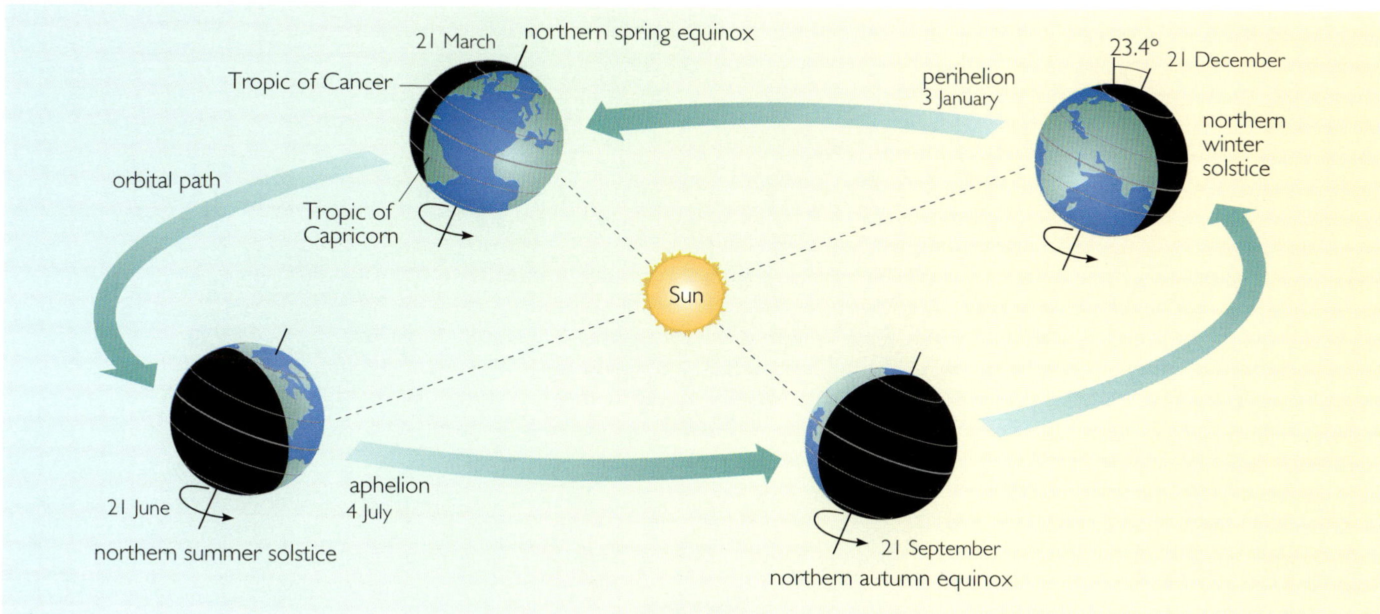

Figure 4.4 The four seasons (here given for the Northern Hemisphere) related to the Earth's orbit around the Sun. The Earth's axis is tilted at approximately 23.4° to a line at right angles to the plane of its orbit around the Sun, with the result that between latitudes 23.4° N and 23.4° S (the Tropics of Cancer and Capricorn, respectively), the noonday Sun will be directly overhead for at least part of the year. When the Sun is overhead one or other of the Tropics, it is the summer solstice (the longest day) in the hemisphere experiencing summer, and the winter solstice (the shortest day) in the other. Poleward of the Tropics, the Sun is never directly overhead.

Figure 4.4 shows the passage of the seasons for the Northern Hemisphere. At the summer solstice (the longest day, 21 June), the noonday Sun is overhead at 23.4° N. Days then get shorter until the winter solstice (the shortest day, 21 December), when the noonday Sun is overhead at 23.4° S; after that, days begin to lengthen again. Figure 4.5b shows the change over the course of the year of the angle that solar radiation makes with the Earth's surface. After the northern summer solstice (1), an observer on the Earth sees the Sun move south. This continues until the southern summer solstice (3), after which the Sun starts to move north again.

Question 4.1 What do you think would happen to the latitudes of the Tropics of Cancer and Capricorn (currently at 23.4° N and 23.4° S) and those of the Arctic and Antarctic Circles (currently at 66.6° N and 66.6° S) if the tilt of the Earth's axis increased from 23.4° (which it is at present) to 30°? *Hint*: Look at Figure 4.5a. ◀

You may remember that in the 'Tidal Seas' video there is a sequence about very high tides flooding into a mangrove swamp. We are told in the narration that 'since this is the equinox, the tide is rising fast', which suggests that the tidal range is particularly large. As you now know, there are in fact two equinoxes each year, one in the spring and one in the autumn (Figures 4.4 and 4.5).

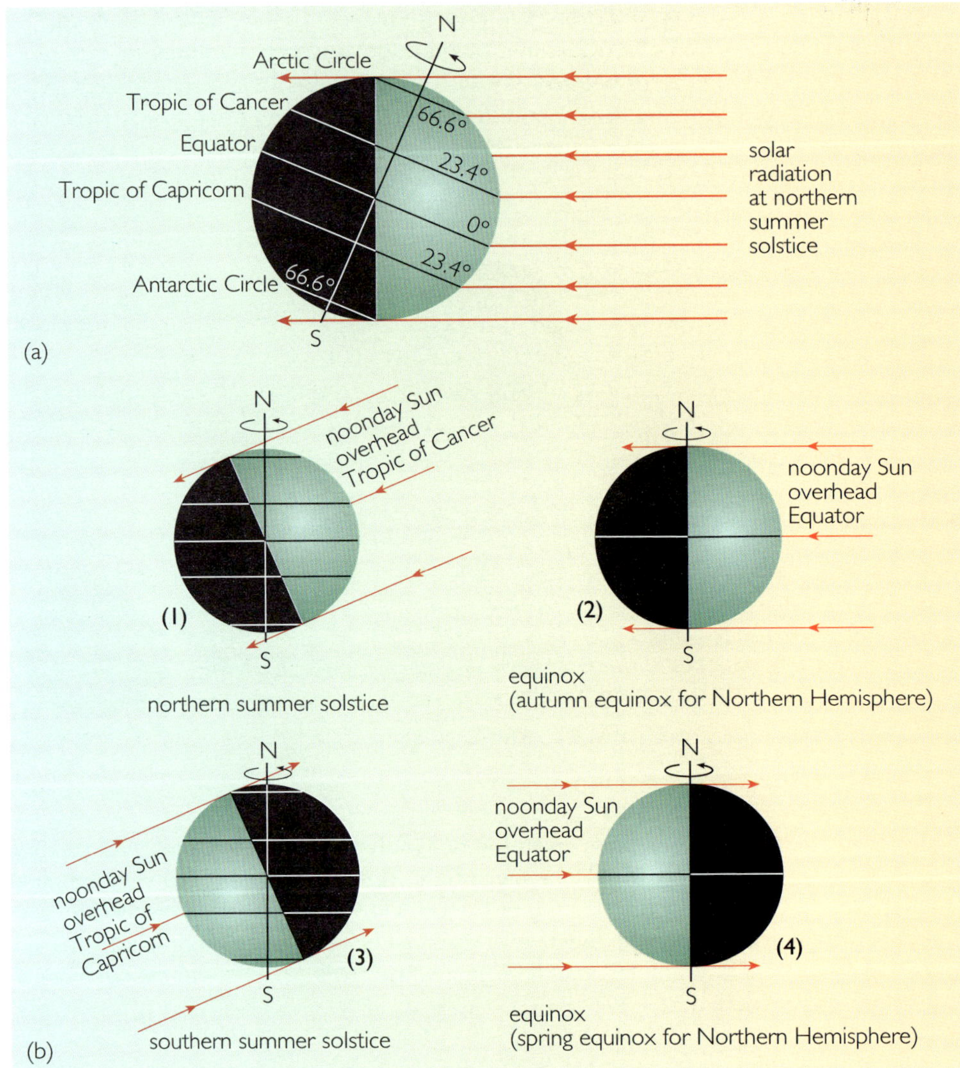

Figure 4.5 (a) The angle of tilt of the Earth's axis (at present 23.4°) determines the latitude of the Tropics (where the Sun is overhead at one of the solstices) and of the Arctic and Antarctic Circles (66.6°, which is 90° minus 23.4°), poleward of which there is total darkness for at least part of the year.
(b) (We recommend you study this in conjunction with Figure 4.4.) The passage of the seasons, shown in terms of the position of the noonday Sun with respect to the Earth. (1) The northern summer solstice, with the noonday Sun overhead the Tropic of Cancer, and (3) the southern summer solstice, when the noonday Sun is overhead the Tropic of Capricorn. In between the solstices are the equinoxes ((2) and (4)), when the Sun is overhead at the Equator, Northern and Southern Hemisphere are illuminated equally, and days and nights are equal at all latitudes.

- So why are tides unusually high around the time of the equinoxes?

- At the equinoxes, the Earth is oriented with respect to the Sun in such a way that the Sun is 'above the Equator', so that the gravitational attraction of the Sun aligns with that of the Moon.

However, things are slightly more complicated than this, because the Moon's orbit around the Earth is *not* permanently above the Equator as Figure 3.1 seems to suggest. Over the course of about 27 days, the plane of the Moon's orbit (and hence that of the 'ellipsoid') tilts, moving between about 28° north of the Equator and 28° south of the Equator. Furthermore, the orbit of the Moon around the Earth is elliptical (like that of the Earth around the Sun) so the very highest spring tides occur when equinoxes coincide with times when the Moon is at its closest to the Earth – a situation known as *perigee*.

4.2 Light in the oceans

While watching the Blue Planet videos, you will probably have noticed that the quality of the underwater light is quite variable, even allowing for the fact that filming requires relatively good light (even artificial lighting on occasions). So why does the quality of light in, say, the open ocean or over a coral reef, differ from that in, say, a temperate shelf sea?

4.2.1 Light penetration, colour and visibility

Visible light is a form of electromagnetic radiation. Light that we perceive as white is made up of a continuum (spectrum) of different colours – violet, blue, green, yellow, orange and red – the colours seen in a rainbow (as shown in the 'Living in the Oceans' module of your CD). When sunlight enters the ocean, its total intensity decreases more or less exponentially, as shown by the black curves in Figure 4.6a and b. In fact, the curves in Figure 4.6 are somewhat unrealistic because they have

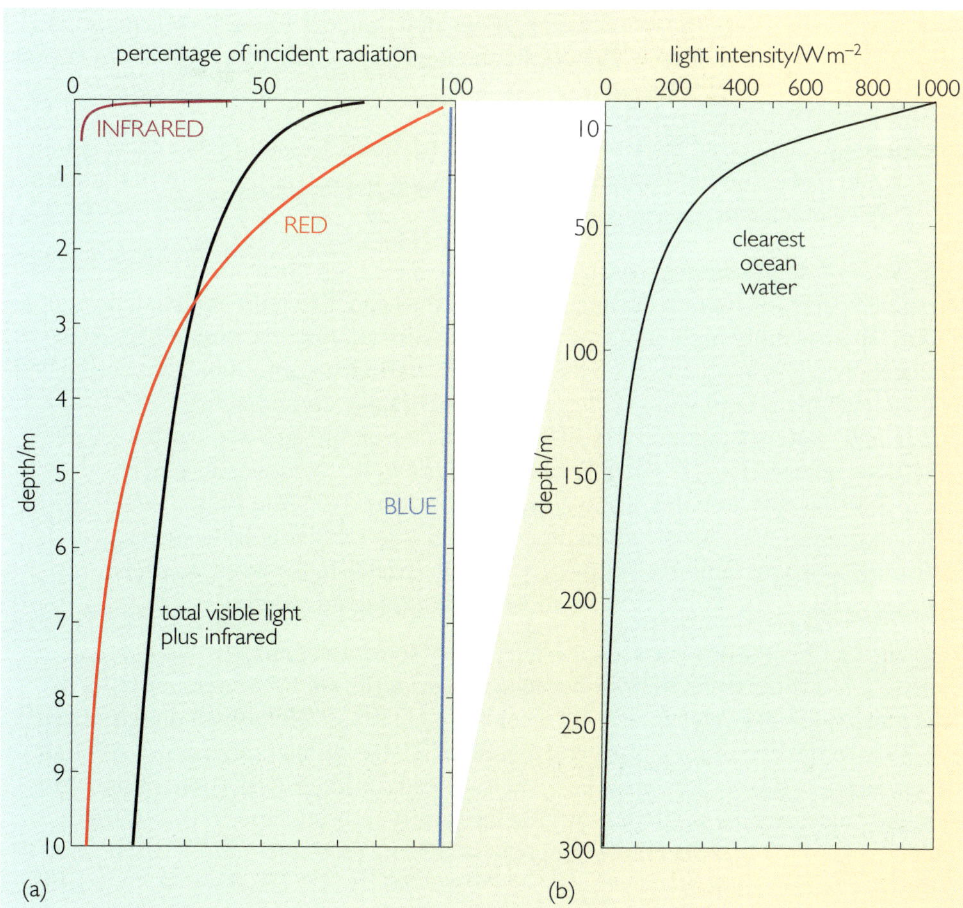

Figure 4.6 (a) Profile showing the variation with depth in the uppermost 10 m of the ocean of total light intensity (black curve), plus profiles for the intensities of red light, blue light and infrared (i.e. thermal) radiation, all plotted relative to their intensity at the surface. These plots have been calculated assuming that the water is clear, and that all of the solar radiation that reaches the sea-surface passes through it, which is not the case (see text). (b) Profile showing the decline of total light intensity with depth in the uppermost 300 m of the ocean, assuming bright sunlight (an intensity of about 1000 W m^{-2} (watts per square metre) at the surface) and the clearest open ocean water.

been plotted assuming that *all* the sunlight that reaches the sea-surface passes through, which of course it does not: some is reflected from the surface, and some is absorbed and scattered by foam, etc. The proportion of incoming sunlight reflected from the sea-surface changes over the course of the day (and with the seasons), because it is significantly greater when the Sun is low in the sky.

The light energy is absorbed by particles in the water column, both non-living (sediment particles) and living (including phytoplankton, which use the light in photosynthesis). Light is also absorbed by seawater itself, and by organic compounds dissolved in the seawater. It is also scattered (deflected 'off course') by multiple reflections from suspended particles; most of the scattering is forward, i.e. the path of most of the scattered light is deflected only slightly from its original direction.

It is important to be clear that the curves in Figure 4.6 show the variation of light intensity with depth *at a single point in the ocean*. This type of curve, often used in oceanographic work, is known as a *profile*.

- According to the black profile in Figure 4.6a, at roughly what depth in the ocean has the total light intensity been reduced to 50% of that incident at the surface? (Ignore the fact that the black profile includes a small contribution from the infrared.)

  (If you need reminding about graphs, practise on this one. Draw a vertical pencil line from the tick mark for 50% down to the black curve. Then, at the point where your pencil line crosses the black curve, draw a horizontal line across the graph until it intersects the vertical axis. You can now read off your answer.)

- Using the method just outlined, we get a value of about 0.6 m, or 60 cm. So, in the topmost 60 cm or so of the ocean, the intensity of sunlight coming down from above is reduced by half.

Question 4.2 Thinking back to both Figures 3.4 and 4.1, would you expect sunlight to penetrate further down through the water column in coastal waters or in the open ocean? Give at least *two* reasons for your answer. ◀

As Figure 3.4 demonstrates, coastal waters may have high concentrations of suspended particles (sediments and phytoplankton) and also tend to have a distinctive colour. Rivers supply high concentrations of dissolved organic ('humic') material produced by decaying plants, and there are also various organic substances produced by the metabolism of plankton. These dissolved organic compounds give coastal (and inland) waters a distinctive yellow–brown coloration, and in older books are sometimes referred to as *Gelbstoff*, which is German for 'yellow substance'. Figure 3.4 suggests how this name arose – the outflow from the Baltic, which has a high concentration of dissolved organic material (but relatively little suspended sediment), looks particularly yellow. By contrast, water in the open ocean is especially clear – the full reason for this will be explained shortly.

Visibility is a matter of contrast – an object may show up against its background because it is a different colour, or because it has a different brightness, or both. An object viewed underwater is seen by means of light rays which travel directly from the object to the eye of the observer. However, like the light coming down through the sea-surface, this will be absorbed and scattered. Furthermore, some of the light from the object will be scattered towards the observer, producing a 'veil of light' behind which the object becomes progressively more indistinct until it disappears against the background.

Except in very shallow water, brightness contrast has a much greater effect on visibility than colour contrast. This is because at depths greater than a few tens of metres, not only has the intensity of the light coming down from above been greatly reduced by absorption and scattering, but the light has become almost monochromatic, i.e. of one colour (cf. the 'Living in the Oceans' module).

- According to the idealized plots in Figure 4.6a, roughly what percentage of blue light passing through the sea-surface penetrates to a depth of 10 m? What percentage of red light penetrates this far?

- More than 95% of blue light penetrates to a depth of 10 m, but only about 5% of red light.

Water molecules themselves preferentially absorb light at the red end of the spectrum, and absorb blue light the least. This is why although a small volume of water appears colourless (e.g. in a kitchen sink), a larger volume (e.g. in a swimming pool) looks blue. In fact, in clear ocean water, light from the blue–green part of the spectrum penetrates furthest, which means that underwater everything has a blue–green hue.

Seawater also often looks greenish because of the presence of phytoplankton containing chlorophyll. Chlorophyll looks green because it most strongly reflects green light (the middle of the visible spectrum), and most strongly absorbs red light and violet–blue light (at either end of the visible spectrum). There are actually a number of different photosynthetic pigments, of which chlorophyll is the most common. The other photosynthetic pigments absorb light in other parts of the spectrum, and as a result some algae look brown, golden or even red in colour.

- Thinking back to Section 3.2.2, does the fact that blue–green light penetrates furthest help to explain why brown seaweeds tend to predominate in deeper water?

- Yes. Fucoxanthin, the main pigment in brown seaweeds, absorbs blue–green light most efficiently and reflects light of other colours (which is why these seaweeds look brown).

Subtidal red seaweeds also contain pigments that absorb blue–green light. In fact, red and brown seaweeds *also* contain chlorophyll, but its colour is masked by the other pigments. Presumably the chlorophyll comes into its own at low tide, when the seaweeds are not as deeply submerged. (Interestingly, in very turbid water, it is red light that penetrates the furthest.)

Figure 4.7 summarizes some of the key differences between coastal waters and those of the open ocean, as far as the penetration of sunlight is concerned. From the point of view of life in the upper part of the ocean, the most important point to note in Figure 4.7 is that phytoplankton can grow at much greater depths in the open ocean. The depth zone within which light is sufficient to support the growth and reproduction of plants is known as the **photic zone** (or, sometimes, the **euphotic zone**). Generally speaking, the depth of the photic zone in the open ocean is usually about 100 m and no deeper than 150 m. In shallow coastal seas it is often only 15 m, or even less (a few metres) if the water is turbid with riverborne sediment.

Between the photic zone and the sea-bed is the **aphotic zone**, where light levels are insufficient to meet the requirements for phytoplankton growth and reproduction (i.e. for primary production).

So would it be correct to describe the aphotic zone as 'completely dark'?

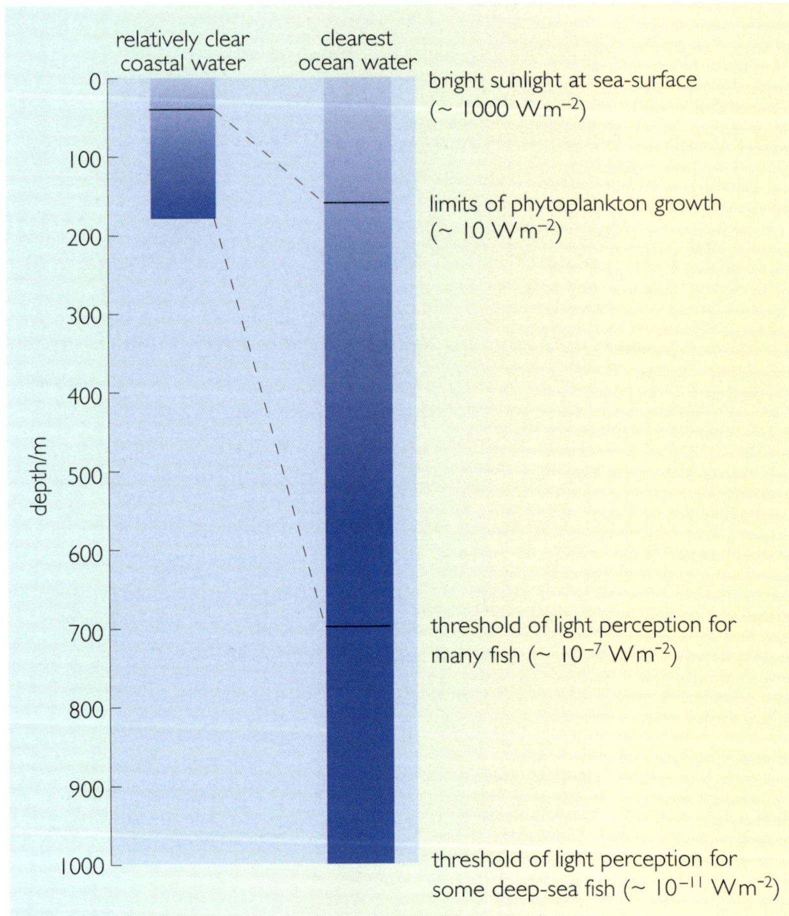

Figure 4.7 Diagram to show some of the implications of the absorption of sunlight in (left) relatively clear coastal water, and (right) the clearest ocean water (corresponding to the situation in Figure 4.6). Note how the depth scale of this figure relates to those in Figure 4.6; 10^{-7} W is one-hundredth of one-millionth of 10 W.

No – at least not as far as marine organisms are concerned. Figure 4.7 shows that the very small amount of light that penetrates to about 700 m can be perceived by many fish, and that some deep-sea fish can even perceive daylight at 1000 m depth.

This dim region between the bottom of the sunlit surface waters and about 1000 m depth is sometimes referred to as the 'twilight zone'.

4.2.2 Hiding in the twilight zone

As you will see shortly in 'The Deep' video, many animals living in the upper part of the twilight zone remain invisible to predators by being transparent – as indeed do some zooplankton living at or near the surface (including jellyfish, some species of mollusc, and other species related to those that appear in 'The Deep'). For both predator and prey alike, remaining unseen is a great advantage. Another way to avoid being spotted is to be small: with increasing depth, and decreasing light levels, organisms that could be food for predators that hunt by sight can be progressively larger without increasing the risk of being eaten.

Yet another technique for avoiding being eaten is camouflage. A fish whose camouflage techniques have been well studied is the hatchetfish, *Argyropelecus affinis*, which lives at depths where daylight is still important. Like a hatchet blade, it is flat and shiny. Viewed from the front or back, it is slim enough to be barely visible. Viewed from the side, it almost disappears, as the light reflected from its 'mirrored' flanks exactly matches the dark blue of the 'background', which grades downwards into darker and darker blue. Viewed from below, the fish is hard to see because its outline is broken up by blue light from lines of **photophores**, or light-producing organs, along its ventral (lower) surface. By having one photophore directed upwards into its tubular eyes (which also receive light from above) it is able to match the light being produced by the photophores to that coming down from above. Fine-tuning of the spectrum of light emitted by the photophores to ensure that it exactly matches the ambient light is achieved by means of adjustable magenta-coloured filters over the apertures of the photophores.

This technique of using photophores to break up the silhouette of the body is used by many fish in the twilight zone. It seems a relatively straightforward adaptation, but there are many aspects of **bioluminescence** that remain mysterious – not least, how it might have evolved in the first place. We will return to this tantalizing subject in Chapter 10.

Question 4.3

(a) Why do you think many fish living in mid-depths (i.e. in the upper part of the aphotic zone) have dark upper surfaces but silvery undersides?

(b) Given what you have been reading, especially in connection with Figure 4.6a, can you suggest why many animals living in mid-depths have evolved black or red coloration? ◀

The highly directional nature of illumination in the twilight zone has affected the types of eyes that have evolved. Animals that live in the uppermost few hundred metres are likely to need to look out for predators or for food particles coming down from above. As a result, many animals at these depths have eyes that look upwards to some extent (the hatchetfish is an extreme example); others have eyes that look sideways, or nearly so. Planktonic crustaceans often have round eyes, providing equally good vision in all directions. There is not space here to discuss this topic further, except to say that the type of eye an animal has depends on the direction(s) in which it needs to look, and the acuity (sharpness) with which it needs to see. For example, the 'alien creature' *Phronima* [1:27:14], which you will see shortly in 'The Deep' video, has double eyes, with a narrow upward-looking field-of-view of high acuity, and a wider lower field-of-view of low acuity.

▶▶ *This is a good point to watch the video on 'The Deep' on VC2, and while you are watching, pay attention to the differently shaped eyes, mentioned above. You should stop the tape at [1:32:11]. You can then leave it at this point, or rewind it to the beginning if you would like to watch the whole of 'The Deep' later.* ◀◀

Notes on 'The Deep' video (first part)

[1.25:28] Sperm whales are *the* champion divers. You will be able to find out more about how they can dive so effectively in the video entitled 'Wild Moves: Water', on VC3.

[1:27:00] The nearly transparent 'frilly' kite-shaped animal with long slender antennae, and multiple swimming legs, is *Tomopteris helgolandica. Tomopteris* is a planktonic polychaete worm, and is about 25 mm long.

[1:27:14] Amphipods are crustaceans. They are distinctive because they are laterally compressed, rather like fleas. 'Amphipod' means 'two types of legs', which distinguishes them from 'isopods', whose legs are all the same (a woodlouse is a terrestrial amphipod).

[1:28:19] You were introduced to squid in the 'Living in the Oceans' module, and will be able to learn more about them in Chapter 7.

[1:28:27] Most of the 'jellies' seen here are comb jellies, such as *Pleurobrachia* which uses two long tentacles to spread its sticky net. Comb jellies are also known as sea-gooseberries. As the video sequence shows, they swim using rows of cilia (fine hairs), reminiscent of those on a gooseberry. As you may have seen in the 'Biological Diversity' module, comb jellies are closely related to jellyfish, but are classed as ctenophores (pronounced 'tenofours') rather than cnidarians (pronounced 'nydarians'), as they do not have the stinging cells known as 'cnidoblasts' ('nettle cells'), possessed by jellyfish and other cnidarians.

[1:29:09] Siphonophores are colonial cnidarians, in which many individuals with specialized functions are combined to make one organism. At first sight, a siphonophore appears to be an ordinary jellyfish, but closer inspection shows that its 'bell' is made up of numerous compartments. The Portuguese man-o'-war (*Physalia physalia*) is a tropical siphonophore famous for its 10 m-long stinging tentacles.

[1:30:03] You can judge the hatchetfish's camouflage for yourself! Note the use of the magenta filters at [1:31:20].

4.3 Heat, light, mixing and nutrients

So far, we have been concentrating on the visible light entering the ocean. Now let's think about the infrared or thermal radiation (i.e. heat). Turn back to Figure 4.6a and study the infrared curve.

● By approximately what depth has the intensity of thermal radiation entering the ocean been reduced to 5% of its value at the surface?

○ Thermal radiation has been reduced to 5% of its value at the surface by a depth of about 0.2 m or 20 cm.

So, thermal radiation from the Sun penetrates into the ocean hardly at all; furthermore, by itself, conduction of heat by water is very, very slow. The way in which heat is carried deeper into the ocean is through *turbulent mixing*. The mechanism for downward heat transport in the ocean is analogous to the method generally used to transport hot tap water from one end of the bath to the other – by stirring! The same is true for water cooled at the surface.

The vertical distribution of temperature within the ocean is therefore a result of two main processes:

1 the warming of surface water by the Sun at low and mid-latitudes, and the limited downward mixing of this warm water to form a distinct upper layer, which is markedly less dense than the water beneath; and

2 the extreme cooling of surface water at high latitudes, so that it sinks and then flows equatorward to occupy much of the volume of the deep oceans.

The processes involved in (2) have important implications for life in the deep oceans, and we will be looking more closely at them in *Discovering the Deep Oceans*. The processes involved in (1) are intimately related to the seasonal cycle of life in the uppermost layers of the ocean, and we will now examine these processes more closely.

In winter, at high and mid-latitudes, storms churn up the surface layers of the ocean (you will see some good shots of this in the 'Seasonal Seas' video). Because the water is being cooled by cold winds, and sometimes also by evaporation (cf. Section 2.1.1), it becomes denser than the water beneath it – this is an unstable situation, so the cooled water tends to sink and displace warmer less dense water, allowing the mixing to reach to great depths. In certain high-latitude areas, winter cooling is so intense that surface water becomes sufficiently cold and dense to sink down to the sea-bed, contributing to the cold dense waters mentioned in (2) above.

In the temperate mid-latitudes, the winter 'overturn' of water may extend down to 800–1000 m, but the well-mixed layer (often referred to simply as the mixed layer) is generally only several hundred metres thick. This situation is shown schematically on the left-hand side of Figure 4.8a (overleaf). The variation of temperature with depth that results – i.e. the **temperature profile** – is shown alongside. This has a near-vertical section at the top, corresponding to the mixed layer (where temperature is more or less constant), then a section where temperature decreases relatively sharply with depth. This sloping section corresponds to the **thermocline**, which is the transition zone between the warmer surface waters above and the cold dense water below, where the temperature profile again becomes near-vertical.

- Does temperature vary markedly with depth in the deep ocean?

- No – the fact that the profile is nearly vertical below 1000 m depth suggests that temperature in the deep ocean is uniformly cold, at 3–4 °C.

The term thermocline means (vertical) temperature gradient or slope. The thermocline we have just been discussing is often referred to as the **permanent thermocline**, for reasons which will become clear shortly. (In practice, the term is used both for the water in question and the part of the temperature profile that corresponds to it.)

Over the course of spring and summer, the weather becomes calmer, and surface waters gradually warm up. The relatively unstable winter situation, where cold surface water is easily overturned by wind and waves, is replaced by a very stable situation in which the uppermost layer of water is significantly warmer and less dense. When the ocean is stably 'layered' like this, it is described as *stratified*. In these circumstances, mixing by wind and waves tends to be confined to the uppermost layer, and so the temperature profile acquires a well-defined **seasonal thermocline**, as well as the permanent thermocline below (Figure 4.8b).

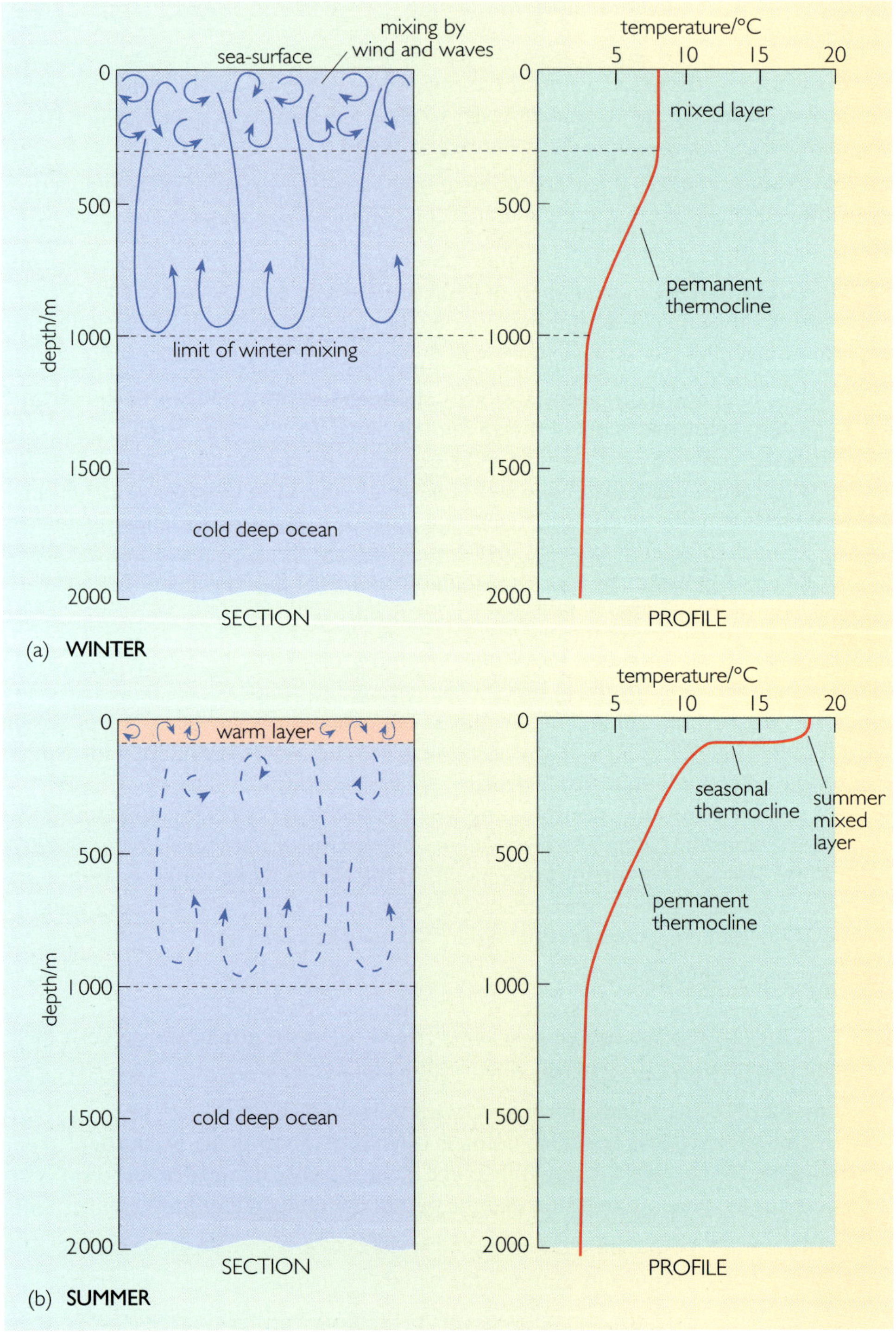

Figure 4.8 Schematic diagrams showing how the vertical distribution of temperature in the oceans in mid-latitudes results from the alternation of winter mixing and summer warming. (a) Cross-section (left) showing winter mixing, and (right) a typical winter temperature profile. (b) Cross-section (left) showing how summer warming produces a thin warm surface mixed layer, and (right) a typical summer temperature profile, with a seasonal thermocline. The effects of winter mixing (dashed arrows) remain, and contribute to the temperature gradient in the permanent thermocline, which is between the well-mixed layer (or seasonal thermocline) and the cold, deep water beneath.

Winter mixing of the surface ocean at high and mid-latitudes is extremely important for life in the oceans, because it mixes up from greater depths substances that are essential for phytoplankton growth, but which have been used up by phytoplankton over the course of the previous summer. These phytoplankton mostly either died or were eaten, and their remains sank down out of the photic zone in small clumps of organic debris known as **marine snow**. The nutrients that had been taken up by the phytoplankton were therefore removed from the photic zone, and were slowly returned to solution in deeper water during decomposition of the organic material they were part of. You might spot some marine snow in the 'Seasonal Seas' video – it can be seen clearly in the sequence about lobsters migrating to breed [1:29:20].

As far as phytoplankton are concerned, the most important (non-gaseous) constituents dissolved in seawater are nitrate (NO_3^-), phosphate (PO_4^{3-}) and silica (SiO_2) – these are known as **nutrients**. Interestingly, these biologically usable forms of nitrogen (N) and phosphorus (P) occur in seawater in the same proportions that they occur in the soft tissues of marine organisms. Nitrate and phosphate are used to make proteins, while silica is used in the external skeletons of certain groups of phytoplankton, notably diatoms.

Light levels permitting, it is the concentrations of the nutrients that determine how much phytoplankton production can take place. Other constituents are also used – for example, calcium is used to build shells and skeletons, and sodium is one of a number of elements used in soft tissues, but calcium and sodium are available in great abundance in seawater, so their precise concentrations have no effect on the growth of living organisms. Nitrate, phosphate and silica, on the other hand, may be completely used up by phytoplankton in surface waters, so their concentration may be the limiting factor determining whether or not phytoplankton can continue to grow. In some parts of the ocean, notably much of the Southern Ocean (i.e. around Antarctica) and parts of the Pacific, a shortage of dissolved iron can be a limiting factor. Iron is known as a 'micronutrient' because it is required by phytoplankton in very small amounts.

The 'Seasonal Seas' video is about the spring bloom in temperate waters, including the northern part of the North Atlantic. The satellite images in Figure 4.9 (overleaf) show dramatically the increase in the amount of chlorophyll – i.e. of phytoplankton – in these waters between December and May. The trigger for the **spring bloom** (as it is often called) is the right combination of sufficiently high light levels, a good supply of nutrients, and a fairly stable upper water column (Figure 4.10 overleaf).

As described above, in winter, nutrients are brought up from deeper in the ocean by vigorous mixing by wind and waves (Figure 4.10a). However, despite the good nutrient supply, phytoplankton cannot grow because light levels are too low. By early spring, light levels have risen sufficiently for the phytoplankton population to begin to grow, although for individual algae there is still a danger of being carried down into waters where it is too dark to photosynthesize (Figure 4.10b). By late spring the bloom is well underway (Figure 4.10c), and because the seasonal thermocline is beginning to become established (cf. Figure 4.8b) phytoplankton are at less risk of being carried down below the photic zone.

- By referring back to the discussion of Figure 4.8, can you explain why the establishment of the seasonal thermocline tends to keep phytoplankton in the photic zone?

- The formation of a warmer, less dense surface layer results in mixing by wind and waves being mainly confined to that layer.

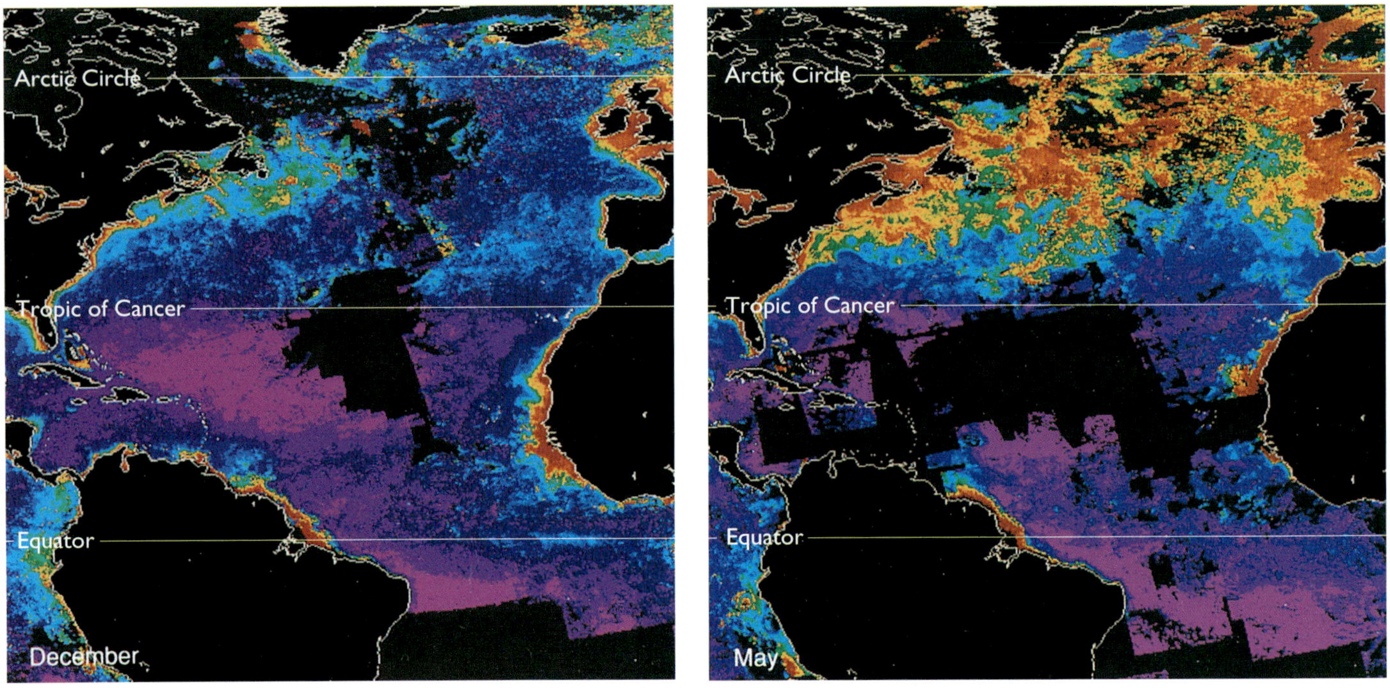

(a) (b)

Figure 4.9 Seasonal changes in primary production in the North Atlantic, as indicated by the concentration of chlorophyll pigment estimated using the satellite-borne Coastal Zone Color Scanner. Colours are artificial: pink corresponds to lowest concentrations, red to highest concentrations. (a) In December, the only red areas are on the continental shelves and close to coasts, and much of this may be due to large amounts of suspended sediment. (b) By May, the spring bloom is at its peak, and there is high primary production over much of the northern part of the North Atlantic. (Some of the red along coastlines may correspond to high production resulting from nutrients in river run-off, including agricultural fertilizers.)

At the seasonal thermocline, there is a sharp density change between the warmer summer mixed layer and the cooler water beneath. This sharp density change acts as a 'floor' to mixing, and phytoplankton are only carried down below it (and out of the photic zone) during exceptionally rough weather.

By now, the population of zooplankton is also growing and is grazing down the phytoplankton (Figure 4.10c). By mid-summer (Figure 4.10d), not only has a good proportion of the phytoplankton population been eaten, but the nutrient supplies above the seasonal thermocline are significantly depleted.

Figure 4.10 shows the circumstances leading to peaks in phytoplankton and zooplankton numbers in the northern Atlantic, up until mid-summer. In the autumn, there is another bloom of phytoplankton and another peak in zooplankton numbers. Peaks in phytoplankton and zooplankton abundances also occur in other mid- and high latitude waters, but there are important differences from region to region. For example, it seems that in the northern Pacific, phytoplankton abundance is restricted by a shortage of iron, grazing by zooplankton keeps pace with the production of phytoplankton, and the rise in phytoplankton abundance is nowhere near as dramatic as that in the northern Atlantic (Figure 4.9).

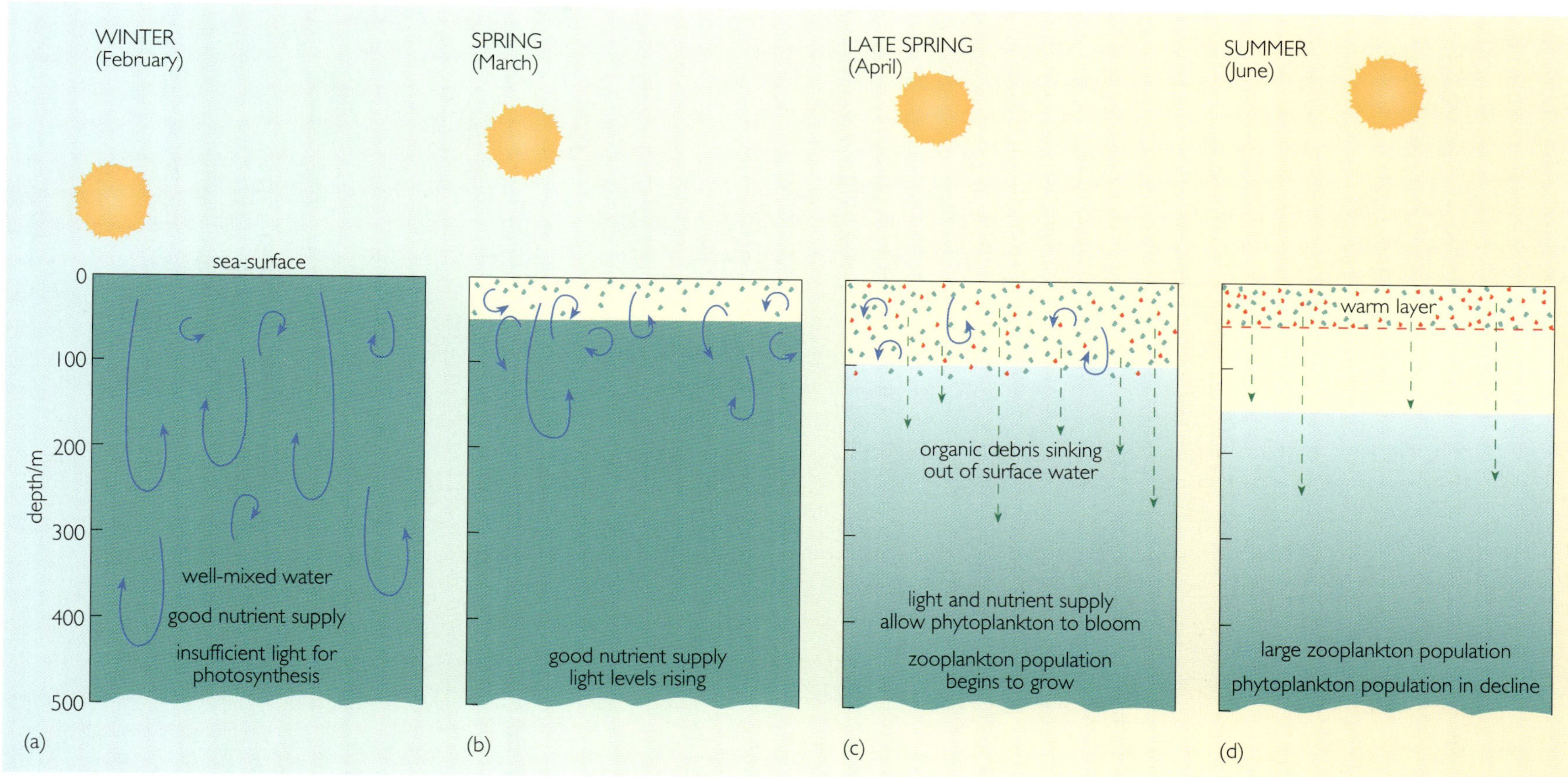

Figure 4.10 Schematic diagrams to show the circumstances that lead up to the spring bloom (a)–(c), and (d) the subsequent depletion of nutrients from surface waters. (a) By February, the water column is well mixed, and surface waters are rich in nutrients (as indicated by the intensity of the green tone). (b) As light levels rise, algae begin to photosynthesize, but tend to be carried down out of the photic zone (shown in yellow) by turbulent mixing. (c) By late spring, phytoplankton are being kept in the photic zone by the existence of the seasonal thermocline. Zooplankton numbers grow, and faecal pellets and remains of dead plankton rain down out of surface waters. (d) By mid-summer, the spring bloom is over, and surface waters have been significantly depleted of nutrients.

- Why are spring blooms a feature of the oceans at mid- and high latitudes, but are not characteristic of tropical waters?

- Because at low latitudes, seasonal variations in conditions are much less marked. There is no winter cooling, and no deep mixing, so the surface layers are permanently low in nutrients.

As a result, primary productivity at low latitudes is generally much lower than at higher latitudes, and the ocean is therefore much clearer (cf. Section 4.2). Indeed, the clear blue of the tropical ocean is sometimes referred to as 'desert blue'.

▶▶ *This is a good time to watch the 'Seasonal Seas' video (VC1). To get the most out of the video, you might find it helpful to first read through the notes below. You can look at them again afterwards, if you wish.*

In Chapter 8, we will be looking at how different types of seal swim. In preparation for this, you might like to pay particular attention to how the swimming technique of harbour seals [1:22:47] compares with that of sea-otters [1:18:58]. Again looking ahead to Chapter 8, you could make a note of any aspects of feeding, or of any other behaviour, that seem to be characteristic of whales and dolphins. ◀◀

Notes on the 'Seasonal Seas' video

This video focuses on the temperate seas that overlie the continental shelves. The temperate zone lies between the warm tropics/subtropics and the cold subpolar/polar seas. Such waters include those over the Grand Banks off Newfoundland, and the coastal waters around the British Isles, including the North Sea. The 'story line' starts in spring and ends during the following winter.

As you know from Chapter 2, continental shelves usually slope very gently, which means that over much of the shelf, the sea-bed is within the photic zone, and seaweeds will be able to grow. The sea-floor sediments are often sandy, with ripples.

[1:07:50] The pillbox-shaped phytoplankton seen here are a type of diatom. Diatoms have outer casings made of silica – in effect, glass. The green structures are chloroplasts, which contain the chlorophyll pigment. Diatoms are often the most conspicuous algae in temperate and high latitudes. The 'swimming' phytoplankton are dinoflagellates.

[1:08:40] Here, jellyfish reveal their close relationship with anemones. Not all jellyfish species go through this 'polyp' stage; the floating stage is known as the 'medusa' stage, after the mythical Gorgon with snakey locks.

[1:09:13] The species of copepod shown here is probably *Calanus finmarchicus*, one of the most abundant planktonic animals of northern temperate and Arctic waters.

[1:15:20] Sea squirts (the vase-shaped animals) are chordates, and have tadpole-like larvae. Gorgonians are soft corals. There are also some sea-urchins (echinoderms) here.

[1:17:00] *Important:* The seasonally high primary productivity off the coast of California is *not* simply the result of the increase in light levels. As you will see in Chapter 5, there is another important trigger here.

[1:17:54] Note how the blacksmith fish are changing the shapes of their tails.

There will be more about tails in Chapter 6.

[1:18:58] Try to make a note of how exactly sea-otters swim, for comparison with the harbour seals later.

[1:20:25] Bryozoans are sometimes called 'moss animals'. In the majority of species, each tiny individual (< 0.5 mm across) is largely encased in an external skeleton of calcium carbonate. As shown in the video, they feed by capturing small planktonic organisms or particles of organic debris, using a special food-trapping device which consists of numerous tentacles with cilia (hairs). There are almost 4000 marine species of bryozoans (a few living at depths of more than 8000 m) but their ecological significance has not really been investigated.

[1:22:39] As mentioned in connection with the 'Tidal Seas' video, seagrasses are flowering plants, not algae. Eelgrass (*Zostera marina*) is very widespread in shallow waters around the Atlantic, eastern Pacific and Mediterranean.

[1:22:47] How does the harbour seal's swimming technique compare with that of the sea-otter? (Don't spend a lot of time on this.)

[1:24:41] Rays are related to sharks (as you will see in Chapter 6). Try to observe the bat ray's swimming technique.

[1:24:50–1:24:57] Note the red and brown coloration of many of the seaweeds, and the sandy nature of the sea-floor. The parallel ripples indicate a gentle current.

[1:26:47–1:27:55] Sea-slugs are molluscs with no shell or a greatly reduced one. Most species are carnivorous, and live near the shore (there are a few species which swim in the water column, e.g. *Melibe*, coming later [1:41:02]).

[1:29:20] Note the marine snow drifting down.

[1:31:31] The seaweed being eaten by the baby crab is sea lettuce (*Ulva*), mentioned in Section 3.2.2.

[1:33:34] Note how the octopus's eyes resemble those of humans more than those of fish.

[1:33:52] Mysid shrimps are crustaceans of the Sub-order Peracarida (encountered in Question 1.2). Peracarids typically have a carapace that projects forward over their heads. They are most common in estuaries and inshore waters (some are harvested commercially in parts of Asia). However, they are not generally abundant in the planktonic community, and many species spend much of their life on the sea-floor or in deeper water.

[1:34:38, 1:34:58, 1:39:34] Sharks and dogfish are closely related. We will be saying more about them in Chapter 6.

[1:41:50] The phytoplankton have mostly 'disappeared' partly because they have been eaten by zooplankton and other animals, and also because the levels of sunlight are now so low that very little photosynthesis can occur. However, a few individuals do survive to form the basis of next year's 'crop'. Also, some types of phytoplankton, including diatoms and dinoflagellates, have dormant stages, known as resting spores. These spores, which have tough shells, sink to the bottom until favourable conditions return.

[1:42:05] The particles in the water column are bits of organic debris, probably mostly from the dying kelp itself.

[1:43:22] The phytoplankton that you can see here (including chains of diatoms) are superimposed artificially – remember that in reality they are microscopically small.

[1:44:00] Note how the squid are propelling themselves along.

[1:45:59] Can you see how the sea dragon is propelling itself along?

[1:49:28] Swimbladders will be discussed in Chapter 6.

4.4 Meroplankton – just passing through

The term meroplankton means 'temporary plankton' and it refers to planktonic stages of animals, both nektonic and benthic, that spend only part of their life cycle as a member of the plankton. (Plants and animals that spend their entire lives floating in the water column are classified as holoplankton.) Meroplankton are most abundant in shelf seas, where about 70% of the larger benthic invertebrates (i.e. those more than 1 mm across) release eggs or embryos into the water column. Depending on the species, these meroplankton may spend a few minutes to several months (or even years, in exceptional cases) as part of the plankton.

As you saw in the 'Seasonal Seas' video, planktonic young come in an amazing variety of shapes, mostly very different from the adult forms. Benthic snails and clams produce tiny shelled young, which have a distinctive membrane edged with tiny hairs, used for 'swimming' and collecting food. Many benthic organisms produce planktonic larvae that go through a number of stages, sometimes separated by moulting. Some animals, including crabs and lobsters, have a final planktonic stage that resembles the adult – this is known as a 'megalopa'; a crab megalopa can be seen in the 'Seasonal Seas' video [1:31:14].

Although some fish species lay their eggs on or within the sea-bed sediment, or attach them to seaweed, many – including tuna, sardines and anchovy – produce free-floating eggs. Fish eggs and fish larvae form an important part of the meroplankton. In a single spawning, one female may produce several hundred thousand eggs. The eggs are tiny transparent spheres, usually only 1–2 mm in diameter. They carry a supply of transparent yolk, and in some cases also a globule of oil, presumably to help keep them buoyant. (We return to the reproductive strategies of different groups of fish in Chapter 6.)

4.5 The oxygen minimum layer

As discussed in Section 2.1, surface waters have a high concentration of dissolved oxygen, partly because oxygen is produced as a by-product of photosynthesis (Equations 1.1a and 4.1), and partly because waves churn bubbles down into surface waters.

- What biological processes remove oxygen from solution?

- Respiration by plants (mainly phytoplankton) and by animals, and decomposition.

Bacterial decomposition of organic matter sinking out of the photic zone (dead organisms, faecal pellets and other organic debris) – i.e. bacterial respiration – means that at some depth below the surface, the concentration of dissolved oxygen begins to decrease. The organic debris tends to sink more slowly through the permanent thermocline because the marked temperature decrease is accompanied by a marked *density increase*. The slowly sinking organic debris attracts large numbers of zooplankton, and the decomposition, combined with respiration by the zooplankton (and other animals feeding on them), means that oxygen concentrations decline to a minimum, usually somewhere between 400 and 800 m depth. Below this **oxygen minimum layer**, the concentration of dissolved oxygen begins to increase again, because the cold deep water which originally sank from the surface at high latitudes carries large amounts of oxygen.

- Thinking back to Section 2.1, can you suggest why this might be?
- Cold water can hold more dissolved gas than can warm water.

The degree of oxygen depletion in the oxygen minimum layer varies from place to place, depending largely on the amount of organic debris falling from surface waters. The greatest depletion tends to occur where the 'oceanic' oxygen minimum layer impinges on the continental shelf or slope, where large amounts of organic debris could be accumulating beneath highly productive coastal waters. This situation is found in the northern Arabian Sea and in association with the Benguela Current off south-west Africa (for reasons that will become clear in Chapter 5).

At depths where there are marked oxygen minima, the biomass of pelagic animals is reduced, and relatively few species can survive in conditions with very little dissolved oxygen. If oxygen-depleted water upwells to the surface, it can cause mass mortalities of fish and other invertebrates. However, low oxygen concentrations do not necessarily mean a shortage of animals – for example, enormous populations of spider crabs have been observed feeding on the organic-rich sediment on the continental margin off Oman, in the lower part of the oxygen minimum layer. In the open ocean, certain species – e.g. the grotesque 'vampire squid' (*Vampyrotheuthis infernalis*) – have become adapted to live permanently within the low-oxygen layer, while other animals migrate in and out of it.

4.6 The sound channel

We mentioned in Section 2.1.1 that sound can travel long distances in the ocean without much loss in intensity. In fact, it can travel 1000 km or more – let's look briefly at how this can happen.

Imagine a sound source (a whale, say), sending out sound waves in the ocean. Some of the sound energy is absorbed by the seawater itself, and some is scattered as a result of bouncing off bubbles and suspended particles. The intensity of the sound also declines with increasing distance from the whale, as the sound energy spreads out over a wider and wider front, in all directions.

However, for reasons that we do not need to go into, sound waves produced at a depth where the speed of sound is at a minimum will remain at that depth, spreading out sideways, but with relatively little spreading up and down. This is therefore the optimum depth for long-distance communication in the ocean.

Question 4.4 The speed of sound in the ocean increases with increasing temperature and with increasing pressure (and is only slightly affected by salinity). Given this information, and the temperature profile in Figure 4.8a, explain why there is a minimum in the speed of sound at around 1000 m depth. Begin by discussing how the speed of sound changes with depth in the thermocline, given the extra information that temperature generally has a greater effect on the velocity of sound than pressure. ◀

This minimum in the speed of sound is known as the **sound channel**. It is not always at exactly the same depth, but it always corresponds roughly with the bottom of the permanent thermocline. Its existence is certainly known about by whales, which use it for communication over distances of 1000 km or more.

We have seen that winds are important for life in the oceans because they generate waves, which mix up the surface layers of the ocean and affect the distribution of nutrients, the supply of dissolved oxygen, the vertical temperature distribution and the stability of the water column. Waves also beat upon the coasts and shoreline, and locally contribute to the patterns of zonation of intertidal organisms. On a global scale, winds are important because they drive the surface currents, which – as you will see in the next chapter – have far-reaching effects on life in the ocean.

Winds, currents and life

5

In the introductory video, we are told that 'currents, more than any other factor … control the distribution of nutrients and life around the globe'. You will now appreciate that mixing by wind, and the establishment of a seasonal thermocline, play an important role in promoting high productivity in temperate waters. Wind also plays a crucial role in driving currents, not only surface currents but also, in certain locations, *vertical* movements of water.

In Sections 5.2 to 5.4, we will look at how wind and current patterns lead to low concentrations of nutrients in the surface waters of the open oceans, as well as at various causes of locally high nutrient concentrations and high biological productivity.

5.1 The global wind system

The uneven heating of the Earth by the Sun gives rise to the global wind system, the large-scale pattern of air movement within the atmosphere which – along with surface currents – redistributes heat from low to high latitudes. Figure 5.1 (overleaf) shows the prevailing winds over the Earth's surface in July and January, along with the mean patterns of high and low atmospheric pressure. These are *average* pictures – on any one day in July or January the wind and pressure pattern could look completely different from either of the patterns shown here. Another important result of averaging is that small-scale features are 'smoothed out', so Figure 5.1 shows only relatively large-scale features of the global wind pattern.

The most persistent winds are the Trade Winds, which can be seen on Figure 5.1 mainly between the Tropic of Cancer and the Tropic of Capricorn, and blow generally westwards and towards the Equator. Winds are named for the direction they blow *from*, so these winds are known as the North-East Trade Winds and the South-East Trade Winds (sometimes 'Trades' for short).

The purple line is the Intertropical Convergence Zone (ITCZ), which is the zone of low pressure where the wind systems of the two hemispheres meet, and where air carried in the Trade Winds rises, before eventually beginning to move poleward. Winds blow from regions of high pressure to regions of low pressure, so if the Earth were not spinning, the Trade Winds would blow directly southwards and northwards (from the high pressures of the subtropics, shown red/pink in Figure 5.1), towards the ITCZ. It is because the Earth is spinning towards the *east* that the air in the Trade Winds moves *westwards* in relation to the Earth (i.e. not simply towards the ITCZ) – you can think of this as the air being 'left behind' by the Earth turning beneath it. Away from the Equator, the fact that the Earth is rotating *combined* with the fact that it is spherical, results in moving air in the Northern Hemisphere tending to be deflected to the right relative to the Earth, and moving air in the Southern Hemisphere tending to be deflected to the left relative to the Earth. This phenomenon is known as the **Coriolis effect**; it influences both winds and currents and, perhaps surprisingly, it indirectly has a profound effect on life in the oceans.

Study the arrows around the regions of high and low pressure in Figure 5.1.

- In which direction, clockwise or anticlockwise, do winds blow around areas of high pressure (1) in the Northern Hemisphere, (2) in the Southern Hemisphere?

- (1) Winds blow clockwise around areas of high pressure in the Northern Hemisphere, and (2) anticlockwise around areas of high pressure in the Southern Hemisphere.

Figure 5.1 The prevailing winds at the Earth's surface, and the position of the Intertropical Convergence Zone (ITCZ) where the wind systems of the two hemispheres meet, in (a) July (northern summer/southern winter) and (b) January (southern summer/northern winter). Also shown are the positions of the main regions of high atmospheric pressure (red/pink tones) in the subtropics, and low atmospheric pressure (blue tones) at low latitudes and in subpolar regions, at those seasons of the year. Note the positions of the Tropics of Cancer and Capricorn (23.4° N and 23.4° S).

- In which direction do winds blow around areas of low pressure? (This is easiest to see in Figure 5.1b.)

- Winds blow anticlockwise around areas of low pressure in the Northern Hemisphere (and clockwise around areas of low pressure in the Southern Hemisphere).

Whichever hemisphere they are in, winds that blow around *high* pressure areas are referred to as **anticyclonic**, and winds that blow around *low* pressure areas are referred to as **cyclonic**. So, if you were watching a storm warning on a TV weather forecast for Australia, the winds around the low pressure centre would be clockwise; whereas in the Northern Hemisphere, we see low pressure centres with anticlockwise winds.

If you compare Figures 5.1a and 5.1b you will see that in summer, atmospheric pressure over the large continental masses tends to be low, whereas in winter it tends to be high. Over the ocean, by contrast, the general positions of the regions of high and low pressure remain in more or less the same place over the course of the year (although their relative strengths vary significantly). This indirectly affects the salinity of surface waters, because while high pressure is associated with dry, settled weather and generally clear skies, low pressure centres – whether tropical cyclones, or the lows (depressions) typical of temperate latitudes – are associated with moist air, clouds and rain. The Intertropical Convergence Zone, for example, gives rise to very heavy precipitation, and this lowers the salinity of surface waters in equatorial latitudes. Being of relatively low salinity, as well as very warm, the uppermost layer of water at extremely low latitudes is markedly less dense than the water below. This gives rise to a strongly stratified water column – i.e. one that is highly stable and not easily mixed – so the surface waters tend not to be replenished with nutrients from below. Thus, the high rainfall at low latitudes indirectly contributes to the 'barren' nature of the waters there (cf. end of Section 4.3).

By contrast, surface waters under the clear skies of the subtropical highs lose much more freshwater by evaporation than they gain from rainfall, and so they have relatively high salinity. In the 'Tidal Seas' video, you saw flamingos and brine shrimps living in the highly saline coastal shallows around the Bahamas. These islands lie just to the south-east of Florida, and so the waters around them are subjected to quite high evaporation, especially under the influence of the North-East Trades (Figure 5.1). However, in this case, the exceptionally high salinity of the waters around the islands is the result of the fact that they are the highest part of a large shallow region known as the Bahama Bank. Because the waters are so shallow, they warm up quickly and are subject to high rates of evaporation; furthermore, the high salinity waters that result tend not to be diluted by less saline waters from adjacent areas.

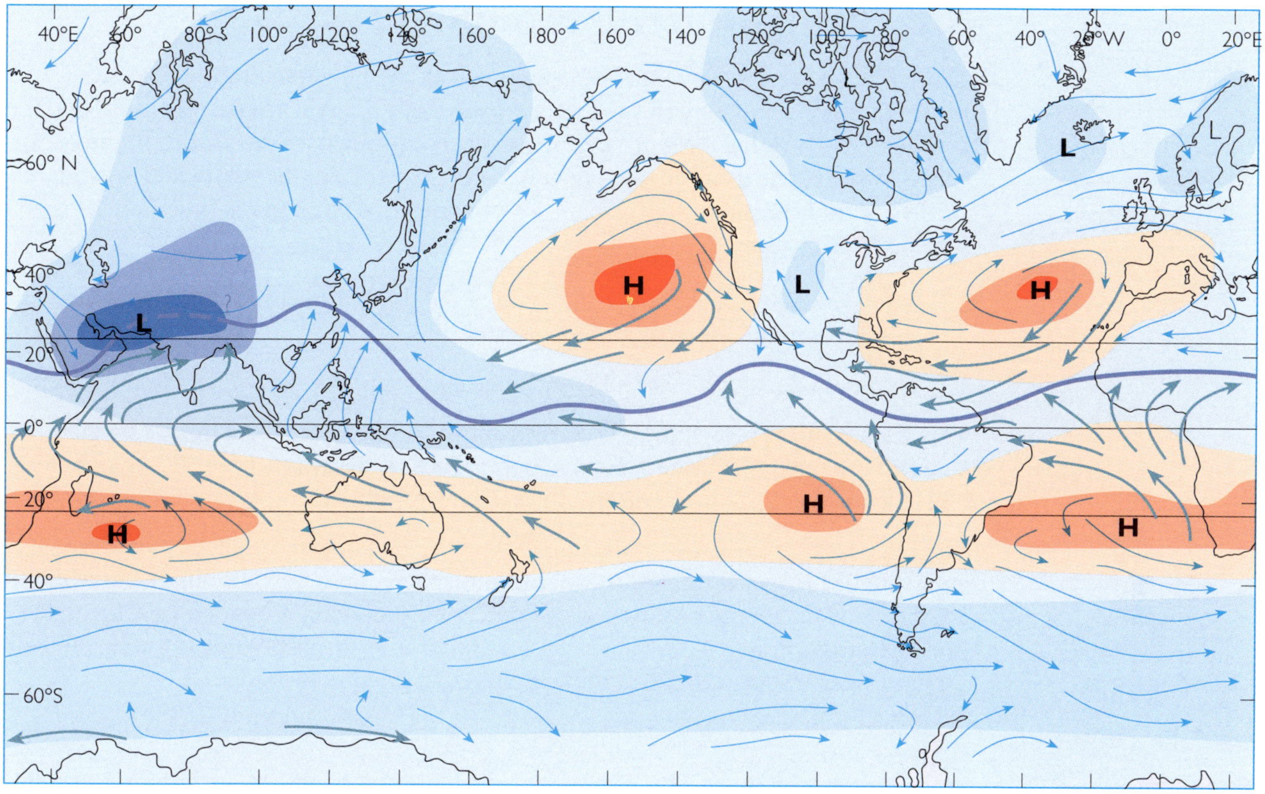

(a) JULY

KEY — mean position of ITCZ; most frequent wind direction; prevailing wind direction (≥50% of observations)

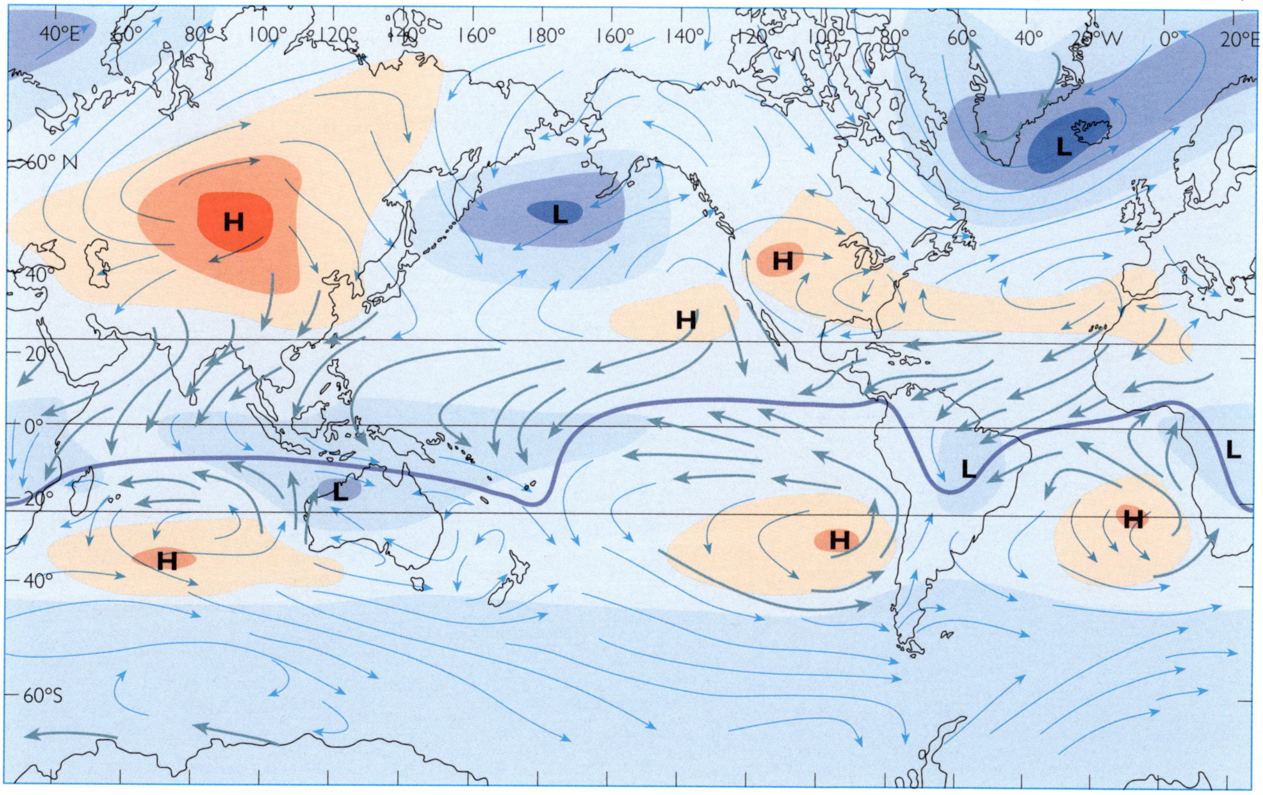

(b) JANUARY

5.2 Wind-driven currents

The surface current system of the ocean is driven by the winds. If you compare Figures 5.1 and 5.2, you will see that there are some general similarities, although the flow patterns of ocean currents are, of course, constrained by the shapes of the ocean basins. Perhaps the most obvious features of Figure 5.2 are the westward-flowing North and South Equatorial Currents, and a number of large **gyres** (i.e. more or less circular flow patterns).

- In the Atlantic Ocean, how is the path of the South Equatorial Current affected by the shape of the coast of South America?

- The South Equatorial Current is deflected northwards by the bulge of South America.

This has the effect of diverting large amounts of warm water from the Southern Hemisphere into the Northern Hemisphere. Much of the warm water flowing in the Gulf Stream has come from the Southern Hemisphere.

The largest gyres are to be seen either side of the Equator in the subtropics. They are anticyclonic (clockwise in the Northern Hemisphere, anticlockwise in the Southern Hemisphere) and are driven by anticyclonic winds blowing around the strong high pressure areas (Figure 5.1). These gyres are known as the **subtropical gyres**; on their western sides, water warmed at low latitudes is carried poleward.

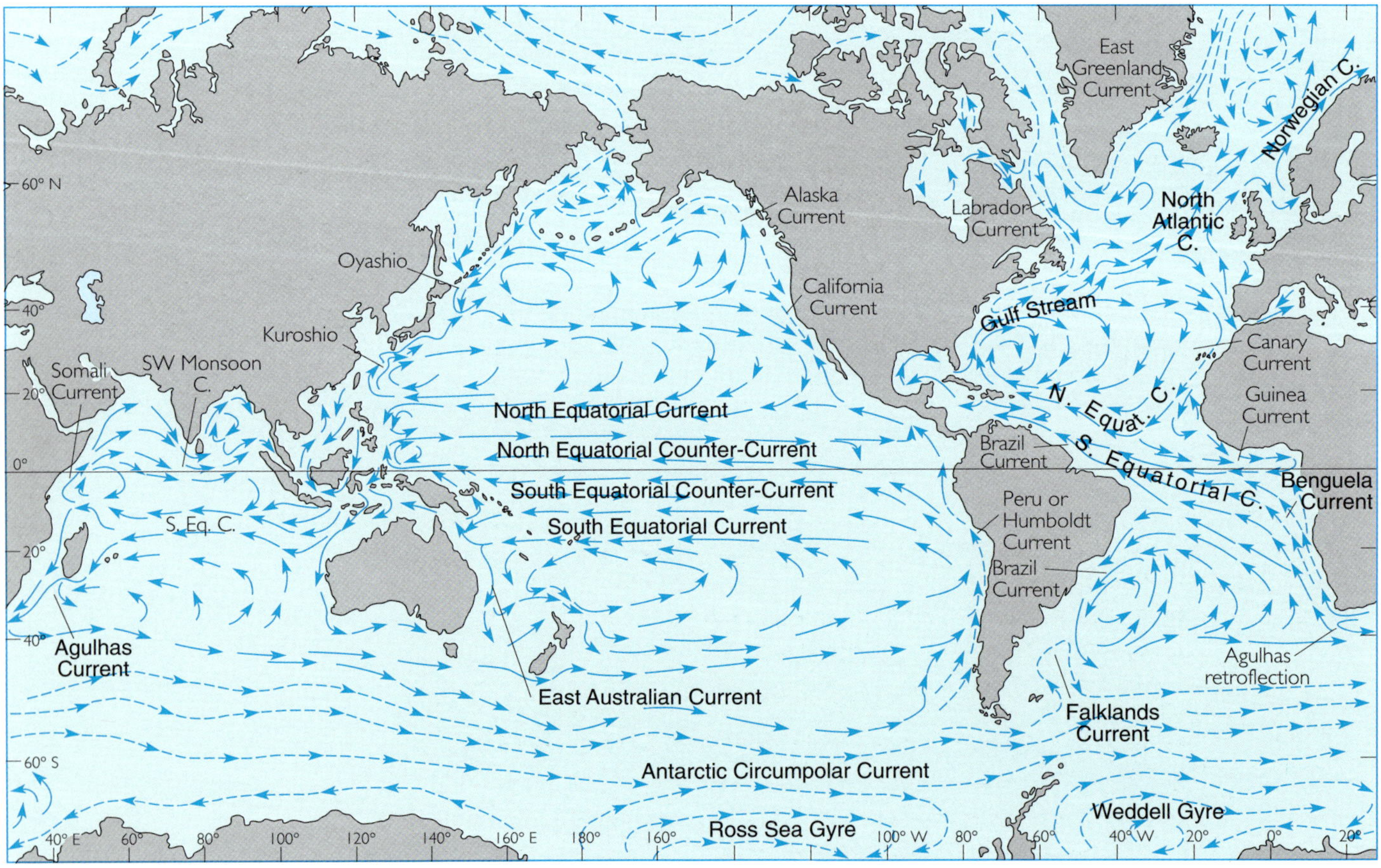

Figure 5.2 A generalized representation of the global surface current system. Cool currents are shown by dashed arrows; warm currents by solid arrows. The map shows average conditions for summer months in the Northern Hemisphere. There are local differences in the winter, especially in regions affected by monsoons (seasonally reversing winds).

Question 5.1 Which poleward-flowing currents carry warm water from equatorial and tropical regions in (1) the North Atlantic and North Pacific, (2) the South Atlantic, and (3) the southern Indian Ocean? ◀

As suggested by the arrows in Figure 5.2, the poleward-flowing currents you have identified are fast and intense (arrows close together), in contrast to the equatorward-flowing currents on the opposite sides of the oceans, which are slow, wide and diffuse (arrows far apart). The former are often referred to as 'western boundary currents', and the latter as 'eastern boundary currents'. Eastern boundary currents are, of course, cold or cool, because they are carrying water from high latitudes, i.e. from polar and subpolar regions.

- Identify the eastern boundary currents in (1) the North Atlantic and North Pacific, and (2) the South Atlantic and South Pacific.

- They are (1) the Canary Current and the California Current, and (2) the Benguela Current and the Peru or Humboldt Current.

In tropical and subtropical regions, the redistribution of heat by the surface current system means that, at a given latitude, water temperatures on the western side of the ocean are typically higher than those on the eastern side of the ocean. This is the reason (alluded to in Section 2.1.2) why temperature-related distributions of species are not quite in zones parallel to the Equator.

5.2.1 Wind-driven upwelling and downwelling

As discussed above, eastern boundary currents are colder than western boundary currents because they flow from high latitudes, whereas western boundary currents flow from low latitudes. However, eastern boundary currents are also cold for another reason. Because of the Coriolis effect, away from the Equator, surface water moving in response to a persistent wind does not flow exactly parallel to the wind, but at an angle to it – to the right of the wind direction in the Northern Hemisphere and to the left of the wind direction in the Southern Hemisphere. The uppermost layer of sea being 'dragged along' by the wind in turn drags the layer of water below it, and that in turn drags the one below, and so on, down to the depth where the effect of the wind is no longer felt (the thickness of the wind-driven layer varies between a few tens of metres and 200–300 m, depending on the time of year). Now, the slower a wind or current is moving, the greater the deflection caused by the Coriolis effect, so the direction of motion of each layer is deflected slightly more than the one above. The overall effect is that, if the wind has been blowing for some time, the *average* motion of the wind-driven layer is at right angles to the wind, to the right of the wind direction in the Northern Hemisphere and to the left of the wind direction in the Southern Hemisphere. This can have dramatic consequences for primary productivity (i.e. the rate of primary production) in coastal waters.

- Imagine a stretch of coastal seas in the Northern Hemisphere. What do you think will happen if a persistent wind blows along the coast, in such a way that the coast is on the left?

- The layer of surface water under the influence of the wind will move to the right (as this is in the Northern Hemisphere), i.e. it will move offshore.

A comparable situation will arise if a persistent wind blows along a Southern Hemisphere coast in such a way that the coast is on the right. In both cases, the surface water moving offshore allows deeper, more nutrient-rich water to rise to take

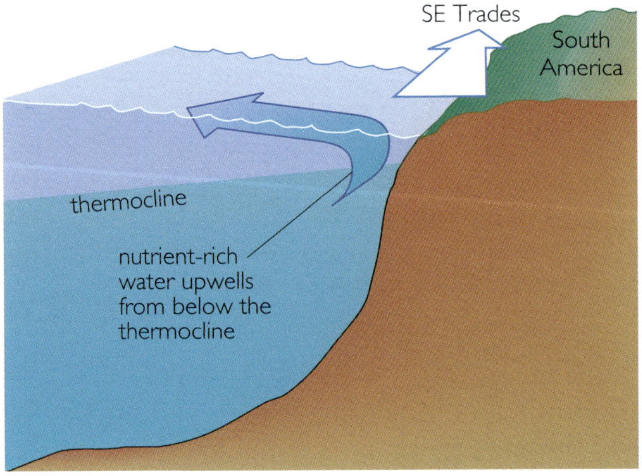

Figure 5.3 Schematic diagram to show how equatorward winds along eastern coastlines give rise to upwelling of nutrient-rich water. Here, the South-East Trade Winds blowing along the coast of Peru and Ecuador give rise to motion of the wind-driven layer offshore. As this is in the Southern Hemisphere, the wind-driven layer moves to the *left* of the wind direction.

its place. Once in the photic zone, this nutrient-rich water will support high levels of phytoplankton growth, and hence also large populations of zooplankton and of animals further up the food chain. (Note: this nutrient-rich water upwells from 100–200 m depth at most; it does *not* upwell from great depths as is commonly supposed.)

Some of the most biologically productive coastal **upwelling** regions are found in the tropics and subtropics on the eastern sides of the oceans where, at certain times of year, the Trade Winds blow along the coast (Figure 5.1). The best known such upwelling region is probably that off the coast of Ecuador and Peru (Figure 5.3). It is this upwelling that fails when the South-East Trades weaken during the climatic fluctuations known as El Niño events. Another rich upwelling region is that within the Benguela Current, off south-west Africa (Figure 5.4).

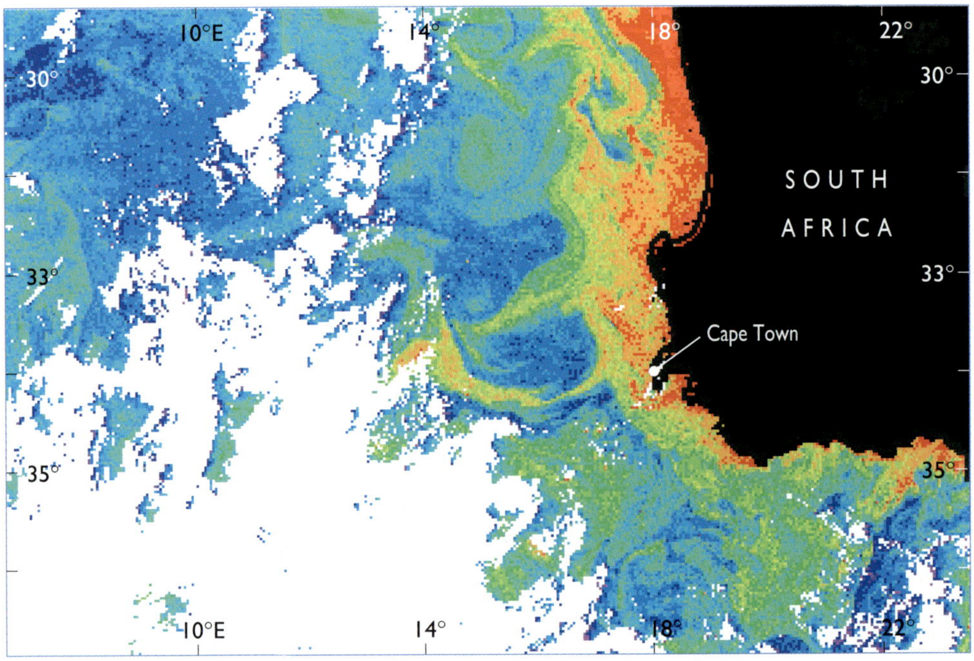

Figure 5.4 Coastal Zone Color Scanner satellite image showing the southernmost end of the zone of upwelling and high productivity which occurs off the coast of south-west Africa, in the Benguela Current. Colours are artificial: red corresponds to high concentrations of chlorophyll pigment, pale blue to very low concentrations (white is cloud). Note how complicated the flow patterns are, with wave-like features and filaments of productive water streaming out into the open ocean.

The dramatic seasonal growth of the kelp forests off the coast of California, seen in the 'Seasonal Seas' video [1:16:12 to 1:27:55], is partly a result of the increased intensity of solar radiation in spring and summer, as suggested by the narration. However, the reason for the exceptionally high productivity is nutrient-rich water supplied from below by upwelling. This occurs all year round off southern California, and peaks in late spring and early summer off northern California (cf. the wind directions in relation to the coast in Figure 5.1).

The video 'Bounty off Natal' (which you can watch shortly) shows huge 'slicks' of sardines. The narration suggests that the sardines are there because nutrient-rich water has flowed into the region as a result of reversal of the Agulhas Current – which is the western boundary current (the equivalent of the Gulf Stream) in the southern Indian Ocean (cf. Figure 5.2). In fact, the Agulhas Current does *not* reverse, but at certain times of year it moves away from the Natal coast, allowing colder, more nutrient-rich water, which usually flows northwards at depth along the continental shelf, to come to the surface. Along the coast, therefore, warm southward-flowing water is replaced by cold, northward-flowing water. It is not known for sure why this situation arises – it may be related to the wind pattern, or perhaps to the effect of **eddies** ('swirls' or vortices) in the Agulhas Current.

►► *You can look at the 'Bounty off Natal' video on VC1 now, if convenient, or save it until later (it lasts about 8 minutes). As usual, make a note of any behaviour which seems to be characteristic of whales and dolphins.*

To get the most out of the video, you might find it helpful to first read through the notes below. You can look at them again afterwards, if you wish. ◄◄

Notes on the 'Bounty off Natal' video

[1:54:34] Gannets are amongst the deepest-diving of those seabirds that catch their prey by plunging into the sea (as opposed to pursuing it underwater as penguins and cormorants do).

[1:56:28] This whale is also known as Bryde's whale. It is a baleen whale, and a rorqual, so is a member of the same taxonomic family as the blue whale (Figure 1.3). Species of rorquals can be distinguished from one another by their size, colour, the number of throat grooves (this species has 47–70), and the number of baleen plates (this species has 250–370). Rorquals live mainly on plankton, and will eat fish only if they are in large schools, as here. Note the way the throat bulges when the whale feeds.

Upwelling of nutrient-rich water also occurs in mid-ocean, away from coasts, again as a result of surface water moving apart, or *diverging*, in response to wind patterns. In the eastern Atlantic and the eastern Pacific, there are extensive bands of upwelling just to the south of the Equator, and parallel to it; these arise because the South-East Trade Winds cross the Equator, leading to a moving apart of surface waters known as the **Equatorial Divergence** (Figure 5.5 overleaf). Ringing the globe in the Southern Ocean is another zone of wind-driven divergence of surface water, which also leads to high productivity. This is known as the **Antarctic Divergence**.

The effects of the Antarctic Divergence and the Equatorial Divergence can both be seen to some extent in the distribution of primary production shown in Figure 4.1. Other areas of high production can be seen in the northern North Atlantic and the

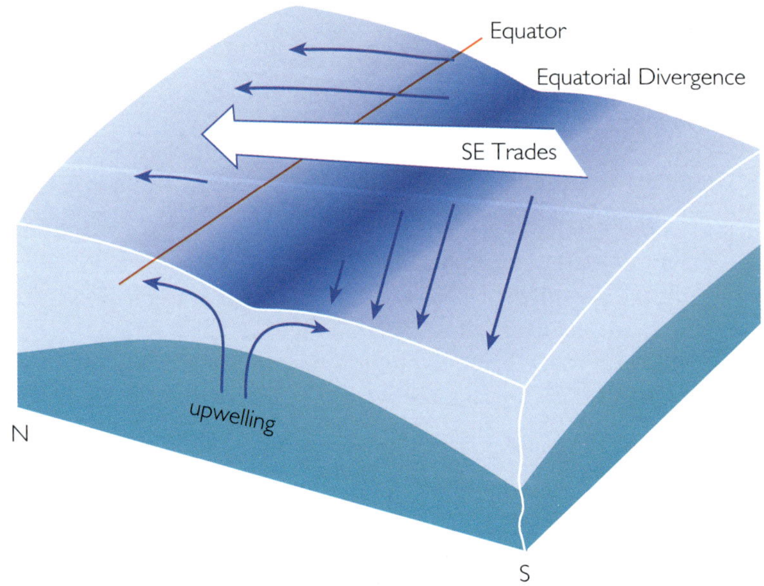

Figure 5.5 Schematic diagram showing why upwelling occurs at the Equatorial Divergence. The South-East Trade Winds blow across the Equator. Because of the Coriolis effect, the wind-driven layer to the south of the Equator moves to the left, at right angles to the wind. However, in the vicinity of the Equator itself there is *no* Coriolis effect, and the wind-driven layer moves in the *same* direction as the wind. As a result, there is a zone parallel to the Equator where surface waters are driven apart, allowing deeper, more nutrient-rich water to rise up into the photic zone. This is the Equatorial Divergence.

northern North Pacific – the areas affected by the spring plankton blooms discussed in the 'Seasonal Seas' video.

- According to Figure 4.1, which regions have the lowest primary productivity of all? According to Figures 5.1 and 5.2, what wind and current patterns characterize these areas?

- The areas with the lowest primary productivity are the central parts of the subtropical gyres, which are driven by the anticyclonic wind systems blowing around the subtropical highs.

Figure 5.6a shows why the central parts of the subtropical gyres have such low productivity. The diagram illustrates the situation in the Northern Hemisphere, where anticyclonic winds are clockwise and the Coriolis effect causes deflection to the right of the wind direction. The result is the same in the Southern Hemisphere, where anticyclonic winds are anticlockwise and the Coriolis effect causes deflection to the left of the wind direction. In summary, in a subtropical gyre the average motion of the wind-driven layer is towards the centre of the gyre. Water converges and 'piles up' in the centre of the gyre and gradually sinks. As a result, the sea-surface is dome-shaped, with the centre of the gyre being nearly a metre higher than the outer parts. The bottom of the mixed layer and the thermocline (Section 4.3) are correspondingly deeper in the middle of the gyre and shallower towards the edge.

A deep thermocline, and a thick mixed surface layer within which water is generally sinking, is not conducive to deeper, more nutrient-rich water being mixed up into the photic zone. This is why the central parts of the subtropical gyres have such low primary productivity. Furthermore, phytoplankton in a thick mixed layer are always at risk of being carried down out of the photic zone by mixing. If this happens, they will not be able to absorb enough light to grow and reproduce, and may even die as a result.

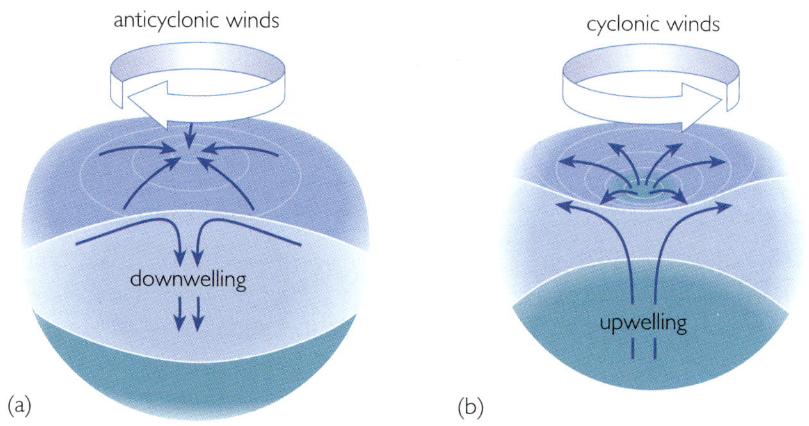

Figure 5.6 Schematic diagrams showing (a) how anticyclonic winds lead to convergence of surface water and downwelling, while (b) cyclonic winds lead to divergence of surface water and upwelling. Although the thermocline is in reality a depth *zone*, here it is shown simply as the boundary between the surface layer (pale blue) and deeper, more nutrient-rich water (turquoise). (Both diagrams are drawn for the Northern Hemisphere.)

The clear waters of the subtropical gyres are the setting for the 'Open Ocean' video. These waters are clear because there are such small populations of phytoplankton and zooplankton. As you will see shortly, open ocean ecosystems function very differently from those of productive upwelling areas.

Earlier, we noted that the high productivity of the spring bloom in the northern temperate seas shows up clearly on Figure 4.1. In Section 4.3, we discussed how the timing of the spring bloom is affected by light levels and the extent to which the upper water column is stratified or well mixed. However, to appreciate fully how the northern parts of the Atlantic and the Pacific come to have such high levels of productivity, we need also to remember their oceanographic setting.

- Look again at Figure 5.2. Generally speaking, how would you describe the surface current patterns in the northern North Pacific and the northern North Atlantic?

- In both areas, surface currents are flowing anticlockwise – in other words, the currents are forming *cyclonic* gyres. (In the northern Pacific, there seem to be two such gyres, linked together.)

Just as deflection of wind-driven currents by the Coriolis effect causes surface water to move towards the centres of anticyclonic gyres, so it also leads to surface water moving *away from* the centres of cyclonic gyres (Figure 5.6b). As a result, the centres of cyclonic gyres – including the subpolar gyres we have just been discussing – are regions where surface waters diverge, the thermocline comes closer to the surface, and deep nutrient-rich water tends to upwell to the surface (especially in winter, when winds are strongest). This helps to ensure that surface waters within cyclonic gyres are 'restocked' with high concentrations of nutrients every winter.

5.3 The effects of islands

Islands and seamounts disrupt current patterns, and may support oases of high productivity in otherwise barren waters. One way in which this occurs is known as the 'island wake effect': surface currents flowing around islands form eddies, and as a result there is vigorous vertical mixing on the downstream side of the islands. Satellite images often show plumes of highly productive water swirling downstream from islands.

Upwelling of nutrient-rich water can also occur as a result of *subsurface* currents encountering islands or seamounts and being deflected upwards. You will be able to see the spectacular results of this phenomenon in the 'Open Ocean' video. Amongst the most persistent subsurface currents are those that flow from west to east along the Equator, in the Pacific and Atlantic Oceans, and – for part of the year – in the Indian Ocean. These currents are known as Equatorial Undercurrents; the one in the Pacific is also known as the Cromwell Current.

The Galápagos archipelago lies on the Equator in the eastern Pacific. Its islands and islets are the tips of volcanic seamounts which together form the Galápagos Plateau. Figure 5.7 shows the topography of the islands and the surrounding sea-bed: note how steep the submarine topography is on the western side of the islands of Fernandina, Isabela and Santa Maria. The Cromwell Current flows eastward as a horizontal ribbon of water which, in the vicinity of the Galápagos is at a depth of about 100 m. On reaching the steep submarine slopes of the Galápagos Plateau, it splits into filaments (blue arrows on Figure 5.7) and is deflected upwards, coming to the surface in some places.

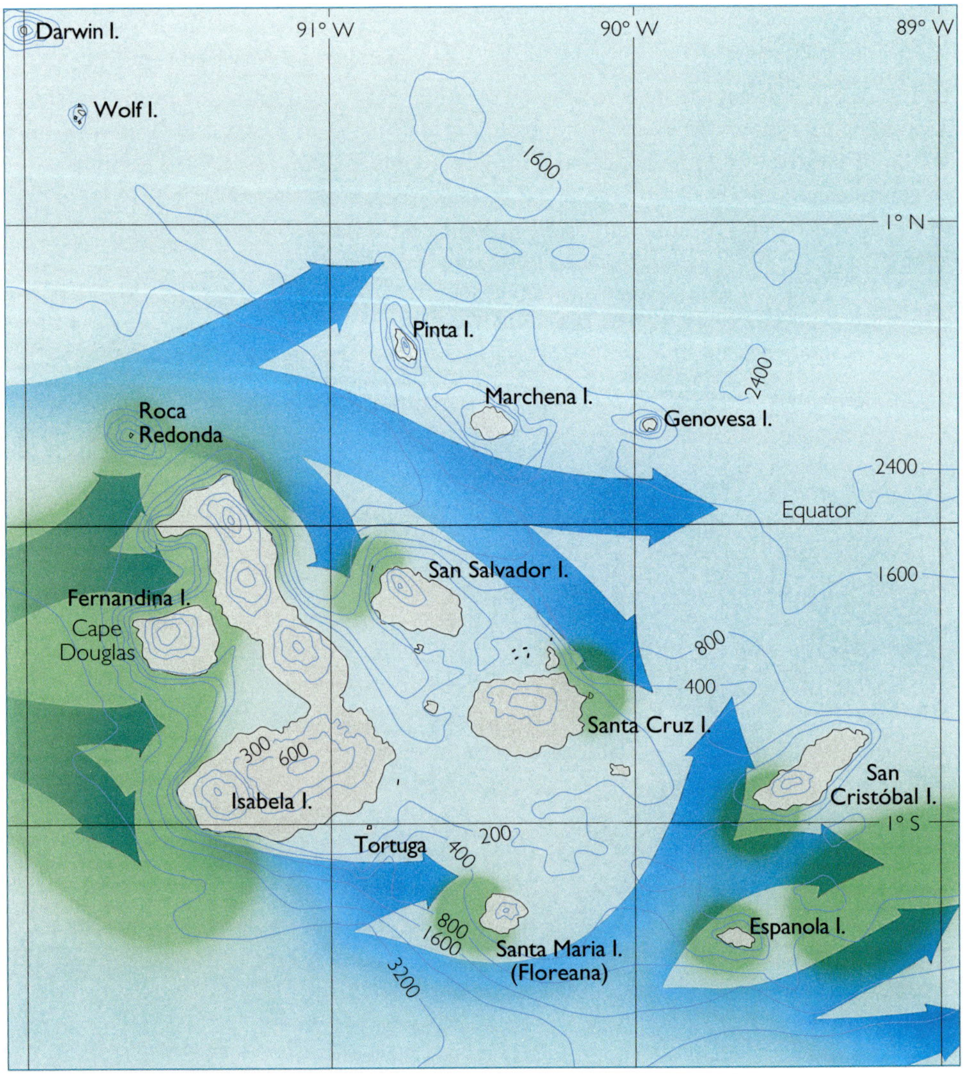

Figure 5.7 The most common flow paths of the Cromwell Current (Equatorial Undercurrent) through the Galápagos archipelago (blue arrows), and the locations of the most persistent upwellings (green areas). The contour depths in the ocean, and heights on land, are given in metres. Note how close together the contours are – i.e. how steep the submarine topography is – on the western side of the islands of Fernandina, Isabela and Santa Maria.

Cape Douglas, home of the marine iguanas seen near the beginning of the introductory video, is on the north-western tip of Fernandina (see Figures 5.7 and 5.8).

Question 5.2 By reference to Figures 5.7 and 5.8, explain why Cape Douglas is a good site for marine iguanas to live. ◀

Perhaps surprisingly, animals like fur seals and penguins, which usually only live at high latitudes, are *also* found on the western side of the Galápagos archipelago. This is partly because the upwelling Cromwell Current water is significantly colder than the surrounding surface water. Another reason is that the Galápagos islands lie at the edge of the zone of equatorial upwelling discussed earlier – the Equatorial Divergence. Furthermore, they lie in the path of the South Equatorial Current (Figure 5.2) – this is cold not only because it comes from the Southern Ocean but also because it carries cold water upwelled along the coast of South America (cf. Figure 5.3). Galápagos penguins now form a distinct species endemic to the islands (i.e. found only there). Being a Southern Hemisphere cold-water group, they would have reached the Galápagos via the coast of South America, in the cold waters of the Peru Current.

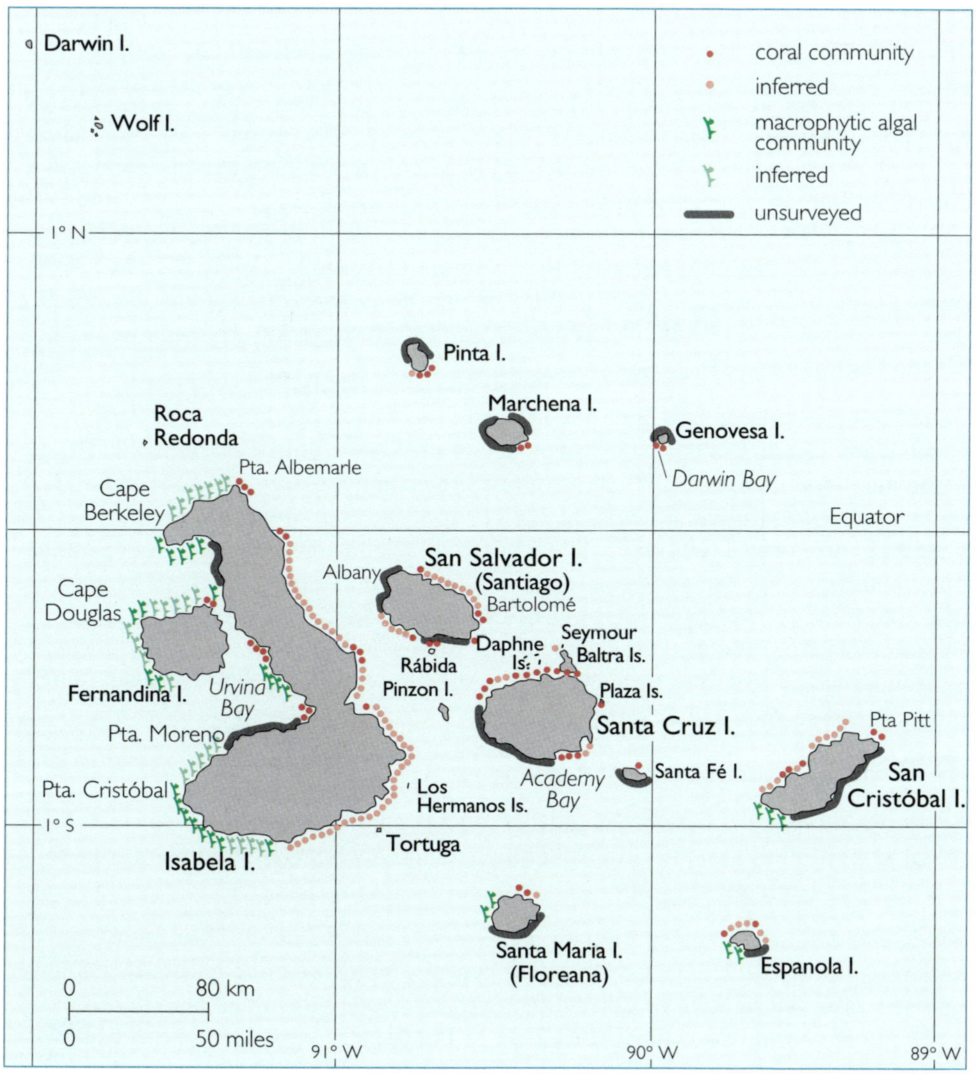

Figure 5.8 Summary map of observed and inferred distribution patterns of coral reef communities and seaweed (macrophytic) communities around the islands of the Galápagos archipelago.

5.4 Fronts

Towards the beginning of the 'Open Ocean' video, the narration refers to 'vast current systems, like immense rivers' and states that 'the boundaries between these masses of moving water form invisible barriers that can trap both plankton and nutrients carried up from the depths'. However, it is important to appreciate that ocean currents are *not* like rivers – maps like Figure 5.2 represent *average* conditions. If you were to measure the surface current somewhere in the region labelled 'Gulf Stream' on Figure 5.2, you might well find that at that moment the current direction at the point in question was quite different from the direction suggested by the arrows in Figure 5.2, perhaps even in the opposite direction. Even powerful, relatively well-defined currents continually shift and change their positions to greater or lesser extents, forming meanders and loops, or splitting into filaments.

5.4.1 Frontal currents and 'rings'

Western boundary currents like the Gulf Stream and the Kuroshio are particularly prone to forming meanders and loops. Such currents are sometimes known as 'frontal currents' because they flow along the boundaries – **fronts** – between different bodies of water, often referred to as 'water masses'. This terminology arises by analogy with that used in meteorology, where fronts are the boundaries between different air masses. Fronts in the ocean are the 'invisible barriers' referred to in the narration.

For reasons we do not need to go into here, it is the difference in density between two adjacent water masses – that is, the density gradient across the boundary zone – that determines the speed of the frontal current which flows along the boundary zone. The Gulf Stream flows along the boundary zone between cold coastal water (which is further cooled by the cold waters of the Labrador Current; cf. Figure 5.2), and the warm water of the Sargasso Sea (the central part of the subtropical gyre, to the east of the Gulf Stream). Gulf Stream water itself is warm, having flowed from low latitudes via the Gulf of Mexico.

Figure 5.9 is a 'false colour' satellite image of the waters off the coast of eastern North America and Canada, showing concentrations of chlorophyll pigment. The warm and unproductive waters of the Gulf Stream and the Sargasso Sea can be seen to the lower right (in blue), while the cool productive coastal water can be seen to the west and north of this (in green, yellow and red). We would like you to focus on the blue feature shaped like an upside-down comma, to the north of the Gulf Stream, near the centre of the image. This is a **Gulf Stream ring**, a meander of the Gulf Stream which has 'pinched off' and become isolated. To the right of this, you can see a meander which had not yet pinched off at the time this image was recorded, but probably did so shortly afterwards.

- In which direction is the water in the ring in Figure 5.9 rotating?

- It is rotating clockwise (i.e. anticyclonically) – you can tell this because of the way it formed from the Gulf Stream, which is flowing (roughly) from west to east (i.e. from left to right).

Rings like these are being continually generated to either side of all strong frontal currents. Biologically, they are important because their formation results in a column of water from one side of the current being transferred to the other side. In this case, a column of warmer, less nutrient-rich water, containing organisms typical of the Sargasso Sea, has formed from a clockwise meander of the Gulf Stream and then been

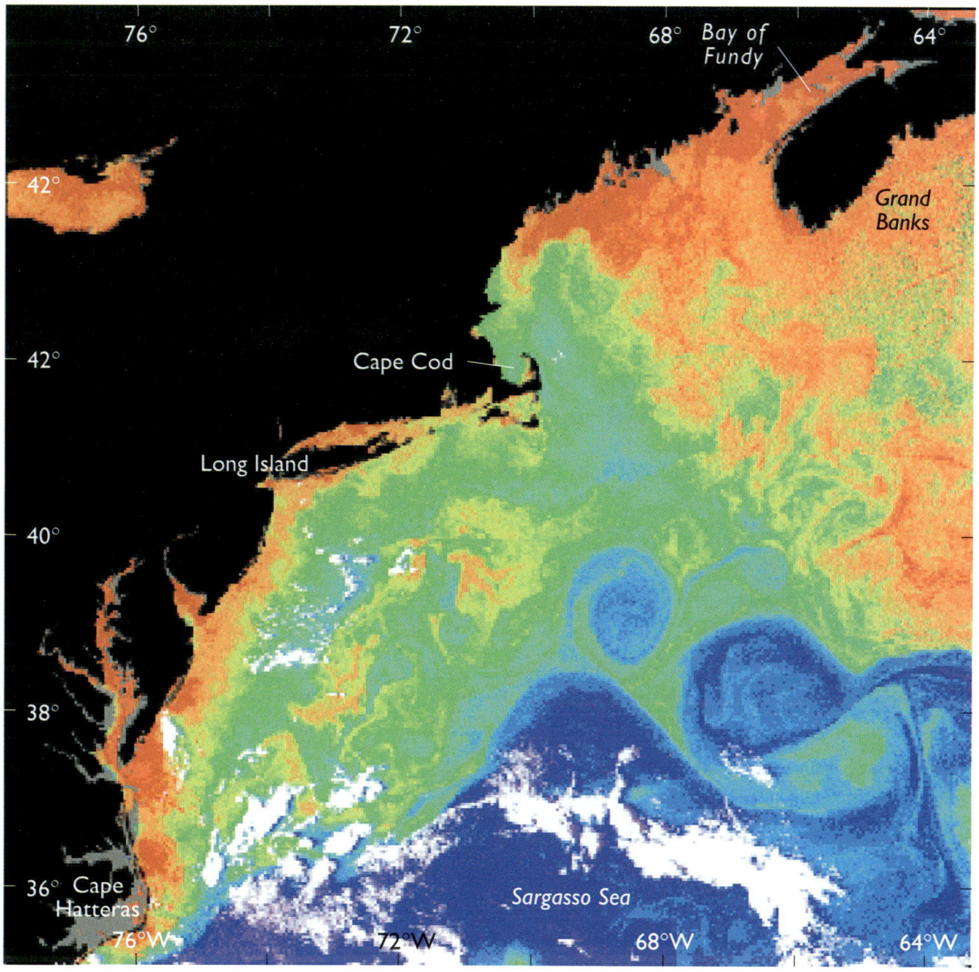

Figure 5.9 Coastal Zone Color Scanner satellite image of the waters off the north-western seaboard of the United States and Canada. Colours are artificial: red corresponds to the most productive water (i.e. that with the highest concentrations of chlorophyll pigment), blue to the least productive water (white is cloud). The red area to the top right is the productive water overlying the Grand Banks, until the early 1990s the site of a major commercial cod fishery. You can also see the Bay of Fundy, whose productive waters were the subject of part of the 'Tidal Seas' video.

left spinning in the cold, nutrient-rich water to the north of the Gulf Stream (which have their own organisms). Similarly, columns of nutrient-rich water may be transferred to the Sargasso Sea side of the Gulf Stream by the formation of an anticlockwise meander. It is not known what the long-term ecological significance of these transfers of water might be, but it *is* known that the rings themselves can persist for months or even years.

5.4.2 Fronts related to sea-bed topography

There are a number of reasons why high productivity can be associated with fronts between different types of water. Sometimes the sea-bed topography plays a role in generating the front and the high productivity. In Chapter 3, we discussed the productive well-mixed water of continental shelves and shelf seas. The boundaries between this well-mixed water and deeper, stratified and less productive waters are often known as **tidal mixing fronts**. Figure 3.4 shows how the water over the continental shelf around the British Isles is more productive than deeper water to the north and west. There is also a clear boundary (front) between the extremely well-mixed water in the shallower, southern part of the North Sea (where the colour of suspended sediment obscures that of the phytoplankton) and the deeper, less well-mixed water in the central and northern part of the North Sea. (As mentioned in the caption to Figure 3.4, the yellowish coloration off the coast of Norway, where the water is deep, is caused by dissolved organic material flowing out from the Baltic.)

- Looking back to Figure 3.4 and its caption, would you say that there is any evidence for increased productivity along the *edge* of the continental shelf?

- Yes, there are blooms of coccolithophores (white areas) along the edge of the continental shelf off Scotland and Ireland (as well as over the continental shelf itself, in some places).

There are various causes of high productivity along the edges of continental shelves. Sometimes, tidal mixing stirs up so much sediment that primary productivity over the shelf itself is restricted by lack of light. In these cases, the highest production tends to occur along the boundaries between well-mixed water and stratified water, i.e. along the fronts. At the very edge of the continental shelf (cf. Figure 2.4), there may be **shelf break fronts**, where deeper nutrient-rich water moves up the continental slope into a more stable, shallower part of the water column, giving rise to high primary productivity. This occurs along the edge of the continental shelf off Nova Scotia, and also along the coast of Natal (seen in the 'Bounty off Natal' video).

Locally, there are often fronts off river mouths, around the edge of the outflowing plume of river water. Being fresher and less dense, the river water flows above the seawater, and tends to entrain deeper water into it. This could be more nutrient-rich than the river water and, if light levels are sufficiently high, could give rise to high primary productivity. Of course, the situation varies from river to river, and the position of the phytoplankton bloom is affected by the strength of the outflow and by local currents. As suspended sediment greatly affects the amount of light available for photosynthesis, the position of the bloom is also affected by how much sediment the river carries and how long it takes to settle out. Of course, river outflows themselves often lead directly to high primary productivity, especially if they carry nitrates leached from fertilized land, or phosphates from sewage effluent.

▶▶ *This is a good time to watch the 'Open Ocean' video (VC1), which looks at life in the clear waters of the nutrient-poor subtropical gyres, and at the isolated 'oases of life' found within them. However, if you have not already watched the 'Bounty off Natal' video, you should look at that first.*

While watching the 'Open Ocean' video, make a note of any features that seem to be characteristic of fast-swimming species like tuna. Pay particular attention to their body shapes and the shapes of their tails. ◀◀

Notes on the 'Open Ocean' video

General note: In this video, we see tuna at different stages in its life cycle – egg, tuna larva, young tuna and adult – and in different parts of its circuit of migration. There will be more about fish migrations in Chapter 9.

[2:00:21] Note how streamlined the Sei whale is while swimming, and not feeding. Note also the water streaming from the whale's jaws, as the sardines are sieved out.

[2:04:19] These eggs form part of the meroplankton. The round object is a globule of oil to help the egg float.

[2:05:43] In Chapter 9, and the next part of 'The Deep' video, you will discover more about these nightly migrations up from the depths. The latest theories about how bioluminescence evolved will be discussed in Chapter 10.

[2:07:35] You will now be well aware that currents are not like rivers, and that these 'invisible boundaries' are fronts!

[2:09:48] As you know from Section 4.6, sound travels through water with very little loss of energy, so the dolphins can detect disturbance in the water some distance away, and use their echo-location to track down the cause. Echo-location involves pinpointing the position of a target by bouncing sound off it. A stream of discrete sounds is emitted and a 'fix' is made using the time taken for the sound to travel to the target, bounce off it, and travel back again.

[2:13:14] The blue-fin tuna's 'special blood vessels' (which all tuna have to some extent) will be discussed in the next chapter.

[2:14:30] This coil is a chain of *salps* (Phylum Chordata). Individual salps have cylindrical gelatinous bodies with an opening either end. Each salp spends part of its life cycle as an individual, and produces a chain by 'budding' to form identical copies of itself. Depending on the species, individual salps may be 1–30 cm long, and chains (which may consist of several hundred individuals) may be as long as 15 m. Salps live in warm surface or near-surface waters and feed on phytoplankton and bacteria.

[2:16:46] Triggerfish are so-called because their forward dorsal fin (i.e. the fin along the back which is closest to the head) consists primarily of a single rigid spine that normally lies against the fish's body, but which can be extended as a weapon if the need arises.

[2:18:23] The significance of 'bony fish' will become clear in Chapter 6.

[2:21:29] This volcano is probably erupting over a 'hot spot' (cf. Section 2.2).

[2:24:37] In this sequence, you can see upwelling generated by steep submarine topography, like that which occurs to the west of the western Galápagos islands (cf. Figure 5.7).

[2:25:51] Characteristic features of sharks will be discussed in the next chapter.

[2:28:66] As suggested above, vibrations in the water are effectively sound waves, which travel through water with very little loss of energy.

[2:31:41] As you will now appreciate, currents shift all the time, in response to fluctuations in the wind or as a result of interactions with other currents. If the current that is being forced up by the seamount moves to one side of it, the upwelling will cease.

[2:35:45] The Azores are steep-sided volcanic islands, so upwelling will be generated off them.

5.5 Ecosystems and food webs

The 'Open Ocean' video covers both the nutrient-poor waters of the subtropical gyres and some isolated upwelling regions. As you will see shortly, open ocean ecosystems function very differently from those of productive upwelling areas like those to the west of the Galápagos archipelago, or coastal upwelling regions in eastern boundary currents such as the California Current and the Benguela Current.

►► *You can now find out more about ocean ecosystems by studying the 'Ecosystems and Food Webs' module on your* Life in the Oceans *CD, and working through Activities 1 to 4. Activities 1 to 3 look at how food webs function, and Activity 4 contrasts four different ecosystems, including two – kelp forests and coral reefs – where the ecosystem habitat is provided by part of the ecosystem itself.*

Before beginning this module, you might find it useful to read through the notes below. ◄◄

Notes for the 'Ecosystems and Food Webs' module

Here are definitions of some of the important terms used in this module, so that you can refer to them later, if you wish. (You can use your *Glossary* if you need to check the definition of terms used earlier in this book.)

biomass Amount of living material, usually in some area or volume. (cf. the discussion in the text relating to Figure 4.1). If quantified, marine biomass is usually expressed in grams of carbon per unit area of sea-surface (or per unit area of sea-bed, in the case of benthic ecosystems), i.e. $gC\,m^{-2}$.

consumer Any member of a food chain or food web, other than the primary producer (see also trophic compartment or trophic level).

ecosystem All the (interdependent) communities of organisms in a particular geographical area, plus the physical environment that they inhabit.

fluxes The amounts of organic material transferred between components of a food chain or food web (or between different trophic levels/compartments – see below).

food chain A linear sequence of organisms in which each organism (or group of organisms) is food for the next member in the sequence.

food web Schematic representation of the feeding interactions within an ecosystem or community (i.e. like a food chain, but in the case of most ecosystems, more realistic).

P : C ratio Ratio of production to consumption – a measure of the efficiency with which food is converted to new 'consumer' tissue.

production Increase in biomass through growth and reproduction (sometimes over the course of a year, by implication). If quantified, production is usually expressed in grams of carbon per unit area ($gC\,m^{-2}$).

productivity Rate of increase in biomass through growth and reproduction. If quantified, productivity is usually expressed in grams of carbon per unit area per unit time (e.g. $gC\,m^{-2}\,day^{-1}$).

top predator Animal at the end of a pathway in a food chain or food web, which is not preyed upon by any other animal.

trophic compartment or **trophic level** The 'position' occupied by an organism in a food chain or food web, e.g. primary producers (plants, or in some unusual circumstances, bacteria), herbivores, carnivores which prey on herbivores, carnivores which prey on other carnivores, top predator. In a food web, an animal can occupy more than one trophic compartment/level.

When you have completed the 'Ecosystems and Food Webs' module, you can check your understanding of Activity 1 (Introduction to ocean ecosystems and food webs) and Activity 3 (Productivity and fluxes in simple and complex food webs) by trying Question 5.3 below, and (a little later) Question 5.4. In your supplementary material, you will also find some exercises which follow up Activity 2 (Quantifying biomass and exchanges in food webs) and Activity 3, and an opportunity to use the spreadsheet provided on the CD.

Question 5.3 Estimates of the annual production of plants on land and in the oceans vary, but all agree that they are of the same order of magnitude. How is it, then, that at any one time the total *mass* of living material (or biomass) in land plants is at least 100 times that of plants living in the ocean (perhaps even 250–300 times, according to some estimates)? ◀

Figure 5.10 (overleaf) shows three representative food webs for three types of marine waters (but laid out in terms of their trophic levels, so they all resemble simple food chains). The topmost food web is typical of the low-nutrient waters of the open ocean, as discussed in the first part of Activity 4 of the 'Ecosystems and Food Webs' module (and the setting for much of the 'Open Ocean' video). The middle one is typical of productive shelf waters, and the bottom one is typical of the highly productive waters found in regions of coastal upwelling, for example in the Benguela upwelling (Figure 5.4) or off the coast of Peru. (You will probably spot that the lower 'branch' of this last example corresponds to the simple food chain shown at the very beginning of Activity 1 of the 'Ecosystems and Food Webs' module.)

Question 5.4

(a) On the basis of Figure 5.10, and what you know about the productivity of different regions of the ocean, would you say that the number of trophic levels in a food chain is related to the productivity of the region concerned? If so, how?

(b) On the basis of what you learnt in Activity 3 of the 'Ecosystems and Food Webs' module, can you explain why the food-web structure in upwelling regions can support enormous planktivorous whales? ◀

It is thought that the lengths of food webs may be at least partly determined by the size of the primary producers. In upwelling areas, colonial (i.e. chain-forming) diatoms are large enough to be eaten directly by large zooplankton such as krill, and even by fish which may in turn be preyed upon by top predators. As you will have seen from the videos, highly productive regions often support large populations of top level predators, such as seals, dolphins and killer whales.

As mentioned in Activity 3, the phytoplankton of the nutrient-poor open ocean are typically very small. These, along with bacteria, are eaten by protozoans (single-celled animals) and other small zooplankton, which are in turn eaten by larger crustaceans such as copepods (e.g. *Calanus*). These are consumed by small planktivorous fishes, which are the prey of squid and larger fish such as tuna.

As discussed in relation to Figure 5.6a, open ocean ecosystems need to function in the absence of a good supply of 'new' (i.e. upwelled) nutrients. In areas where there is deep mixing by storms (Section 4.3), as in upwelling areas, the nitrogen used by phytoplankton is in the form of nitrate (NO_3^-). In the open ocean, phytoplankton rely largely on nutrients recycled *within* the photic zone. In these circumstances, the nitrogen is in the form of ammonia (NH_3) and urea – waste from zooplankton

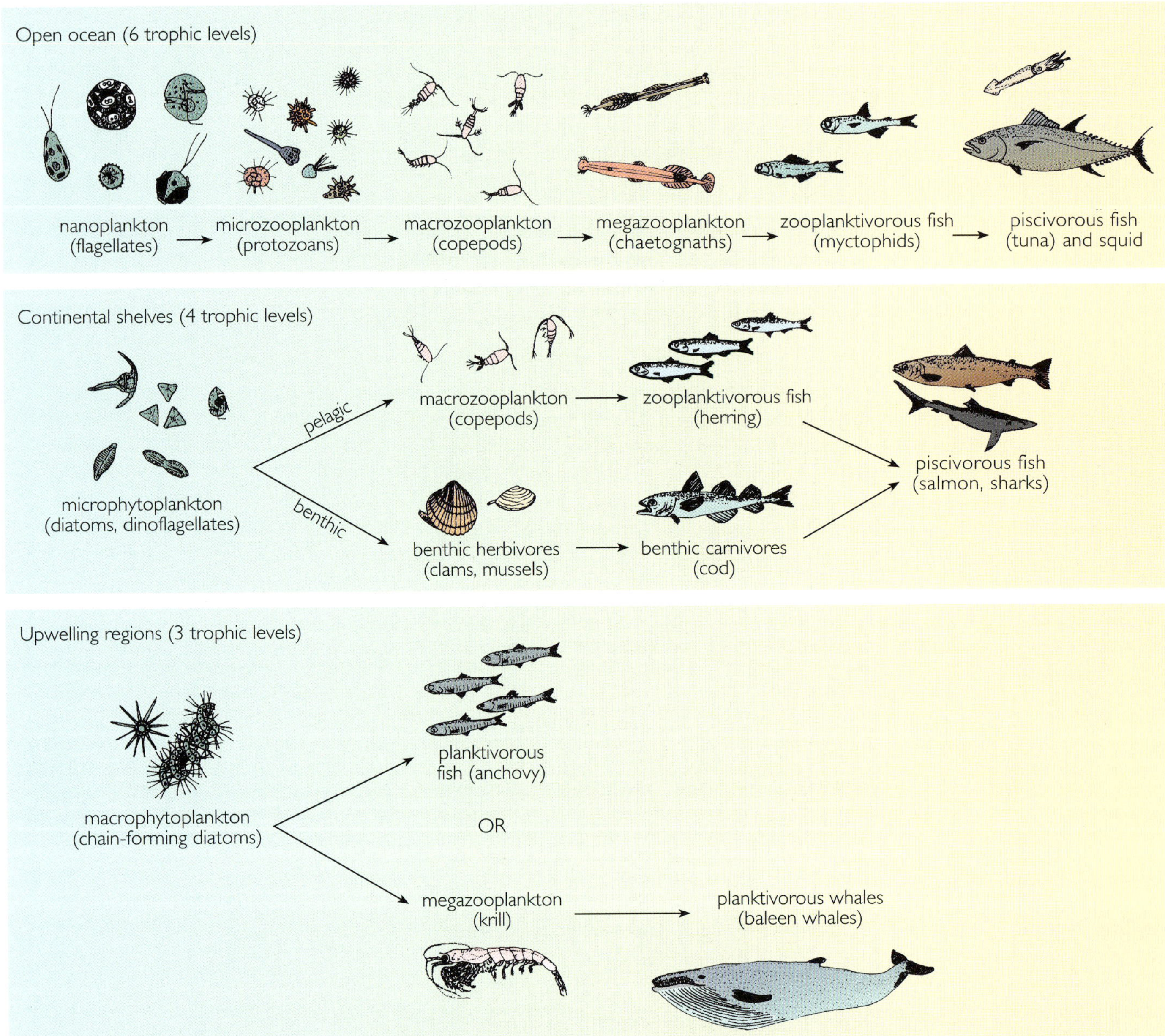

Figure 5.10 A comparison of food chains in three different marine habitats. Note: The organisms representing each trophic level are selected examples of the many marine species that could be present at that level. Note also the prefixes indicating different size ranges: nanoplankton (phytoplankton and zooplankton) are 2–20 µm across (µm = micrometre, i.e. one-millionth of a metre, 10^{-6} m); microplankton are 20–200 µm across; macro- and megaplankton may be millimetres to centimetres across/long. Piscivorous fish are fish that eat other fish.

metabolism, and (in the case of NH_3) decomposition of dead material by bacteria (cf. Activity 3 of the 'Ecosystems and Food Webs' module).

Don't worry if you find this material quite difficult. The main thing to remember is that the open oceans are low-nutrient environments – although as the 'Open Ocean' video makes clear, that does not mean that they are devoid of life!

Fish design

6

In previous chapters, we have been examining the various factors that affect the oceanic environment – light levels, the shape of the sea-bed, mixing, currents and nutrient concentrations – and we considered how these factors influence biological productivity in various parts of the ocean. In this chapter, we will be concentrating on one group of animals – fish – and look in particular at how fish swim and at their buoyancy. The subject of how fish swim is also covered in the two videos which accompany this chapter (on VC3). However, marine mammals are not completely neglected because the second of these videos also looks at what makes dolphins particularly good swimmers and sperm whales such efficient divers.

6.1 Different classes of fish

Fish come in an enormous variety of shapes and sizes, depending on where and how they make their living. Fish are craniates (i.e. vertebrates) and most belong to the Class Osteichthyes ('bony fish'). In modern seas, the great majority of the more than 22 000 species of marine fish are **teleosts** (or 'complete bones'). Teleost fishes have adapted to live in an enormous variety of different environments, in freshwater, shallow marine waters, the open ocean and the deep seas.

- Can you recall from the 'Biological Diversity' module what the other classes of fish are?

- They are the Agnatha (jawless fish) and the Chondrichthyes (cartilaginous fish) – and for completeness we should mention the 'lungfish' which live in freshwater, and do not appear in the CD module.

There are only a few species of jawless fish, including the hagfish which you will see in 'The Deep' video. Of the cartilaginous fish – also known as **elasmobranchs** – the best known are the sharks and rays.

Question 6.1 Think back to the various video sequences showing sharks, for example the blue shark, hammerhead sharks, white-tip reef sharks and the silke shark in the 'Open Ocean' video [2:12:14, 2:25:53 and 2.27:51]. Can you name at least three distinctive physical features that seem to be characteristic of sharks? ◀

Because of their different evolutionary histories, elasmobranchs and teleosts have many differences, some more obvious than others. Some of the most notable contrasts between them are as follows:

- Teleosts have bony skeletons, with many more separately moveable parts than the skeletons of elasmobranchs, which are made of cartilage (a firm elastic tissue which, unlike bone, is not calcified).
- Teleosts have evolved a variety of jaw mechanisms, allowing a great diversity of feeding habits and diets. (The Blue Planet videos – especially 'The Deep' – provide some striking examples of jaws adapted to allow survival in particular ecological niches.)
- Most teleost fishes have neutral buoyancy (i.e. they tend to neither sink nor rise in the water column) mainly as a result of having a swimbladder. Elasmobranchs do not have a swimbladder, although some species come close to achieving neutral buoyancy as a result of having large livers which store considerable amounts of oil. (Buoyancy will be discussed in Section 6.3.)

- Elasmobranchs are typically good swimmers, but their manoeuvrability is limited and they cannot swim backwards or hang motionless in the water as many teleosts do.
- Elasmobranchs produce small numbers of relatively large yolky eggs. Fertilization is internal and the eggs are either laid in protective cases or retained in the mother's body until they are ready to be born. In some elasmobranch species, embryos are fed by the mother while they are developing inside her. In contrast, the vast majority of teleost species lay large numbers of small eggs that float in the water and are fertilized externally. They hatch into tiny larvae which join the meroplankton.

You may remember the video sequence of the baby dogfish growing in its egg capsule attached to a strand of kelp, towards the end of the 'Seasonal Seas' video [1:39:34]. On the basis of this sequence, would you say that dogfish are teleosts or elasmobranchs?

The egg capsule, and the hatching of a fully developed fish rather than a fish larva, both tell us that dogfish are elasmobranchs.

In the 'Open Ocean' video, we effectively followed the life of a yellowfin tuna, from egg to young adult.

Do you think that tuna are teleosts or elasmobranchs?

They are teleosts. As shown in the video, tuna develop from large numbers of small eggs that have been released to float in the ocean.

We suggested that, while watching the 'Open Ocean' video, you made a note of any characteristic features of fast-swimming fish like tuna (or indeed marlin, mackerel, trevally etc.), paying particular attention to the body shape and shape of the tail. Later in the next section, you will be able to compare your notes with our illustrations.

6.2 Fish shape, fins and tails

In all fish, the main body of muscles is arranged in distinct overlapping segments or layers, situated on either side of the spinal column and enclosing the body cavity which contains the stomach, liver, intestines etc. These overlapping layers of muscle make up the white or light-coloured flesh used in many fish dishes: when fish is lightly cooked, the muscle segments can be easily separated. Perhaps surprisingly, in most fish species living in the upper 500 m or so of the ocean (i.e. the fish with which we are most familiar), this white muscle is used only in fast 'bursts' of swimming. For normal cruising speeds (i.e. during steady energy-efficient swimming), these fish use a thin layer of red or brown muscle (which is also in a series of segments) situated along the flanks close to the skin.

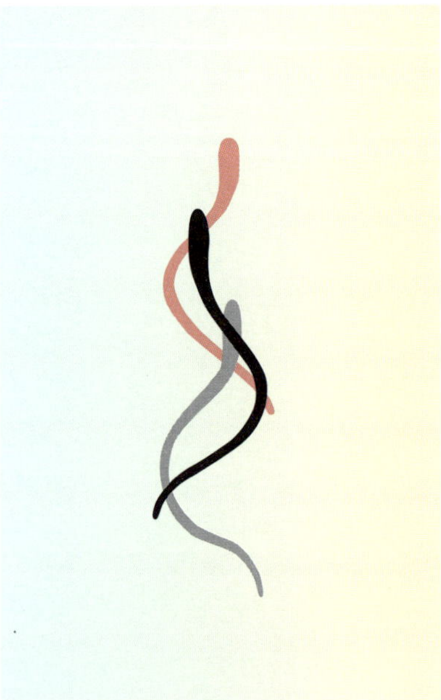

Figure 6.1 The mode of swimming used by the eel (seen from above). The grey, black and red silhouettes show the eel at intervals of 0.3 seconds.

Now imagine the type of swimming seen in eels (*Anguilla anguilla*) and some fish larvae. Here, the animal moves forward as a result of a succession of waves moving down the body from head to tail (Figure 6.1). The bending of the body in the backward-travelling wave is achieved by muscle contractions on one side of the spinal column being accompanied by relaxation and slight stretching of muscles on the other side. Because the bent portions of the body wall push against the water, as the wave moves backwards the animal is propelled forwards. The final thrust is provided by the tail.

- Thinking back to the 'Open Ocean' video, would you say that tuna, marlin and mackerel swim in this manner?

- No, the bodies of these fish remain quite stiff during swimming, while the large tail moves vigorously from side to side, generating the thrust which propels them forward.

In the case of tuna, the major body muscles deliver the propulsive force to the tail by means of large tendons which pull the tail from side to side on a hinged joint. This contrasts with the eel-like style of swimming, which is very inefficient as a lot of energy is expended on side-to-side movement of the head and body, as well as of the tail. Most fish have a mode of swimming which is intermediate between these two extremes.

A fish moving through water experiences a force opposing its motion. This force, known as **drag**, is approximately proportional to the *square* of its speed in relation to the water.

- So what will happen to the drag experienced by a swimming fish if it trebles its speed?

- The drag will become nine times greater. (As the swimming speed increases 3-fold, so drag will go up by $3^2 = 3 \times 3 = 9$-fold.)

This illustrates how important it is for swimming animals to keep drag as low as possible. The total drag acting on a swimming animal is made up of two components: *pressure drag*, which is the opposing force experienced as it 'pushes' its way through the water, and *skin friction drag*, which is the frictional force generated by the water moving over the surface of the animal. Pressure drag is reduced by having a long, thin body with a pointed front. However, long thin shapes have a large surface area relative to volume, and this increases skin friction drag. For fast swimming, therefore, a compromise is needed. It will probably not surprise you to learn that the smallest possible total drag is achieved by having the torpedo-like shape of fast-swimming fish like tuna, as well as many whales and dolphins.

Drag can be further minimized by increased streamlining through reduction of protuberances on the body. Some fish, including tuna, can fold their fins into grooves and recesses on their bodies. Even the eyes of tuna are flush with the head and covered with a layer of fatty tissue.

In the case of a streamlined fish swimming at low speeds, the flow of water around the body is smooth and laminar, i.e. in layers. The thin layer of water adjacent to the surface of the fish moves *with* the fish, and each succeeding layer is influenced by the motion of the fish slightly less. So if the fish were swimming through still water, the layer of water closest to the fish would move at the speed of the fish, the next layer out would move slightly slower, the next one out again would move even more slowly, etc. This situation results in low drag. If the fish speeds up, there will come a point when the smooth flow of water over its body begins to break down and turbulent eddies start to be generated. The onset of turbulence results in about a three-fold increase in drag, and fish that need to swim fast have strategies to delay this, which include keeping side-to-side motion to a minimum (as noted above). Only slow-swimming fish make large side-to-side movements. In the case of tuna, the little fins on the slender part of the body near the tail are thought to help delay the onset of turbulence.

The skin of the fish may itself be adapted to reduce drag. The skins of some fish species produce mucus, which helps reduce friction and promotes laminar flow. This is probably most effective at slow speeds. By contrast, the scales of some fish, such as sharks, have tiny tooth-like protuberances which generate small vortices or eddies, producing a layer of 'microturbulence' which acts as a kind of lubricant, reducing friction and delaying the onset of fully developed turbulence. (This principle has been adopted by designers of racing yachts and suits for competitive swimming.) Some marine fish have a porous skin so that seawater can pass into and out of a 'canal' system just under the surface; this can also help to produce a layer of microturbulence close to the skin.

Fishes make forward progress against drag by generating **thrust**. Just as jet engines expel hot gases backwards in order to move forward, so fish send 'parcels' of water backwards to propel themselves forward. In fact, the water sent backwards by a swimming fish bears more resemblance to the vortices sent back from a propeller than to the jet from an engine (Figure 6.2). A tail beat to the right generates anticlockwise vortices (seen from above in Figure 6.2a), and a tail beat to the left generates clockwise vortices. The amount that a fish moves forward as a result of one to-and-fro sweep of the tail is known as its 'stride-length'. In most normal fish, one stride-length is about 0.7 of the length of the fish.

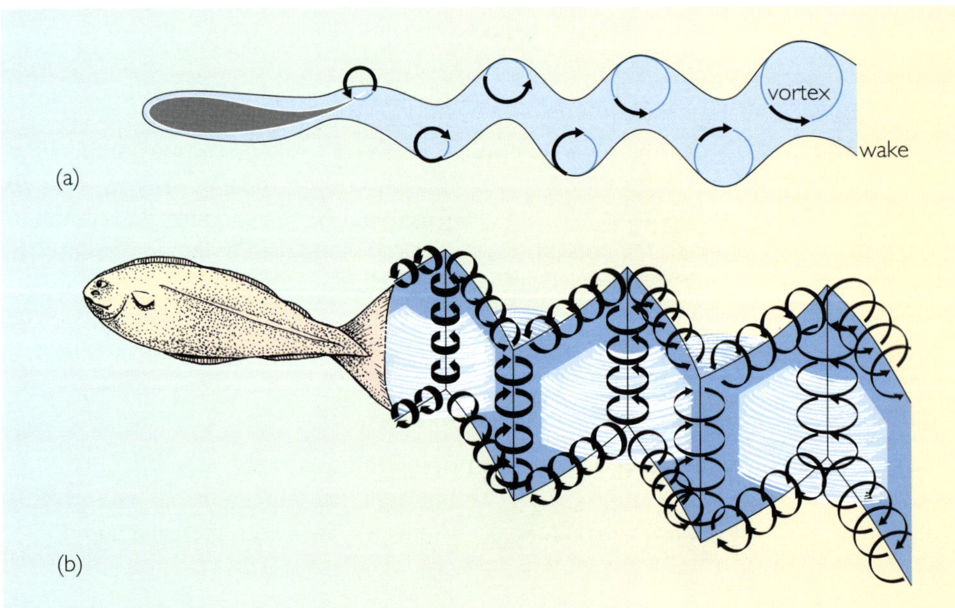

Figure 6.2 (a) A two-dimensional view of the wake of a swimming fish viewed from above, showing the vortices released at the end of every stroke of the tail to the right or left. (b) An impression of the vortex flow system behind a swimming fish, seen from the side. The tail is shown in the middle of a stroke towards you. The 'tightness' of the vortices and the speed of the water flow (indicated by the thickness of the arrows) decrease as they spiral out behind the fish.

For many fish, habitat and lifestyle mean that being able to cruise efficiently is not a high priority. Instead, they may need to accelerate quickly, or be able to manoeuvre well. Fish that specialize in short bursts of speed (for striking at prey or escaping from predators) are generally long and thin, which (as mentioned above) maximizes the surface area in contact with the water and so also maximizes the thrust that can be generated by the body. These darting fish also have a lot of muscle relative to their size (making them rounded rather than oval in cross-section) and have strong tails. Fish that specialize in quick turns are somewhat flattened and disc-shaped, which gives them a more flexible body. Most fish species have a shape that is a compromise between these three extremes (Figure 6.3), but there are also specialists, such as plankton-feeders and those that hunt by stealth and rely on camouflage, and these may have very bizarre shapes indeed. (You will see some good examples of this last category in the 'Coral Seas' video.)

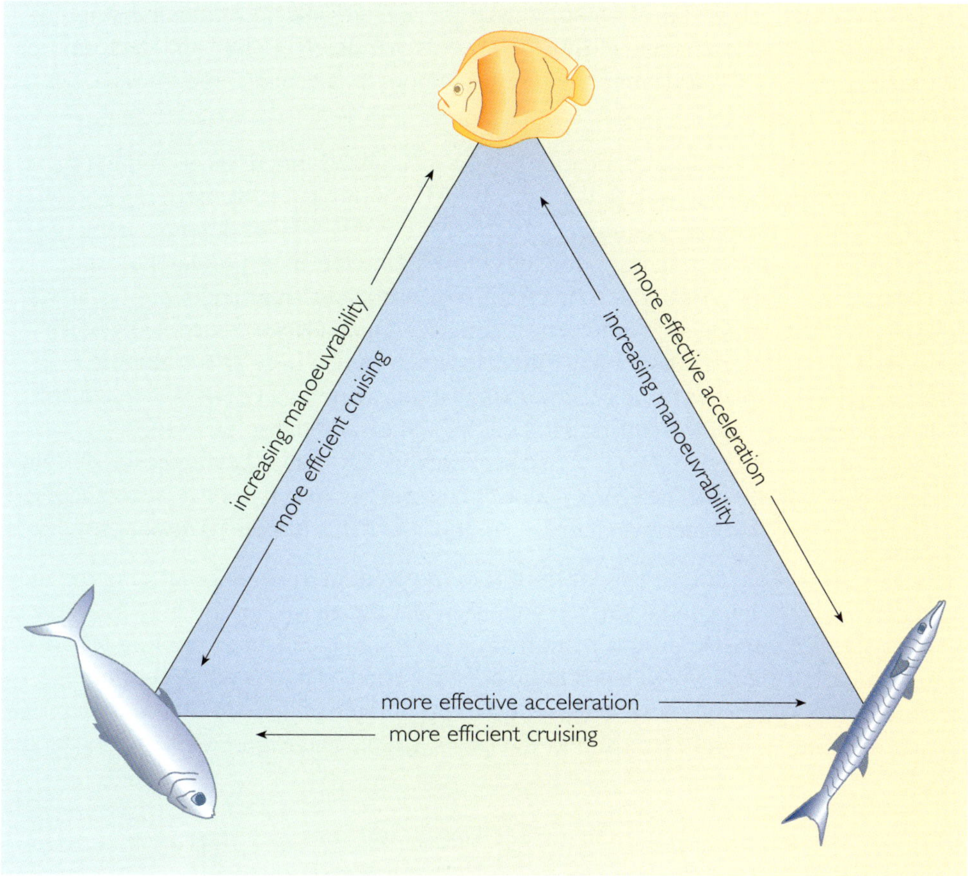

Figure 6.3 The 'fish triangle', showing ideal shapes for efficient cruising (torpedo-like), good acceleration (low drag, but well-muscled), and manoeuvrability (disc-shaped and flattened). Most fish have a body shape that is a compromise between these three extremes.

Fins also play an important role in swimming and turning, and are supported and moved by means of fine flexible rods or spines known as fin-rays, or simply rays. Fish generally have a pair of pectoral fins (one either side, behind the head), two dorsal fins along the back, an anal fin beneath the rear half of the body, a pair of pelvic fins on either side of the lower body (forward of the anal fin), and a caudal (tail) fin (Figure 6.4). The size, shape and position of these fins varies greatly between species, and in certain species some types of fin may be absent altogether.

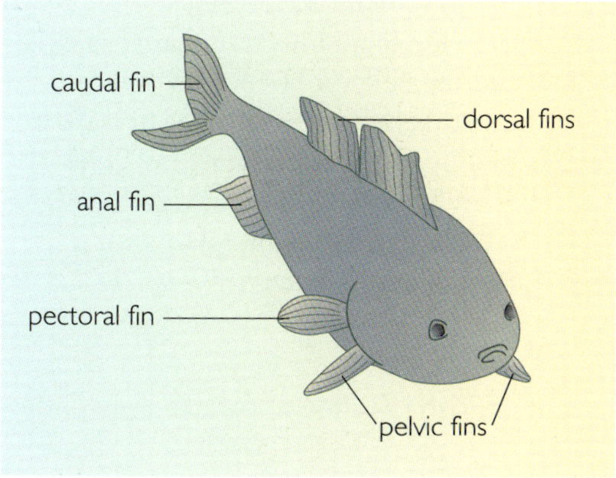

Figure 6.4 The different types of fins, shown on an imaginary fish.

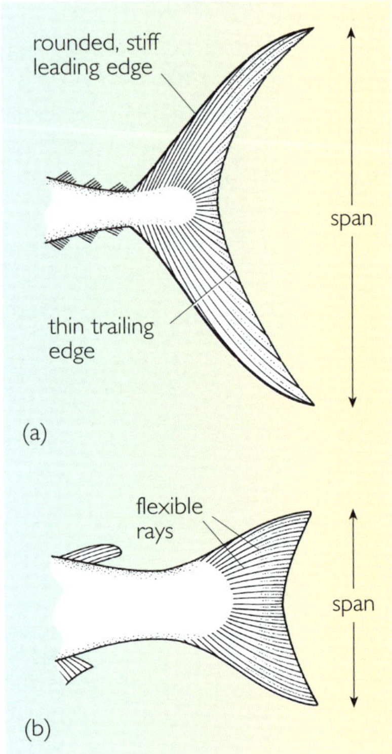

Figure 6.5 Two similarly shaped tails of different aspect ratios: (a) is a tuna (note the small fins just forward of the tail, which are thought to delay the onset of turbulence), and (b) is a cod.

The pectoral and pelvic fins are mainly used for manoeuvring, turning and stopping, while the vertical dorsal and anal fins are used as stabilizers. Pelvic and pectoral fins can usually be folded flat against the body when not in use, and sometimes so can the dorsal and anal fins.

Many fish species have fins adapted to highly specialized functions. A number have dorsal fins adapted to act as defensive or offensive weapons, with sharp rays or spines that may contain a venom. A number of reef fish use this type of defence, including lionfish which swim with their undersides close to the reef when threatened, and stonefish and scorpion fish which lie on the reef or the sea-floor and ward off attack from above. As mentioned in connection with the 'Open Ocean' video, triggerfish have highly specialized dorsal fins (triggers) which can be used as formidable weapons. Certain species of reef triggerfish use this spine as a defence mechanism. When chased, they swim headfirst into a hole, and extend the spine to lock themselves in. In the case of angler fish (which you met in the 'Living in the Oceans' module, and will see in 'The Deep' video), the front ray (or rays) have been adapted to become 'lures' that can be dangled in front of the fish's mouth to attract prey.

Now let's look at the tail, or caudal fin. From the point of view of generating the most thrust on a tail stroke, a large surface area is an advantage (cf. Figure 6.2). However, a larger surface area also produces more drag, so in practice fast swimming requires a compromise tail shape which has a large **aspect ratio** (AR), where aspect ratio is defined as the *square of the span* (from tip to tip of the fin) divided by the *area of the fin*, i.e. $span^2/area$. Figure 6.5a shows the tail of a tuna, and Figure 6.5b shows the tail of a cod.

- Which of the two tails has the greater aspect ratio?
- Not surprisingly, it is that of the tuna.

Relatively speaking, the area of the tuna tail is somewhat bigger than that of the cod, but the span, and especially the *square* of the span, is a lot bigger, making $span^2/area$ significantly bigger. Tuna tails have an AR of about 6, which is as high as it can be before strength begins to be sacrificed. Broader, low AR tails, like those of cod, are more suited to slow speeds, and good acceleration from a 'standing start'. Note, however, that fish can to some extent *change* the aspect ratios of their tails to suit the speed, by separating the rays of the fin or bringing them together. (Blacksmith fish could be seen changing the shapes of their tails in the 'Seasonal Seas' video [1:17:54].)

However, swimming fast is not always the main requirement, so tail fins are highly variable in shape. For ease of discussion, we can divide them into five main types, as shown in Figure 6.6: rounded, truncate, forked and lunate ('moon-shaped'), plus asymmetric (see below). The aspect ratios of these tails increase from left to right in Figure 6.6 (i.e. from rounded to lunate), and as mentioned above, lunate tails like those of tuna provide good thrust. However, they are very stiff, and provide little help in manoeuvring, so although a predatory tuna could easily outswim a fish with a rounded or truncate tail, the prey might well escape by outmanoeuvring the tuna.

- Do you recognize the type of tail shown at the far right?
- Asymmetric tails are typical of sharks and dogfish (as shown, for example in the Open Ocean' video [2:25:51]).

Asymmetric tails have a special function, discussion of which is reserved to the next section.

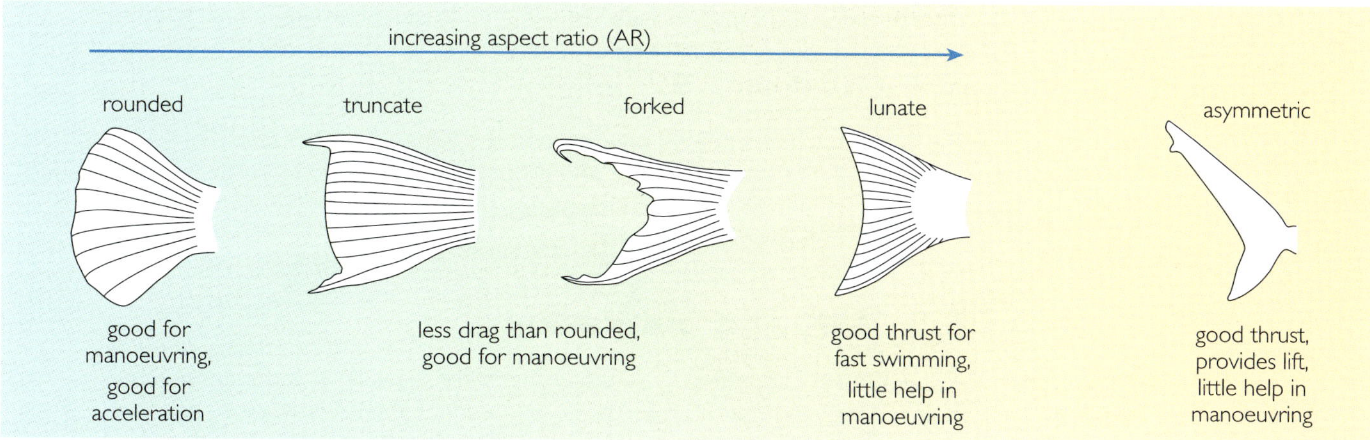

Figure 6.6 The five basic types of tail fin, the first four arranged in order of increasing aspect ratio. Many fish species have tail shapes that fall between these categories.

Some fish have fins that undulate (i.e. have a wave-like motion), which are used either as the main method of propulsion – as in the case of sea-horses, for example – or as an extra method, in addition to movement of the tail and body (Figure 6.7). Use of undulating fins confers excellent manoeuvrability. The 'wings' of rays are greatly enlarged pectoral fins, and rays propel themselves along by means of undulations passing back along the margins of the fins (this can be seen best in the 'Seasonal Seas' video [1:24:41]. (There are also some good examples of propulsion by undulating fins in the 'Coral Seas' video.)

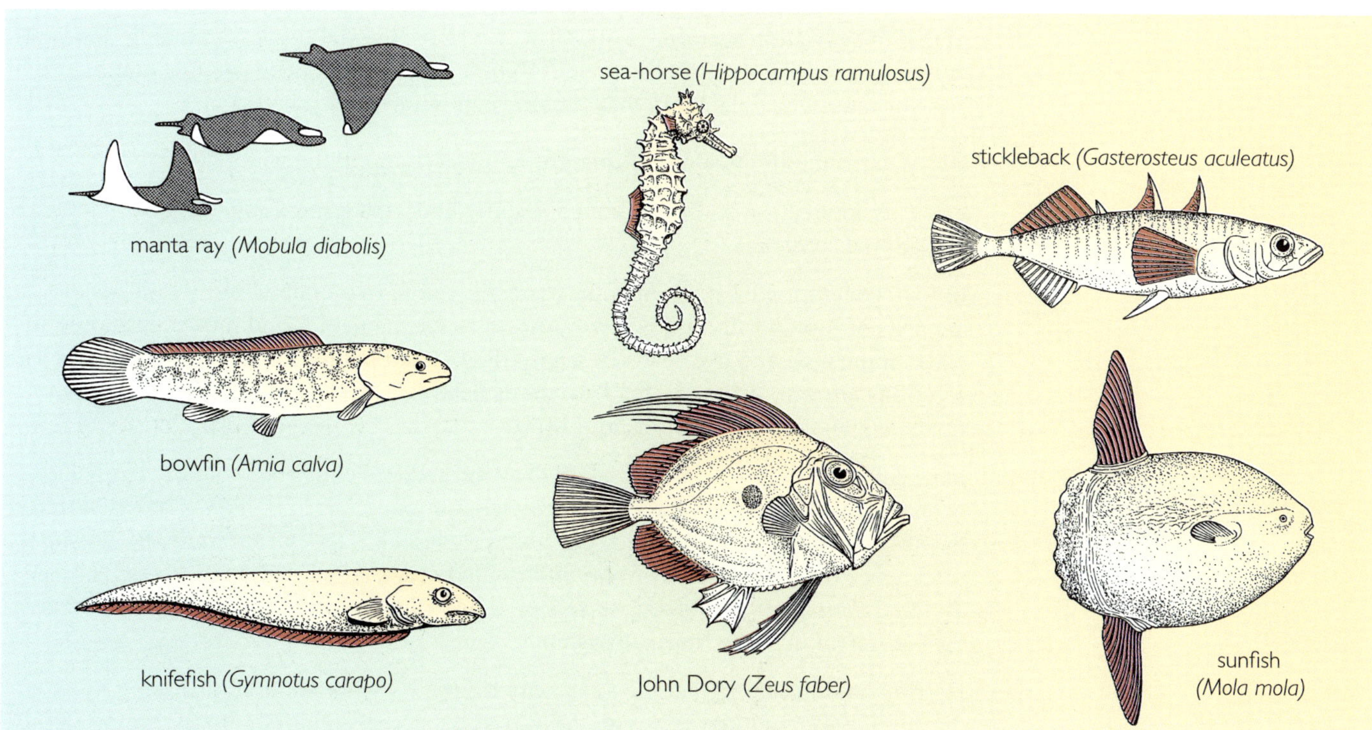

Figure 6.7 Examples of fish that use undulating fins for locomotion (the fins in question are shown in red). The fish are not shown to scale: sea-horses are only centimetres long, while sunfish may be 4 m from fin tip to fin tip.

Question 6.2 In Figure 6.7, the fins that undulate are toned in red (with the exception of the ray). Referring to Figure 6.4 as necessary, identify the type of fin involved in each case. ◀

The sunfish, which you will have seen in the 'Open Ocean' video [2:18:17], uses its flap-like tail as a kind of rudder, and propels itself forward by means of side-to-side motion of its unusual dorsal and anal fins (both of which have very high aspect ratios) (cf. Figure 6.5).

6.3 Lift and buoyancy

As mentioned in Section 2.1, the fact that salty seawater is more dense than freshwater means that it provides more buoyancy than freshwater. The buoyancy we experience when swimming at the sea-surface is a result of the fact that the force of our weight acting downwards is counteracted by an upwards force, known as **upthrust**, which is equivalent to the weight of the volume of water we have displaced. This is why people with a relatively large proportion of body fat (which has a low density) float higher in the water than people with little body fat – they do not have to displace as large a volume of water to generate sufficient upthrust to balance their weight.

Of course, most marine animals spend their lives completely submerged, so the volume of water that they displace is always the volume of their body. Their effective weight in water is their actual weight minus the weight of seawater they displace, i.e. minus the upthrust. To be neutrally buoyant (i.e. to be effectively weightless), and neither rise nor sink in the water column, they need an average density that is equal to the average density of the water they are in. For most fish, average body densities are reduced to some extent by the fact that the salt content of their blood is only 30–50% of that of seawater (Section 2.1.2). However, most animal tissues – notably bone and muscle – have a density that is greater than that of seawater (i.e. a cubic centimetre of bone or muscle weighs more than a cubic centimetre of seawater).

- What is the implication of this, for animals living in the water column?

- The implication is that without some method(s) of generating extra buoyancy, the animals will sink.

In fish, generation of extra buoyancy is achieved in two main ways: by means of deposits of low-density lipids, i.e. fat or oil (a mechanism found more commonly in elasmobranchs), and by means of a gas-filled swimbladder. As you will see, these two solutions are very different, because gases behave differently under pressure from lipids, which are solid (fat) or liquid (oil).

Most teleost fish have elastic gas-filled swimbladders which are roughly oval and lie beneath the spinal column and above the abdominal cavity. Oxygen is released into the swimbladder via a so-called 'gas gland', which has an extraordinary blood supply (and hence oxygen supply) of two intertwined networks of perhaps 100 000 (i.e. one hundred *thousand*) tiny blood vessels or capillaries. This blood supply is known as the *rete mirabile* – the 'miraculous net'.

Herring are unusual in that they can only fill their swimbladders by gulping in air at the surface. Herring are relatively primitive, as are eels and fish of the salmon family, which also have 'open' swimbladders with a duct to the oesophagus or gullet. Most advanced teleosts, however, have closed swimbladders. Swimbladders normally contain nitrogen, oxygen and carbon dioxide in varying proportions. In fish that live near the sea-surface, the proportions of gases in the swimbladder are close to those in the atmosphere, but for reasons that will become clear, the proportion of oxygen in the swimbladder increases with the depth at which the fish lives, and the swimbladders of deep-sea fish contain almost pure oxygen.

Having a closed swimbladder imposes constraints on how fast and how far it is possible to swim up and down the water column. In gases, the constituent molecules are widely spaced, with the result that – in contrast to liquids and solids – gases are very compressible. The volume occupied by a given mass of gas can therefore change greatly in response to changing pressure, becoming smaller under increased pressure, and larger under reduced pressure. (You might remember the stream of bubbles rising from the shoal of herring being driven up towards the surface by killer whales in the 'Seasonal Seas' video – as the pressure on the herring decreased, the air in their swimbladders expanded and escaped through their mouths.)

- For a fish with an elastic swimbladder (containing a fixed amount of gas), what danger might there be in swimming rapidly up through the water column?

- As the fish swam upwards, the pressure acting on it would decrease, and the volume of the gas-filled swimbladder would increase. This in turn would reduce the average density of the fish as a whole, making it still more buoyant, and causing it to rise faster. (Such a situation is known as a 'runaway positive feedback effect'.)

This expansion of gas under the influence of decreasing pressure is the reason that the swimbladders of fish caught at depth and brought rapidly to the surface using long lines or trawls, often explode or can be seen protruding from their mouths. The reverse problem would arise if our hypothetical fish swam downwards – its swimbladder would be compressed, the average density of the fish as a whole would increase, and it would sink still further.

Maintaining neutral buoyancy despite changing depth can be achieved by varying the amount of gas in the swimbladder so that its volume remains constant, regardless of the external pressure acting on the elastic swimbladder. The total amount of gas in the swimbladder may be increased by supplying extra oxygen from the blood, and, as you will probably have realized, this is where the gas gland and the *rete mirabile* come into play. The mechanisms whereby the oxygen content of the swimbladder is regulated are very complicated and we cannot go into them here. One aspect we *can* look at is how oxygen can pass into the swimbladder simply by *diffusion* from the *rete mirabile*, i.e. individual oxygen molecules passing from high-oxygen blood to a lower-oxygen swimbladder *without* being pumped in, even though the pressure in the swimbladder is very high. At first sight this does indeed seem miraculous!

- Can you suggest why the networks of thousands of tiny capillaries allow the *rete mirabile* to supply oxygen so efficiently?

- It is the large surface area of the mass of tiny capillaries, or strictly the large diffusion area in comparison with the volume of blood in the capillaries.

If you have ever gutted fish, you will have seen swimbladders, though perhaps without realizing what they were. Sometimes they have not completely collapsed, and sometimes (as in the case of herring, for example) they are easy to spot as they appear silvery. This is because they are covered by a continuous layer of overlapping crystals of a substance known as guanine. The crystals themselves are impermeable, and as they overlap, and lie closely together, any escape of gas occurs only very slowly. Even when the surface of the swimbladder is stretched or contracts, the overlapping crystals provide an effective barrier to gas escape.

Question 6.3 Some marine animals, including cuttlefish (*Sepia*), do not have swimbladders that can vary in size. Instead, the gas is effectively enclosed in a rigid 'box'. Can you suggest (1) any advantages, or (2) any disadvantages of this? ◀

As mentioned earlier, the other method of generating extra buoyancy, found more frequently in elasmobranchs such as sharks, is the accumulation of low-density lipids. Ordinary fish oils (e.g. cod liver oil) have densities of around 930 kilograms per cubic metre (kg m^{-3}), significantly less than the density of water, but lipids used to increase buoyancy have lower densities than this: around 860 kg m^{-3}. Even so, to achieve neutral buoyancy, enormous deposits of these substances need to be synthesized (or consumed in prey species); and more needs to be added as the animal grows.

- Do you think that the lift provided by accumulations of lipids will be affected by the depth of the fish in the water column, in same the way that lift from gas-filled swimbladders can be?

- No, because unlike gas, lipids are relatively incompressible, so their volume (and hence their density) is not markedly affected by pressure.

The basking shark and the whale shark, plankton feeders which cruise slowly along with their mouths open ('Open Ocean' [1:14:13]), are both close to neutral buoyancy as a result of huge stores of lipids (fat) in their livers. Many deep-sea sharks can also be neutrally buoyant for the same reason – their livers can occupy 30% of the volume of their bodies and cause them to look quite corpulent.

However, the great majority of elasmobranchs do not store enough lipids to achieve neutral buoyancy. For dogfish and some sharks that spend a considerable proportion of their time resting on the bottom, being neutrally buoyant is not as important as for most other fish. However, all sharks and dogfish benefit from extra lift generated by their asymmetric tails (Figure 6.6). As well as moving from side to side, the tail twists, and generates a net upward force; you will learn more about this in the 'Wild Moves: Water' video, which you will see shortly.

Lift generated by relative motion between the water and an animal's body is known as **dynamic lift** to distinguish it from lift resulting from buoyancy, which is known as **static lift**. The commonest type of dynamic lift is generated by the flow of water over pectoral fins. If you study the extended pectoral fins of active fish such as tuna and mackerel, you will see that they are inclined to the horizontal, with the leading edge higher than the trailing edge. This, combined with the 'hydrofoil' shape of the fins, leads to a variation in pressure over the upper and lower surfaces of the fins which results in a net upwards force. As discussed in the video 'Wild Moves: Water', it was thought that sharks also used their pectoral fins to generate lift in this way, but it now seems that (at least at normal swimming speeds) the lift provided by the tail is more important. This lift force acts upwards at the tail end of the shark and, on its own, would tend to tilt the shark's body downwards. To counter this, the shark swims with its body at an angle.

Mackerel – which as mentioned above, *do* generate lift using their pectoral fins – may also swim with their bodies at an angle to avoid sinking when swimming at low speeds. When the body is tilted, the thrust from the tail, which acts along the body of the fish, also has an upwards component. In other words, the tilted body of the swimming mackerel itself generates lift.

- If a mackerel was swimming very fast, would you expect its body to be tilted more than usual or less than usual?

- It would be tilted less than usual.

Like drag forces, lift forces increase with the square of the speed, and are very small when the swimming speed is small. Because of this, there is a minimum swimming speed below which a shark or tuna would begin to sink. Large and active swimmers like sharks and tuna already expend a considerable amount of energy in swimming, so the small amount of extra energy involved in swimming to avoid sinking is negligible. The same is true of mackerel.

- Can you suggest why it is important for the plankton-feeding basking shark and whale shark to be neutrally buoyant, i.e. be able to avoid sinking without the help of lift generated by fins or tail?

- Collecting and sieving plankton can only be done efficiently by swimming relatively slowly (in these cases, at speeds of about 1 metre per second, 1 m s^{-1}). This is too slow for the flow of water over the pectoral fins or tail to generate much dynamic lift.

Figure 6.8 shows the approximate distribution of fish with and without swimbladders at different depths in the ocean. As you can see, there is not really a clear-cut distribution pattern of fish with swimbladders and without. Some of the reasons for

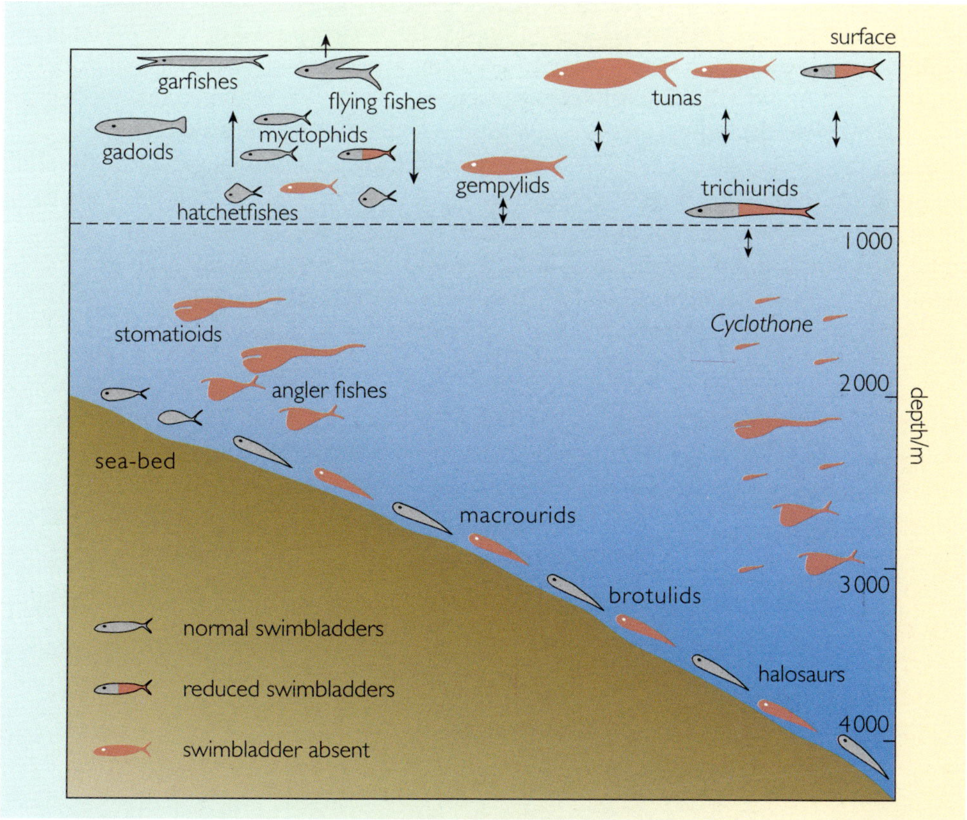

Figure 6.8 Diagram to show the distribution of fish with and without swimbladders at different depths in the ocean (see key). You should imagine the sea-bed to continue up to the left into shallow water. Do not worry about not knowing some of the fish names; myctophids are also known as lanternfish. (The dashed line indicates the bottom of the twilight zone; it does *not* indicate a sharp cut-off in the distribution of fish with swimbladders, as some mid-depth fish *do* have swimbladders. Vertical arrows indicate groups that undergo vertical migrations, a topic that will be covered in Chapter 9.)

this probably relate to the issues we have been discussing. Another reason might be that over millions of years, certain fish groups may have changed the depth ranges at which they live, and some which lost their swimbladders on moving down into the deep sea subsequently moved back up into mid-depths.

The compressibility of gas means that with increasing depth in the ocean, gas-filled swimbladders become increasingly inefficient. Furthermore, with increasing pressure, gas becomes more soluble, so producing gas for the swimbladder, and retaining it there, becomes more expensive in terms of energy. Therefore, the swimbladders of many mid-water and deep-sea fish contain not gas, but lipids. Many deep-sea fish with swimbladders cruise slowly just above the sea-bed, and use their swimbladders to detect low frequency (low pitch) sound.

There are also some good reasons for bottom-living fish *not* to have a swimbladder.

- What advantages might there be for flatfish like plaice (*Pleuronectes platessa*), that normally rest on the bottom, not to have a swimbladder?

- Fish that normally rest on the bottom need to be able to resist being swept along by bottom currents, and often need to be able to settle into the bottom sediment to hide. For both of these reasons, it would be advantageous to be denser than water.

6.4 Swimming muscles

As mentioned at the start of Section 6.2, most of the muscle of fish is white muscle which, in fish living in the upper 500 m of the ocean, is used only in fast 'bursts' of swimming. For normal cruising – that is, highly efficient steady swimming, the equivalent of jogging – these fish use a thin layer of red or brown muscle which is usually situated along the flanks close to the skin. Figure 6.9 shows how individual white and red muscle fibres (within the muscle segments) are arranged in a typical teleost fish. Note the helical arrangement of the white muscle fibres, which are arranged rather like the twisted fibres of a rope. This helical arrangement effectively multiplies the effect of a muscle contraction by about four, i.e. it causes the body to curve much more than a similar contraction of the red fibres along the flank. The white muscle thus allows swimming in 'low gear' compared with the 'high-gear' swimming ('cruising') attained using red muscle. (Note, however, that for reasons which will become clear in Chapter 10, most deep-sea fish have *no* red muscle.)

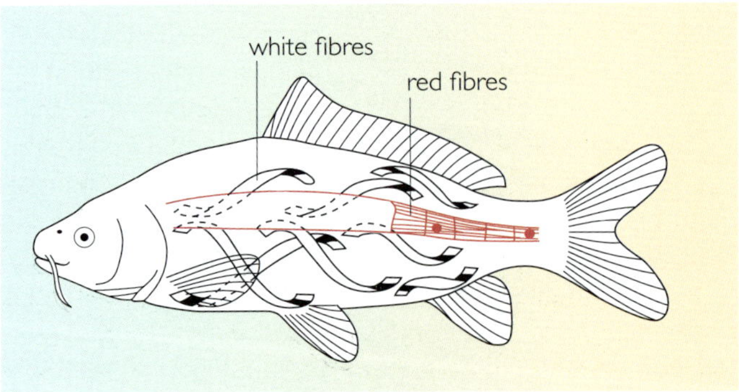

Figure 6.9 Arrangement of superficial red muscle fibres and deeper white muscle fibres (within overlapping muscle segments). The white muscle fibres account for about two-thirds of all the muscle.

The differences between red and white muscle go much further than their arrangements in the body of the fish. Red muscle fibre contracts slowly, and has a high density of blood capillaries, while white muscle has a meagre supply of blood. The energy to activate red muscle comes mainly from respiration in the presence of oxygen from the blood supply, i.e. aerobic respiration (or aerobic metabolism). White muscle, by contrast, is activated through energy released using only the first stage of the metabolic processes usually involved in respiration, which saves time and does not need oxygen (i.e. is *an*aerobic). For this reason, in the 'Wild Moves: Water' video, which you will see shortly, white muscle is referred to as 'anaerobic muscle'. Although anaerobic metabolism/respiration is fast, it has the disadvantage that it produces a waste product known as lactic acid, which is not produced in aerobic metabolism/respiration. Lactic acid tends to accumulate in the muscles and must be removed (oxidized or excreted) before the muscle can be activated again (it is accumulation of lactic acid which sometimes causes us cramp during vigorous exercise). This is why white muscle can only be used as an 'emergency power pack' and why fish need time to recover after white muscle has been used (as you will see in the videos 'Swimming in Fish: an experimental approach' and 'Wild Moves: Water'). (Don't worry if you did not fully understand this discussion of red and white muscle. It was provided as background to some of the video sequences.)

6.4.1 Warm-bodied fish

As the 'Open Ocean' video showed, tuna are fast and tireless swimmers. They do not undertake 'burst' swimming, but maintain high speeds for long periods of time – more like a middle-distance runner than a sprinter. They are able to maintain higher swimming speeds than most other teleosts, and for much longer.

Question 6.4 On the basis of what you have read so far in this chapter, list at least three adaptations of the tuna that help it to swim fast and efficiently. ◀

Rapid swimming in large fish is very expensive in metabolic terms – most large fish can only keep up high-speed swimming for a few minutes. In the case of some of the larger tunas (and some sharks), part of the explanation for their spectacular swimming performance probably lies in the fact that – unlike other fish, which are cold-blooded – they can maintain the temperature of their muscles significantly above the temperature of the water in which they are swimming. The muscles of bluefin and skipjack tuna, for example, are both normally 5–10 °C above the water temperature. This seems to allow the metabolic rate of tunas to approach that of mammals (cf. Section 2.1.2), so allowing sustained swimming.

These relatively high muscle temperatures are achieved by an arrangement of blood vessels that reduces heat loss to the environment from certain areas of the body. In most fish, the blood is delivered through main vessels that lie just beneath the spinal column, with branches delivering the blood to the outer parts of the body. Tunas, by contrast, have their blood vessels just below the skin, with smaller vessels delivering blood into the interior. This allows heat generated within the body to be conserved. In tunas, the heat generated by the red muscle is also conserved because it is positioned either side of the spinal column, an arrangement which again differs from that in most other fish (Figure 6.10 overleaf), where the red muscle is along the flanks. (This central position of the red muscle in tunas could also help explain their efficient 'stiff-bodied' swimming.)

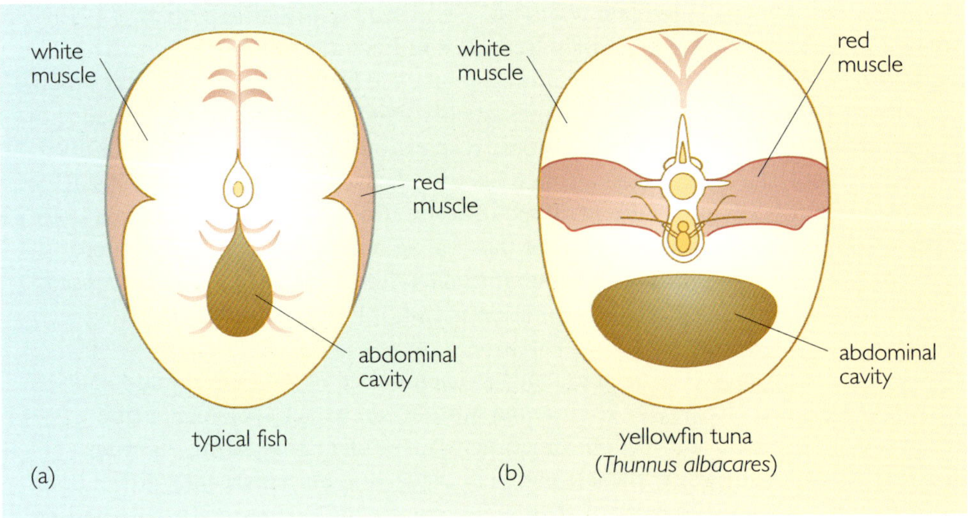

Figure 6.10 (a) Idealized cross-section of a typical fish body showing the large mass of white muscle and the mainly superficial layers of red muscle. (b) Idealized cross-section of the body of a yellowfin tuna, showing the distinctive distribution of red muscle on either side of the spinal column.

In most fish, body heat is lost to the surrounding seawater from the blood passing through the gills (where oxygen is taken up from the water). Tunas have an arrangement of blood vessels that greatly reduces this heat loss from the gills. Throughout the whole body there is a series of arteries where the blood flow is in the opposite direction to the flow in veins lying close to them. This 'countercurrent heat exchanger' ensures that most of the heat produced in the muscles and warming the blood in the veins, is passed directly into the adjacent arteries. It therefore does not get carried to the gills, and instead is trapped in the tuna's body.

6.5 Schooling

Unfortunately in this short course, it is only possible to touch on a few of the more interesting aspects of fish behaviour and physiology which relate to the Blue Planet videos. However, there is one type of behaviour that we cannot ignore, not least because it is very obvious in a number of video sequences – this is *schooling*. Schooling is the intentional massing together of large numbers of fish (or squid), rather than the crowding that may occur as a result of many animals being attracted to (say) a particularly good feeding area, or being pushed together by current patterns (as occurs, to some extent, in the case of the sardines off the coast of Natal).

Although feeding schools may consist of more than one species, schools of actively swimming fish are nearly always of one species only. The 'bait balls' of small fish that appear in the videos (e.g. anchoveta, 'Open Ocean', [2:28:54]) appear to have formed as a defence against predation.

- How might the formation of a tight 'bait ball' reduce predation?

- As suggested by the narration, the fish in the centre of a tight 'bait ball' are (relatively) protected. Those on the outside of the school are most vulnerable to predators (each fish spends a fairly brief time on the outside) and those individuals that become isolated are picked off first.

It is also possible that schooling is intended to confuse predators. Schooling fish may swim towards predators or even form rings around them, presumably to make it difficult for them to concentrate on any particular fish. Tightly schooling fish usually have silvery sides and (as in the case of the anchoveta) may swim so as to produce a wave-like effect on the outside of the school, and this may further confuse predators.

As suggested in the 'Wild Moves: Water' video, schooling may also allow swimming to be more efficient, because in a school, each fish swims in the 'slipstream' of the fish in front. In other words, it makes use of vortices produced by the fish ahead (cf. Figure 6.2), rather in the way that birds flying in a 'vee'-formation use vortices shed by the wings of the bird in front.

▶▶ *This is a good time to watch the two videos entitled 'Swimming in Fish: an experimental approach' and 'Wild Moves: Water' on VC3. The first of these was made some time ago, but all the principles described in it remain valid. 'Wild Moves: Water' briefly revisits the topics covered in detail in 'Swimming in Fish: an experimental approach', and revises much of what you have read in this chapter. It also looks at the results of some recent research which casts light on how dolphins manage to swim so much faster than their muscles should in theory allow, and includes video footage which reveals some of the deep-diving techniques of marine mammals.*

While watching these videos, jot down some notes to enable you to answer Questions 6.5 and 6.6 (relating to 'Swimming in Fish'), Question 6.7 (relating to both videos) and Question 6.8 (relating to 'Wild Moves: Water'). ◀◀

Notes on the 'Swimming in Fish – an experimental approach' video

[0:02:34] The word for blocks of muscle is spelt 'myotomes'.

At the very end of the video, the narration says: 'Certainly, more sophisticated transmitters will be one major avenue of advance, so that fish can be studied in the best possible environment – their own.' Such transmitters ('smart tags') have now been developed and transmit information relating not only to the fish's physiology, but also to the surrounding environment.

Note on the 'Wild Moves: Water' video

[0:42:15–0:42:49] The 'baby shark' is in fact a dogfish. The vortices spinning off its tail (made visible by the reflective particles and represented in colour on the computer screen) are equivalent to the vortices shown in Figure 6.2b, but are different because of the asymmetric tail of the dogfish and the way the tail moves.

Questions 6.5 and 6.6 relate to 'Swimming in Fish'.

Question 6.5 For each of the two statements below, say whether it is true or false, and why.

'As swimming fish increase their speed, there is a definite point where white muscle takes over from red muscle.'

'White muscle is particularly useful for outswimming predators because it can be used for sustained periods.' ◀

Question 6.6 What fundamental (potentially problematic) aspect of their bodies affects the swimming styles of both mackerel and sharks? Do mackerel and sharks use the same techniques to combat this potential problem? ◀

Question 6.7 relates to both 'Swimming in Fish' and 'Wild Moves: Water'.

Question 6.7 Why don't marine mammals need buoyancy aids, like swimbladders or accumulation of low-density fats? ◀

Question 6.8 relates to 'Wild Moves: Water'.

Question 6.8 Dolphins swim much faster than their muscles should (in theory) allow. Briefly outline at least three possible contributory reasons for this. ◀

▶▶ *If you have the time, you might like to watch the 'Open Ocean' video again, bearing in mind what you have learnt in Chapter 6.* ◀◀

Coral reefs

7

In Chapter 4 and the 'Seasonal Seas' video, you saw that temperate waters teem with life every spring because surface waters have been 'restocked' with nutrients mixed up from below during the winter storms. The corollary of this is that, except in areas of upwelling, tropical waters, which are rarely turned over by storms, are mostly very poor in nutrients. They therefore support very low primary productivity and hence low productivity generally, despite the fact that they receive high levels of sunlight all year round.

So this invites the following question: how is it possible for coral reefs, found only in tropical waters, to be almost bursting with life, supporting not only a wide variety of species but also extremely large numbers of individuals?

The answer is that coral reef ecosystems conserve and recycle nutrients very efficiently. Before we go into how this achieved, we should explain what coral reefs are.

7.1 What is a coral?

Although coral *reefs* are found only in the tropics, corals themselves are very widespread organisms. Solitary corals (i.e. those which do not form colonies) are found in shallow waters (e.g. around the British Isles) and large solitary species are also found on reefs. There are also deep-water corals which form mound-like colonies,* but not reefs of the type that grow in tropical waters.

- Thinking back to the third activity of the 'Biological Diversity' module, would you say corals are ancient animals, or did they evolve relatively recently?

- Corals are very ancient animals – they were represented on one of the lowest branches of the tree (cf. Figure 1.1).

As you may remember from Question 1.1, corals are closely related to sea-anemones, and both belong to the Class Anthozoa. An individual coral animal, known as a polyp, looks very much like a sea-anemone, and consists of a tubular body with a central mouth surrounded by a crown of tentacles. The fact that polyps are tubular (i.e. radially symmetric) tells us that the first corals existed before the Cambrian 'explosion' in diversity. They were probably anemone-type animals which did not produce calcium carbonate skeletons.

So, modern reef-building corals are effectively colonial sea-anemones which secrete supports (skeletons) of calcium carbonate (i.e. limestone) into which they can withdraw for protection. The living colony forms a thin layer over a limestone foundation which has been almost entirely produced by previous generations, and may be thousands of years old.

Each coral polyp sits in a cup-like depression in the skeleton, which has ridges or plates radiating from the centre. This ridged cup is known as a calyx. Depending on the species and the time of day, the polyp will be extended out of the calyx to varying degrees, and at times of danger or physical stress it contracts down into the bottom of the calyx. As you will see in the 'Coral Seas' video, most reef coral species feed at

* You may have seen news reports about possible threats to such 'reefs' growing along the continental slope to the north and west of the UK, from deep-water oil exploration and exploitation.

night. They capture zooplankton with their tentacles which have stinging cells ('nematocysts') and carry them to their mouth and central gut, which is folded into pleats that fit between and around the plates of the calyx (there is an animation showing this in the 'Coral Seas' video).

Reef-building coral colonies can be divided into massive and branching forms. Massive corals tend to be mound-shaped and somewhat irregular, while branching corals may look like tree branches or have a more-flattened shape like elk horns. Massive corals tend to grow slowly, no more than about 1 cm per year in any direction. Branching corals grow much faster, of the order of 10–15 cm per year. You will be able to see time-lapse footage of a growing branching coral in the 'Coral Seas' video.

The shape of the colony is to a large extent determined by where the new 'buds' form and the degree of separation of the resultant polyps. An extreme example is provided by the massive 'brain corals' (*Meandria*), where the polyps grow side by side but do not separate, resulting in rows of mouths fringed by rows of tentacles. It is the intersection of rows of polyps and tentacles that produces the pattern which looks like a human brain. In branching corals, the new polyps form at or towards the top of an existing polyp.

Budding is a form of asexual reproduction, and produces identical individuals or clones. As you will see in the 'Coral Seas' video, corals also reproduce by sexual reproduction, i.e. by producing eggs and sperm. The resulting coral larvae then drift as members of the plankton until they find suitable substrates on which to develop into new coral animals.

7.2 Where are coral reefs found?

Reef-building corals can only live where water temperatures never fall below about 18 °C, and grow best at temperatures of 25–29 °C. They do not thrive in water with low or variable salinity and cannot tolerate low light levels and turbid water. Reef-building corals are therefore found in shallow, clear, warm waters in the tropics.

They are widespread throughout the tropical Indian Ocean, in the western tropical Pacific, in the Caribbean and along the coast of southern Brazil, but are found only in restricted areas in the eastern Pacific and the eastern Atlantic.

Question 7.1 By reference to Figure 5.2, can you explain why conditions on the western sides of the Atlantic and the Pacific are more conducive to coral-reef growth than conditions on the eastern side? ◀

We mentioned above that reef-building corals only grow in clear shallow water, and it might have occurred to you that these are conditions which favour plant growth. At first sight, this could seem strange because corals are animals. In fact, they grow only in well-lit waters because (as you will see in the 'Coral Seas' video) they have a symbiotic – i.e. mutually beneficial – relationship with single-celled algae that live within their tissues. These algae, known as **zooxanthellae** (pronounced 'zoo-zanthelleye'), are a special form of a particular species of dinoflagellate (Section 1.2). Dinoflagellates living in the water column can 'swim' using two whip-like structures known as flagellae, and coral algae removed (or ejected) from a coral change to this swimming form. It seems that although all zooxanthellae are the same species of dinoflagellate (*Symbiodinium microadriaticum*), each species of coral 'host' has its 'own' strain of this species.

Coral seems to benefit from the presence of the algae in two main ways. Like planktonic algae, the zooxanthellae use carbon dioxide and water to manufacture carbohydrate, to which the coral also has access. This 'free' carbohydrate makes up more than 90% of the coral's nutritional needs. Photosynthesis by the zooxanthellae also increases the rate at which the corals can produce their calcium carbonate skeleton (although exactly how this works is not clear). In their turn, the zooxanthellae benefit from the partnership by being protected (to some extent) from grazing by reef animals, and also through access to nutrients excreted by the coral.

Apart from warm, clear shallow water, reef-building corals need a hard substrate on which to establish themselves in the first place. There are three basic types of reef: fringing reefs, barrier reefs and atolls. Fringing reefs develop in shallow water along the shore, and thrive best in arid regions, where river outflow and freshwater run-off are limited. They are usually less massive than barrier reefs and atolls, and are generally patchy because they are easily damaged by sediments (in river outflows or stirred up by storms) and by human activities.

Barrier reefs and atolls are found in areas where the sea-level locally has been rising and/or the sea-bed has been sinking. Since the end of the last glacial period about 11 000 years ago, melting of the ice-caps has meant that sea-level has been rising world-wide. At the same time, movements of the Earth's crust, either upwards or downwards, have meant that locally, sea-level may have gone down as well as up. Barrier reefs (where there is a lagoon between the coast and the reef) and atolls (which encircle a lagoon) start life as fringing reefs, along mainland coastlines (in the case of barrier reefs) or around islands (in the case of atolls). Corals grow best within about 10–20 m of the sea-surface and active reef-building ceases below 25–50 m (cf. Figure 4.7). If (as is generally the case) sea-level above the reef is rising, the reef must build upwards to remain in conditions that enable the zooxanthellae to function well. As a result of continued upward growth over perhaps thousands of years, barrier reefs can be many tens of metres thick.

Many reefs have characteristics of fringing reefs and barrier reefs. Fringing reefs may grow to great thicknesses if the coastal margin is subsiding. In this case, there is a 'reef flat' between the coast and the reef crest (the highest and most vigorously growing part of the reef), rather than a lagoon as in the case of a barrier reef. There are also reefs described as 'platform reefs', which are complexes of corals found on continental shelves and shallow platforms like the Bahama Bank. The Great Barrier Reef off the eastern coast of Australia is not a barrier reef of the type described above, but is an enormous aggregation of reefs of different types, shapes and sizes.

Atolls develop from reefs that have built up around volcanic islands (most of which are no longer active volcanoes). Some are millions of years old.

- By reference to Chapter 2, especially Figures 2.1 to 2.4, can you suggest why volcanic islands might have a tendency to subside over the course of millions of years?

- As ocean crust moves away from the spreading ridge where it originally formed, it cools, becomes more dense, and subsides (Figure 2.3). As a result, volcanic islands that rest upon that crust also subside, and many eventually become seamounts.

The edifices of coral that have grown up around the seamounts over thousands to millions of years may be hundreds to thousands of metres thick. Many are now substantial islands, with terrestrial vegetation and human populations. As Figure 2.1 shows, the western Pacific Ocean has a very large number of volcanic islands, which is another reason why it has many more coral reefs than the eastern Pacific.

- Apart from the isolated mid-ocean islands and seamounts, what other volcanic features are common in the western Pacific?

- The western side of the Pacific is characterized by island arcs, which erupted on the landward side of subduction zones (Figures 2.2 and 2.3).

Figure 2.2 shows that the Caribbean also has a number of island arcs. The corals you will see in the 'Coral Seas' video were filmed in a wide variety of locations – including the Caribbean, the Red Sea and the Great Barrier Reef – and on different types of reefs.

▶▶ *You should now look at the sequence on coral reefs in Activity 4 of the module on 'Ecosystems and Food Webs' in your* Life in the Oceans *CD, if you have not already done so.* ◀◀

7.3 The reef community

The sequence on coral reefs in Activity 4 of 'Ecosystems and Food Webs' emphasizes that, as in the case of kelp forests, the habitat of the coral reef community is provided by members of the ecosystem itself – mainly the coral. However, much of the physical structure of a coral reef is also provided by other reef inhabitants. For example, there may be mounds of bivalves, and of a type of gastropod whose tubular shells are cemented together by 'coralline algae'. Coralline algae are so called because, to deter grazers, they secrete calcium carbonate, and this means that they make a rock-like substrate. These algae, which are very often red, have both branching forms and encrusting forms. Indeed, as corals themselves do not thrive if battered by waves, the topmost part of the reef tends to be dominated by coralline algae. As well as cementing themselves to the reef surface, these algae also cement to the reef chunks of coral broken off by waves, building up what is known as an 'algal ridge'. Below the surface of the algal ridge is a labyrinth of tunnels and cavities which harbour many types of small molluscs and crustaceans.

Like the coral-reef habitat, the sea-bed sediment on and around the reef is provided by the organisms themselves. In the 'Coral Seas' video, we see parrotfish adding to the coral sand, but they are not alone – sponges living within the carbonate skeleton break it down, and coralline algae, molluscs, sea-urchins and many other organisms contain calcareous components that are added to the sand when they die.

7.3.1 A riot of colour – but no green!

Although coral reefs are so colourful, corals themselves have subdued hues of brown, green or blue imparted by the zooxanthellae. The bright colours are provided by the other members of the reef community – especially sponges, anemones, gorgonians (sea-fans) and fish, but also molluscs, crustaceans, echinoderms (e.g. starfish and sea-urchins) and polychaete worms.

But given that phytoplankton are not abundant in these nutrient-poor waters, where are the green plants – the primary producers – supporting this ecosystem?

- Can you suggest one or more reasons for the lack of visible plants?

One reason is that some of the reef algae – the zooxanthellae – are hidden in the corals. Another reason is that coralline algae, which make up a significant proportion of the plants on the reef, are not green and so do not look like plants.

Yet another reason for the apparent lack of primary producers is that the filamentous green algae that do grow on the hard surfaces of the reef are grazed down by herbivores (particularly fish) at such a rate that the amount present at any one time (the 'standing stock') is small – this is clear from several sequences in the 'Coral Seas' video. It has been shown that if grazers are excluded from part of a reef, it quickly turns green.

However, we have still not explained how reefs can have such enormous productivity, given that they are found in the nutrient-poor waters of the tropics. Part of the reason is that the zooxanthellae–coral partnership is very efficient, and so most of the nutrients that the algae need are supplied by the coral polyp. Indeed, corals are not the only reef animals to have symbiotic relationships with zooxanthellae – there are many others, including soft corals, colonial anemones, and the giant clam. It is also advantageous to the system as a whole that corals can obtain food by capturing zooplankton (they cannot digest phytoplankton); they can also absorb organic substances directly from the surrounding water, as well as collecting food particles by means of mucus threads (which are also used to clear sediment particles away).

Furthermore, the structures of reefs themselves, particularly atolls, tend to trap nutrients. On death, the reef fauna decomposes within the reef system, and the nutrients released by this decomposition can be taken up by the zooxanthellae and other reef algae, rather than being carried away to be used by phytoplankton elsewhere.

As the 'Coral Seas' video makes clear, every square centimetre of the convoluted surface of the reef structure, and every nook and cranny within the reef, provides living space for some type of organism. In the crowded reef environment, there is a great deal of interaction between organisms – symbiotic, predatory, reproductive, social and competitive. There is not space to discuss such interactions at length here, but the video shows some fascinating examples, both cooperative and competitive.

Corals themselves are continually in competition with one another, both for light and for space. Because they grow faster, branching corals tend to overshadow slower-growing forms, preventing them from flourishing, with the result that there may be patches consisting only of branching corals. However, slow-growing massive corals have a way of retaliating, as explained below.

In the video, you will see a coral of one species digesting its neighbour, of another species. The polyps of the 'aggressor' coral extrude filaments of their gut through their mouths and through temporary openings in their walls, and literally digest the soft tissue of the neighbouring coral, exposing the skeletons beneath. It seems that there is a coral 'pecking order', in that each coral species only attacks certain other species, and is itself only attacked by certain other different species. Corals of a species that is intermediate in the aggression pecking order may be consuming their neighbours on one side, while themselves being consumed by neighbours of a different species on the other side!

▶▶ *You should now watch the video on 'Coral Seas' (VC2). While doing so, make a note of the different ways in which colour and patterns may be used (this will be followed up in Question 7.6). Also, make a note of any echinoderms that you spot. If you need to be reminded about echinoderms, have another look at the second activity of the 'Biological Diversity' module on your* Life in the Oceans *CD.*

During the video, you will see sequences showing reproductive behaviour of (1) surgeonfish [0:13:15], (2) banded pipefish [0:31:39], and (3) corals [0:36:31]. Make brief notes about the strategies used by each of these animals to maximize the number of offspring.

Also, to apply some of the ideas introduced in Chapter 6, try the following exercises, which are followed up in Questions 7.2 to 7.4:

- *When you get to the sequence showing butterflyfish [0:07:11], pause the tape and sketch the overall shape of the butterflyfish and the shape of its tail.*
- *Similarly, sketch the shape of the tails of the parrotfish [0:12:15].*
- *Sketch (or make notes about) the shape of the jacks [0:14:42].*

You might prefer to watch the video right through and replay it later to do your sketches. Either way, you might find it helpful to read the notes below before viewing. ◀◀

Notes on the 'Coral Seas' video

General note: Most of this video was filmed during daylight, when the coral polyps were withdrawn into their calyces, so the radiating ridges of the calyces are clearly visible.

[0:01:25] As this branching coral grows, note how the position of the new buds determines the overall shape of the coral.

[0:02:27] The Christmas tree worm is a polychaete (its bristles are obscured by its tube). Its spiral of tentacles is covered with cilia that filter suspended particles from the water.

[0:02:54] The animal extending feathery appendages from amongst the tentacles of a soft coral is a small crab.

[0:03:36] When watching this animation, remember that it represents a journey down into a single small polyp and the limestone skeleton beneath. The 'pleats' of the gut can be seen (although in the animation they look hard, rather than like soft tissue). At the edges of the pleats are cells producing digestive enzymes, and at the bottom of each pleat the gut becomes highly convoluted, forming the filaments that are extruded in 'intra-coral warfare', coming later. (In the video, these filaments are shown simply as curled protrusions.)

[0:05:44] The narration states that '98% of the food that the corals consume is produced by the algae'. This is misleading, as the only food that the corals actually *consume* is that captured by the tentacles and trapped on their mucus threads (not seen in the video). The useful organic compounds produced by the zooxanthellae are absorbed directly into the coral tissue. The 2% of food that the corals *do* consume provides nutrients for the algae. (In Section 7.2, we say that 'more than 90% of the coral's nutritional needs' are provided by the algae – the precise percentage will vary from species to species, and will change with light levels, etc.)

[0:06:03] The light against which corals need to protect themselves (and perhaps more importantly, their algae) is ultraviolet light, which can damage cells and cause mutations. This is a particular threat in clear tropical waters where all solar radiation can penetrate to greater depths. The reason that the pigments show up in ultraviolet light is that they have absorbed the light and so look different from adjacent areas of the polyp. (This sequence was filmed using different filters – the dramatically contrasting colours are not natural.)

[0:07:11] Butterflyfish eat the soft coral tissue (i.e. they do not feed by grazing on algae).

[0:07:30] For completeness, we should mention that many species of soft corals feed by capturing zooplankton and detritus, both by day and night.

[0:07:45] Capture of food by the coral tentacles can be seen clearly here. Note that the plankton being eaten is zooplankton – the green that you can see is the zooxanthellae showing through the translucent coral tissue.

[0:08:35] In this sequence about 'territorial disputes', you can clearly see how the soft tissue of the coral relates to the limestone calyces.

[0:09:09] Look out for the 'tube feet' or suckers of the crown of thorns starfish. As will be discussed shortly, starfish are echinoderms – the 'spiny skins'.

[0:13:49] Note that the guano provides the nutrients – nitrate and phosphate – that plants (in this case, land plants) need.

[0:16:02] Sponges are the most primitive animals of all. They have no nervous system, no gut, and no distinct tissues or organs.

[0:17:18] This worm is recognizable as a polychaete by the bristles down either side – you may recognize the similarity with ragworms, which are also polychaetes. While this polychaete has an apparatus for seizing prey, others have external feathery gills, or feathery extensions for collecting food from the water column.

[0:19:28] The lionfish seems to be using fake 'angelfish' to add to its camouflage.

[0:21:14] In this sequence about fish grazing on the green algae, you can also see quite a bit of red coralline algae.

[0:21:21] Again, look out for the starfish's tube feet or suckers.

[0:24:23] Believe it or not, basketstars are echinoderms, like starfish. Basketstars are by no means alone in coming out to feed at night. Generally, the animals that are active at night are different from those that are active during the day. This is partly because zooplankton from deeper waters migrate to shallower levels and so are more abundant on the reef; filter-feeding therefore becomes more worthwhile. (We will come back to the topic of vertical migration in Chapter 9.)

[0:25:44] Here, and in the later sequence showing pipefish larvae [0:34:16], you can see the style of swimming illustrated in Figure 6.1.

[0:26:30] The way in which rays swim by means of backward-moving waves passing along their enlarged pectoral fins (Section 6.2) can be seen clearly in this sequence.

[0:27:04] In this sequence showing white-tip sharks hunting, you can also see how accretions of molluscs (here mussels and other bivalves) form part of the reef structure.

[0:31:55] As you will probably guess, sea-horses and these pipefish are closely related (male sea-horses also brood their young). During this sequence, you can see the undulating pectoral and (especially) dorsal fins being used for propulsion while conferring great manoeuvrability.

[0:34:54] The relationship between cuttlefish, squid and octopus will be covered later in the text.

[0:35:56] The eerie sound you can hear in the background is a male humpback whale singing to establish his seniority over other males. Whales visit reefs at certain times of year when wind-driven upwelling increases the nutrient content of the water and makes then temporarily more biologically productive.

[0:35:59] The narration says: 'Corals also reproduce sexually …'. This is because reproduction by budding is *a*sexual reproduction.

[0:36:31] The narration says: 'A few days after the Full Moon in late spring when tidal currents are at their weakest …' but as you know from Chapter 3, this is not correct! It should simply say 'about a week after Full Moon'.

[0:38:59] In the Caribbean, the stormy hurricane season is the end of summer, when the surface of the ocean is at its warmest. (This footage of the storm shows well how waves result in mixing.)

[0:39:36] These spiny lobsters (actually a kind of crayfish) are walking across flats of coral sand.

[0:40:45] During the following sequence, you can just about see how the corals near the surface are more massive while those deeper down are more delicate. (The topic is discussed in Section 7.5.)

Question 7.2 While watching the 'Coral Seas' video, you sketched the shape of the butterflyfish's body and the shape of its tail. Where does this shape fall with respect to the 'fish triangle' in Figure 6.3? What advantages do these body and tail shapes confer on the butterflyfish, and why are these particularly useful in a coral reef? ◀

Question 7.3 How is the shape of the parrotfish tail classified, according to Figure 6.6? How does the parrotfish appear to be swimming? ◀

Question 7.4 What features of the jack allow it to be one of the key predators on the reef? ◀

Now try Question 7.5, which will revise your understanding of tidal cycles (Section 3.1).

Question 7.5 Why might it be advantageous to corals to spawn together? And can you suggest why mass spawnings occur at night and about a week after Full Moon? ◀

7.3.2 Fish, cephalopods and echinoderms

In this short course, there is not room to discuss all the organisms that appear in the Blue Planet series. However, the 'Coral Seas' video highlights some groups of animals that are prominent in the course as a whole, so we will use this opportunity to say a little more about them here.

Reef fish

The most striking feature of coral reef fishes is their diversity, although the greatest diversity is developed in relatively few groups – it is estimated that 3000 species of fish live in association with reefs in the Indo-Pacific alone. In addition to those fish that graze the filamentous algae living on the reef – including parrotfish, surgeonfish, damselfish and rabbitfish – there are fish that eat the living coral, or *corallivores*. The corallivores include triggerfish, pufferfish and butterflyfish. As you will have seen in the 'Coral Seas' video, both corallivores and herbivores contribute to the erosion of the reef and augment the supply of coral sand.

Reef fishes and other reef animals tend to be brightly coloured and distinctively patterned, presumably because in the clear waters of the reef, colours and patterns are easily seen, even some distance below the sea-surface.

Question 7.6 To what uses can colours and patterns be put? Make a list of as many functions as you can, especially bearing in mind what you have seen in the 'Coral Seas' video. ◀

Reef fish have very good vision, upon which they rely heavily for complex social and ecological interactions, as well as for avoiding predators. Amongst reef fish (as in many other animals), it is generally the males that have the bright colours and distinctive patterns.

- Would you say that the breeding strategy used by surgeonfish to maximize the number of offspring has more in common with that of banded pipefish, or that of corals?

- The breeding strategy used by surgeonfish is closer to that of corals than to that of pipefish. Both surgeonfish and corals undertake mass spawnings, releasing large numbers of eggs and sperm into the water column (cf. Question 7.5). Although a large proportion of eggs will be eaten, some will be fertilized, survive predation and develop into young. Pipefish, by contrast, produce a relatively small number of eggs, which are closely guarded until the young hatch.

You may remember from the sequence about spawning corals that some of the corals were female (producing eggs), some were male (producing sperm), and some were both male and female – i.e. hermaphrodite – producing eggs 'pre-wrapped' in sperm. Invertebrate animals that cannot move (or cannot move far) are often hermaphrodite – limpets are a good example. This ensures that there are always suitable breeding partners nearby. By contrast, many territorial reef fish are *sequential* hermaphrodites, beginning as small, drab females and later becoming brightly coloured males. For successful breeding, male reef fish must not only compete with other males to mate with females, but also guard breeding sites and sometimes also guard the fertilized eggs, so it pays to be big, fast and impressive. The most effective way to produce a large number of progeny is therefore to be female when small, and male when bigger, older and more experienced.

Cephalopods

In the 'Coral Seas' video, you saw some brightly coloured cuttlefish and, slightly later on, an octopus. You may also remember a school of colour-changing squid (mating adults and babies) in the 'Seasonal Seas' video. You will probably not be surprised to learn that cuttlefish, squid and octopi are related to one another. Their ability to change colour is often used for camouflage against visual predators.

(In the second part of 'The Deep', you will see that squid can also produce some spectacular bioluminescence.)

- You met squid in the 'Living in the Oceans' module. Do you recall what phylum they belong to?
- Squid belong to the Phylum Mollusca.

Squid, octopi and cuttlefish are all molluscs, and are known as cephalopods (cephalopod = head–foot).

Cephalopods are the most sophisticated of the invertebrates in terms of their nervous organization and muscular co-ordination, and the complexity of their behaviour. They have well-developed eyes, with some similarities to those of vertebrates, having iris, retina, cornea etc. They are nearly all predators, seizing prey with their circle of arms (which often have suckers), and carrying it towards their powerfully beaked mouth. While octopi have eight arms, squid have ten, including two long suckered tentacles.

For completeness, we should also mention the pearly *Nautilus*, which (sadly) does not appear in any of the videos. The *Nautilus* is more primitive, and has changed little over millions of years. It has a spiral chambered shell, swims at several hundred metres depth, and varies its buoyancy by controlling the proportions of gas and fluid in the chambers of its shell. It does not have any suckers, but has over 90 arms.

Cuttlefish live in relatively shallow water, and may dive from the surface down to depths of about 200 m. As mentioned in Chapter 6, when swimming up and down in the water column, they regulate their buoyancy by varying the amount of gas in their cuttlebone (which is enclosed in a membrane).

Squid have a horny translucent structure known as a 'pen', which provides support but does not play a role in buoyancy control. They have evolved to catch their prey using speed, and so have lost all heavy shell-like structures. In terms of speed and manoeuvrability they are nearly the equal of fish. The smallest squid are a few centimetres long, and the largest – the legendary deep-sea squid *Architeuthis* – may be 20 m long, including its outstretched tentacles. *Architeuthis* is the largest of all living invertebrates.

- Can you remember (from the 'Living in the Oceans' module) the two ways in which squid move through the water?
- They can swim by undulating the fins along the sides of the body, which propels them forward, i.e. 'feet first' (this can be clearly seen in the 'Seasonal Seas' sequence mentioned above). To escape from predators, they squirt a jet of water from the siphon near the head, which drives them backwards.

Octopi have no internal rigid structures and so can squeeze through surprisingly small openings. There are two groups of octopus, of which the more common type appears in the 'Coral Seas' video. It lives on the sea-bed around the coast and in deeper water, can be various colours, and has a muscular body and an ink sac. The other type of octopus, sometimes known as a 'sea-bat', was only discovered in the early 1960s. It lives along the continental slope, and spends much of its time drifting over the sea-bed, with its arms spread so that fine membranes between them form a parachute. It is always red or orange, has fins, and a jelly-like body which provides neutral buoyancy.

Echinoderms

In the 'Coral Seas' video, you also saw several echinoderms – animals in the Phylum Echinodermata (cf. Figure 1.1, and the tree in the 'Biological Diversity' module). All echinoderms have a spiny skin which encloses an internal skeleton of interlocking calcium carbonate plates. They have a five-fold symmetry, which is not always obvious, and move around and feed using the tube feet (seen in the video) which are controlled using water pressure (like the corals expanding their tentacles in the video).

- Which echinoderms did you see in the 'Coral Seas' video?

- The echinoderms that were fairly easy to spot were the crown of thorns starfish [0:09:09] and the orange starfish which was being carried away by the harlequin shrimps [0:20:39]; and (as mentioned in the accompanying notes) the basketstar that emerged from a crevice in the coral at nightfall [0:24:23].

  You may have realized that the black animals clambering over coral, after the sequence showing the Christmas tree worm, are also echinoderms [0:02:40]; and in the sequence about corals overgrowing one another there is a very brief glimpse of a type of echinoderm known as a brittlestar [0:08:33] – if you spotted these, you were doing very well. (Strangely, there are no shots of sea-urchins, which are usually the most abundant echinoderms on coral reefs.)

It is easy to see that starfish (and brittlestars) have a five-fold symmetry, but in the case of the basketstar this is nowhere near as clear! In these echinoderms, the five arms have branches, and these in turn have smaller branches, which is why the overall effect is of a mass of coiled tentacles. In the daytime, they tend to hide with the arms wrapped into a compact ball. At night, they spread out their arms and use their tube feet to catch zooplankton. Other echinoderms include sea-cucumbers, sea-lilies and feather stars.

7.4 The influence of wave action on reefs

As discussed in Section 7.3, coral reefs grow up towards the light while being continually eroded by members of the reef community. This erosion weakens the reef structure, with the result that a large storm can wreak havoc. Towards the end of the 'Coral Seas' video, there are some spectacular scenes of storms battering a coral reef, and of crayfish evacuating the reef top and moving down into deeper water.

It is quite hard to see in the video, but the crayfish are moving down through different zones, which are found to a greater or lesser extent on most reefs. These zones are analogous to those on a rocky shore but in this case they are determined by the depth *below* the waves.

Seaward of the algal ridge, which is the highest part of the reef, there is a 'buttress zone' where the coral is subjected to extremely vigorous wave action. Usually, wave-cut channels extend down from the top, and sand and coral debris are transported down these channels into deeper water. This is sometimes called a 'spur and groove' formation, and the channels are known as 'surge channels'. Coral growth is limited in the grooves, but many invertebrates and fish feed on the organic debris that is travelling down them. The relatively high ridges are free of sediment, and do support corals.

- Would you expect these to be branching corals or massive corals?

- Because of the vigorous wave action, these are robust massive corals, like brain coral (Section 7.1).

In this buttress zone, which extends down for a few tens of metres, there are also encrusting corals and algae. Further seaward down the slope, there is a zone of relatively robust branching corals, and then at about 50 m depth there is a change to more delicate corals – including the so-called black corals – which have long slender branches that extend out beyond the shadows cast by other corals. Here are also soft corals and sea-fans, which extend their delicate feathery branches out into the current to capture food particles and plankton. As you might expect, it is not only the coral that shows a vertical zonation – this is also seen in the invertebrate community and the fish that live amongst the coral.

As the depth zonation is largely determined by the intensity of wave action, and most reefs are in regions affected by a prevailing wind direction (often easterly, because of the Trade Winds; Figure 5.1), the precise depths at which the changes occur depend on whether the reefs are exposed to the prevailing winds (i.e. are facing to windward) or are more sheltered (facing to leeward) – of course, atolls have both windward and leeward sides. So, more delicate corals are found at shallower depths on the leeward side of a reef. Interestingly, in the Caribbean (and possibly in other areas too), the change from more robust to more delicate corals is largely a result of the same species of corals changing their shape, being more stumpy at shallower depths, and with more horizontal flat 'leaves' in the lower light levels further down.

7.6 Does coral have a long-term future?

While tropical storms may wreak havoc on coral reefs, the reefs usually recover surprisingly quickly, especially as the most rapidly growing corals are found in areas most frequently affected by such storms. Even if a reef is completely devastated by a storm, it is rarely killed completely, because fragments survive and regenerate. The real threats to coral reefs are human activity and climate change.

A common cause of coral mortality is high sediment loads in the water, often from development along the coast or as a result of clearing land for agriculture. As you know, corals are threatened by turbidity because their zooxanthellae need high light levels in order to photosynthesize. Sediment can cause large-scale destruction of reefs – for example, the islands of Okinawa to the south of Japan used to have reefs comparable to the Great Barrier Reef, but after the Second World War the islands were stripped of their vegetation for pineapple growing, and the increased sediment in run-off from the islands all but wiped out the reefs.

Question 7.7 Development also threatens coral reefs because sewage and agricultural activity result in increased nutrient supplies in coastal waters. Thinking back to Sections 4.2 and 4.3, and Figure 3.4 (the satellite image showing the colour of water around the British Isles), can you suggest why increased nutrient concentrations pose a threat to corals? ◀

In this chapter, we have been considering coral reefs as if they were independent habitats, but of course this is not the case. For example, in many tropical areas, reefs lie offshore from mangroves (seen in the 'Tidal Seas' video). These form nursery areas for many reef fish and play a vital role in trapping sediment, preventing it from damaging the reefs. When mangroves are destroyed for development or (often) shrimp farming, coral reefs may be smothered with sediment and killed.

Reefs and their inhabitants are also under serious threat from direct onslaughts on the habitat. As the reefs are made up largely of calcium carbonate (i.e. limestone), they may be exploited for building materials, obtained by dynamiting the reef. Dynamiting is also used as a crude fishing technique, along with indiscriminate use of cyanide. This disturbing topic will be looked at again in the 'Deep Trouble' video, in the final part of the course.

While legislation and change of attitude could in theory prevent or limit damage to reef ecosystems by people, there is little we can do to control the climate. We know from recent climatic fluctuations that corals are very vulnerable to changes in environmental conditions. During the climatic fluctuations known as El Niño events, warm, nutrient-rich water invades the eastern tropical Pacific, and areas that are usually dry receive extremely heavy rainfall. Corals around the Galápagos islands (cf. Figure 5.8) have fared very badly, partly because of the lowered salinity of surface waters brought about by the heavy rainfall, and partly, it seems, because of the increased water temperature.

When water temperatures exceed 28 °C, zooxanthellae lose their photosynthetic pigment and become less productive. Corals atrophy, the zooxanthallae die or are expelled from the corals in streams of mucus, and the corals – now devoid of pigment, or 'bleached' – may themselves die. During the 1982–83 El Niño event, many Galápagos corals suffered bleaching, and by the end of 1983, 95% of these had been destroyed. Their demise was hastened by the activities of other organisms. Bleaching corals were quickly colonized by filamentous algae, which spread over corals and rocks down to a depth of 20 m. Sea-urchins fed on this algae, at the same time eroding the coral. As the El Niño event waned, new coral larvae began to settle and become established, but for a colony to survive, the addition of new coral organisms has to keep pace with erosion by foraging sea-urchins and other coral grazers such as parrotfish, surgeonfish and damselfish. The activities of these grazers meant that some reefs have never recovered.

Many climate scientists expect that the recent trend of more frequent El Niño events will continue along with increased global warming, in response to rising concentrations of carbon dioxide in the atmosphere. This does not bode well for coral reefs. What is more, it is also possible that the increase in carbon dioxide in the atmosphere will of itself eventually lead to a global decline in coral reefs. An increase in the concentration of carbon dioxide in the atmosphere is leading to an increase in the amount of carbon dioxide in the oceans, and this in turn is gradually increasing the acidity of seawater. In more acid seawater, it will be harder for corals to extract the carbonate ions they need to precipitate their calcium carbonate skeletons.

However, the fact that reef-building corals could no longer build skeletons would not necessarily mean their extinction. It is possible that they could continue as non-reef-builders, and eventually, perhaps many thousands of years hence, reef-building could begin again.

8 Polar seas

The 'Frozen Seas' video concentrates very much on marine mammals, which we will discuss in some detail later. However, first we should look at what we mean by 'polar' or 'frozen' seas.

8.1 Arctic and Antarctic: poles apart

The Arctic and Antarctic regions are geographically completely different (Figure 8.1): the Arctic is a largely enclosed ocean, with a very narrow connection to the Pacific (through the Bering Straits) and a somewhat larger connection to the Atlantic via the Nordic Seas and the Fram Strait. By contrast, at high southern latitudes the Southern Ocean encircles the continental landmass of Antarctica (which in places extends as far north as ~ 65° S).

- The continent of Antarctica is the coldest place on Earth. By looking back at Figure 5.2, can you suggest why the pattern of ocean currents contributes to Antarctica being colder than the Arctic?

- In the Northern Hemisphere, poleward-flowing currents – in particular, the Gulf Stream, and its extension, the North Atlantic Current – carry heat to polar latitudes. In the Southern Hemisphere, by contrast, the great size of Antarctica, and the broad (cold) Antarctic Circumpolar Current that flows around it, prevent warm currents (e.g. the Agulhas Current and the Brazil Current) from penetrating much further south than 50–55° S.

In fact, there is some transport of warm water southwards, and of cold water northwards, by means of eddies or rings like those which transfer water across the Gulf Stream (Figure 5.9), but as far as heat transport in ocean currents is concerned, the Antarctic continent is largely isolated.

Sea-ice is formed by the freezing of seawater. Ice crystals are almost pure water, so their formation increases the concentration of salt in the seawater that is left behind. Young sea-ice therefore contains droplets of brine, but because salty water remains liquid at lower temperatures than pure water, these droplets gradually melt their way through the ice into the seawater below. As a result, old sea-ice is nearly pure water.

As a result of the contrasting settings of the Arctic and Antarctic, the ice cover of the two regions is very different, as is the amount that the ice-extent changes over the course of the year. Figure 8.1 shows the seasonal differences in the extent of sea-ice in the Arctic and Antarctic, as measured in 1982. The first thing to note is that the Arctic Ocean is largely covered by floating sea-ice or pack-ice.

Figure 8.1 Seasonal changes in sea-ice cover in northern and southern high latitudes, determined using data collected by the *Nimbus* satellite programme in February and September, 1982. (a) and (b) show near-maximum and near-minimum ice cover in the Arctic, and (c) and (d) show near-minimum and near-maximum ice cover around the Antarctic. Purple and red colours correspond to complete or near-complete ice cover, pale blue corresponds to low or zero ice cover. (The orbit of the satellite is such that no data can be collected immediately over the pole, hence the black area in the centre of images (a) and (b).) Lines of latitude (shown as circles when looking down on the poles) are every 5°.

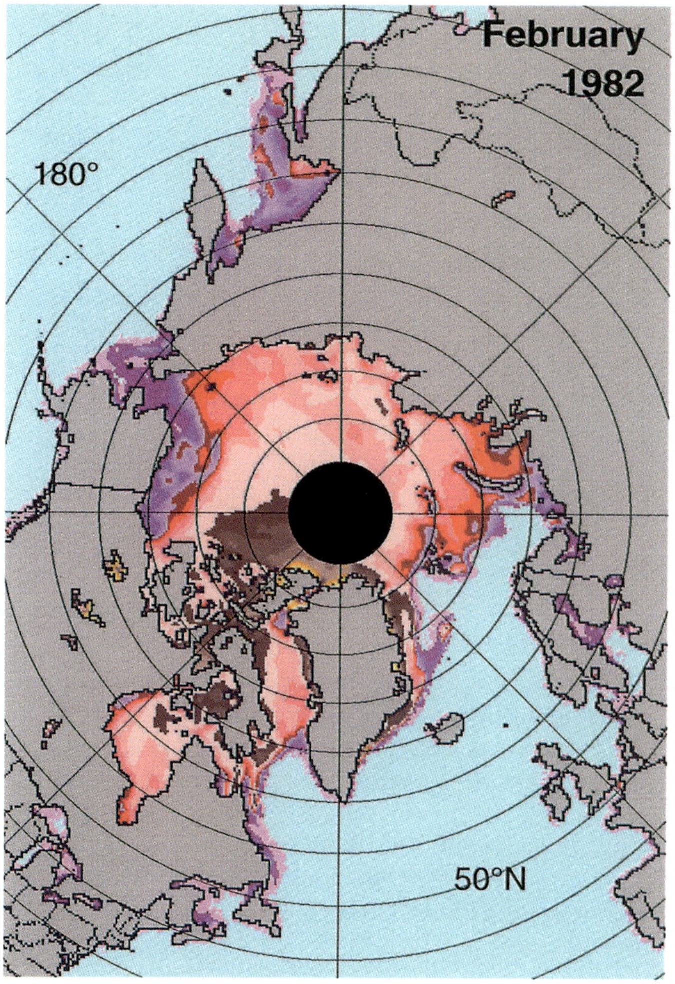
February
1982
180°
50°N

(a)

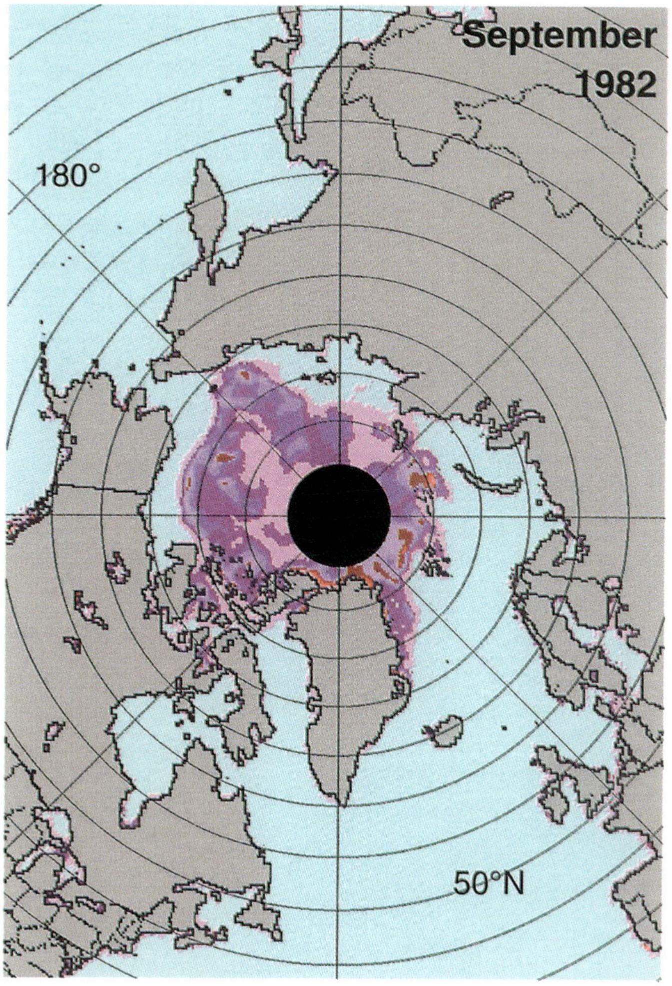
September
1982
180°
50°N

(b)

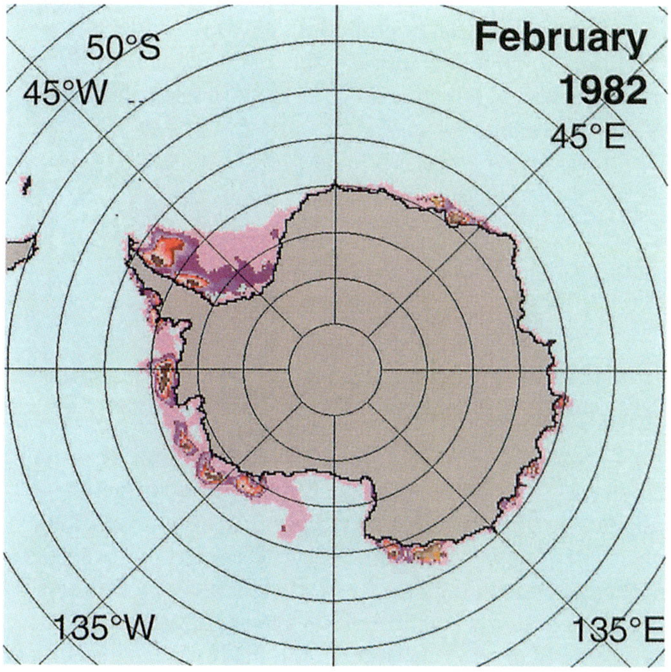
February
1982
50°S
45°W
45°E
135°W
135°E

(c)

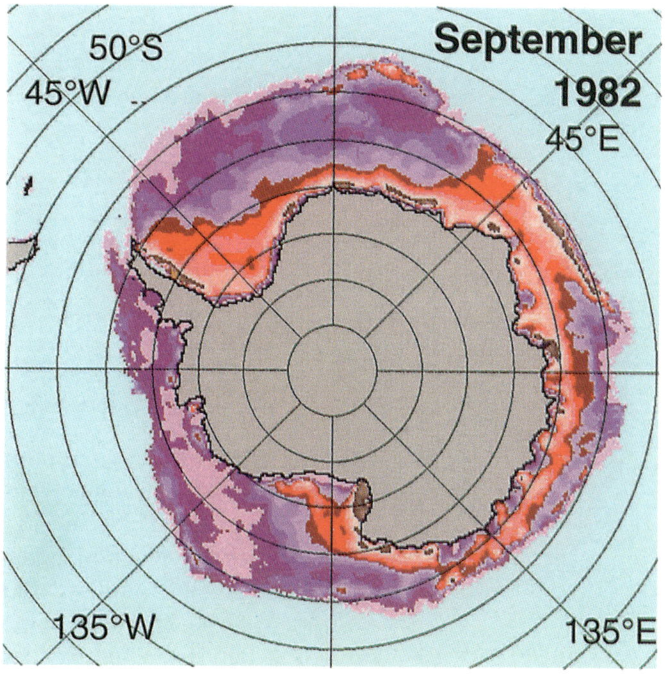
September
1982
50°S
45°W
45°E
135°W
135°E

(d)

- Which region shows the greatest change in ice extent between summer and winter?

- The Antarctic – here the ice edge shifts over about 15° of latitude, whereas in much of the Arctic it moves over only 5–10° of latitude.

In terms of ice area, this corresponds to an increase from about 8.5 to 15 million square kilometres (km^2) in the Arctic, and from about 4 to 20 million km^2 in the Antarctic.

Another difference between sea-ice cover in the two regions is how old the ice is. Ice tends to circulate in the Arctic for several years, and only a small proportion is carried south every year. It moves in response to the ocean currents beneath, and (on shorter time-scales) in response to the wind; as a result, the ice-floes jostle and grind together, or 'raft' over one another. Sometimes, the ice is pulled apart, forming linear regions of open water, or leads (pronounced 'leeds'). When the leads refreeze, and the ice-floes are pushed together again, 'pressure ridges' can form. These may be 10–30 m high, but are actually several times thicker than this, as they also have 'keels' extending down into the water (you will be able to see some pressure-ridge keels in the 'Frozen Seas' video). For these reasons, and the additional ice provided by snowfall, Arctic 'multi-year ice' (as it is called) can be quite thick, even in those areas that are ice-covered for only part of the year.

In the Antarctic, by contrast, the sea-ice is largely re-formed from seawater every winter and melts every spring. Given this information, you may well be wondering where the enormous Antarctic icebergs come from. The answer is that these icebergs are chunks of the Antarctic ice-shelf that have broken off. The ice-shelf is the floating extension of the glaciers which flow down from the Antarctic ice-cap – in other words, icebergs are *land ice* (i.e. originally snow) and do not form from seawater. If you look carefully at the Antarctic icebergs shown in the 'Frozen Seas' video, you will be able to see some indications of yearly snow layers within them.

In the 'Frozen Seas' video, you will see some strangely shaped icebergs in the Southern Ocean. In fact, because they have broken off from the ice-shelf, large newly 'calved' (i.e. newly broken off) Antarctic icebergs are tabular (i.e. flat-topped). The ones in the video must have tipped up at some stage, and been eroded by the waves. Icebergs in the Arctic are much smaller and tend to be more irregular than Antarctic icebergs. Because they mostly calve from glaciers moving down over Eastern Greenland, they often carry fragments of rock and gravel and so tend to be darker in colour.

8.2 Ice and productivity

At high latitudes, algae can only grow for a very short period each year.

- Why is this?

- Even in the half of the year when days are long, the intensity of solar radiation is relatively low because the Sun is so low in the sky (cf. Figures 4.2 to 4.4).

There are two different kinds of algae: the phytoplankton living in the water column and the ice algae, which are generally concentrated in the lowest few centimetres of the ice. These ice algae are adapted to photosynthesize at very low light levels, and have a much longer growing season than the planktonic algae. Different types of ice (notably multi-year ice versus annually forming ice) support different communities of algae, but they are mostly species of diatoms normally found in shallow-water benthic environments. You can see these clearly in several sequences in the 'Frozen Seas' video.

The ice algae use nutrients which leach down through the ice in the droplets of concentrated seawater, and from dust and other particles deposited from the atmosphere onto the surface of the ice. The ice algae are grazed by small invertebrates, as well as swarms of large copepods and amphipods, which in turn are eaten by Arctic cod and other fish (see later). In the Antarctic, ice algae are the main food source for krill overwintering under the ice. (You may remember the krill 'staining the sea red' in the introductory video – you will see krill feeding on ice algae in 'Frozen Seas'.)

Ice clearly cuts down the primary productivity of the water beneath, especially when there is also a covering of snow. Under the thick Arctic pack-ice, it is always too dark for planktonic photosynthesis to occur.

However, in spring and summer, along the margins of the ice, the opposite is true. For centuries, navigators have recorded how, as their ships drew near to the ice-edge, they observed a marked increase in the numbers of whales, seals and birds. In the Southern Ocean, the zone of high productivity can be clearly seen to follow the retreating pack-ice; this also occurs in Arctic waters but the effect is not as marked.

The melting ice produces a layer of low-salinity water, perhaps 50–75 m thick. Where the low salinity water meets the adjacent water, there is a front, and some of the causes of the high productivity may be similar to those that occur at other fronts (Section 5.4). The main reason, however, is probably that the less dense, low-salinity water floating on markedly more dense water beneath is a very stable situation.

- By reference to Figures 4.8 and 4.10, can you recall why such a stable situation would favour a phytoplankton bloom when surface waters were no longer shaded by ice?

- A stable upper water column favours a bloom because it means that phytoplankton are in less danger of being carried down out of the photic zone. In effect, the bottom of the low-salinity (i.e. low-density) layer acts as a 'floor' to downward mixing.

High productivities are also found in upwellings around glaciers entering deep water and around large icebergs.

- Thinking back to Section 5.4.2, can you suggest any possible mechanism for upwelling in the vicinity of glaciers entering deep water?

- One possibility is that subsurface currents, carrying water with high nutrient concentrations, are forced upwards by the presence of the glacier tongue, rather in the way that water is deflected upwards at shelf break fronts.

Icebergs have most of their volume underwater and could in theory act like small islands (Section 5.3), were it not for the fact that they are carried along in the water. In fact, so much of their bulk is under water that they tend to move with *subsurface* currents. As discussed in Section 5.2, wind-driven flow at depth is at a greater angle to the wind than surface wind-driven flow, so icebergs move at an angle to the direction of surface flow. When an iceberg is surrounded by pack-ice, it may be clearly seen to be moving *across* the direction in which the ice is moving. Therefore, it is the upper layers of water that are disturbed by the passage of the iceberg, which stirs nutrient-rich water up into the photic zone.

Upwelling of deeper water is thought to be responsible for the high productivity of extensive areas of open water within the pack-ice, known as **polynyas** (pronounced 'poleenyas'). Polynyas tend to occur in more or less the same place each year, and in the Arctic they are often connected by linear open channels known as shore leads. They seem to be maintained at least partly by current patterns, and the upwelling that makes them such biologically productive regions may also play a part in keeping them open. In polar regions, water at depth is generally warmer than that at the surface, and a supply of upwelled warm water could keep the polynyas open. (It is possible for cold seawater to lie above warm seawater because the density of seawater is determined by its temperature *and* its salinity. The relatively low salinity of surface water, mentioned earlier, allows it to be sufficiently less dense to float upon warmer, more saline water.)

As you will see in the 'Frozen Seas' video, polynyas provide winter refuges for whales, and feeding places for walruses, polar bears and some species of seal.

8.3 Coping with cold

Around Antarctica and in the waters at northern high latitudes, temperatures are always low, and in winter often hover just above the freezing temperature of seawater at −1.9 °C. However, we should not fall into the trap of thinking that the polar regions are necessarily a more harsh environment than any other. The animals that live there have evolved to suit their surroundings and the food available to them, just as animals living in less extreme environments have done.

However, the possibility of freezing does present a problem for animals in polar seas in winter. Even if the animal were not killed by the cold itself, the formation of ice crystals could damage the soft tissues, both through mechanical damage, and because the formation of crystals of pure water from salty body fluids would raise the salt content of the body fluids that remained.

The presence of dissolved salts in water lowers its freezing temperature (this is why salt is often put on icy roads). Nevertheless, in winter, surface polar waters may cool to their freezing temperature and to the freezing temperature of the body fluids of many invertebrates and fish.

- By reference to Section 2.1.2, can you explain why teleost fish (i.e. bony fish) are at a greater risk of freezing than are sharks and rays, and most marine invertebrates?

- Elasmobranchs, and most marine invertebrates, have blood and body fluids with salt concentrations comparable to those of seawater. Teleosts, by contrast, have blood with salt concentrations only 30–50% of that of seawater. The blood of teleosts therefore freezes at higher temperatures than the blood of elasmobranchs and of most marine invertebrates.

The bodies of deep-water fish out of contact with ice can be cooled below their usual freezing temperatures (i.e. they can be 'supercooled'), but fish living near the surface are at risk of freezing through drinking seawater containing tiny ice crystals, which can trigger freezing in their body fluids. The ice-fish, seen in the 'Frozen Seas' video, is shallow-living but survives because it produces a kind of antifreeze which lowers the freezing temperature of its body fluids.

As you know, most marine mammals maintain their body temperatures at about 38 °C, by means of their high metabolic rate and by adaptations that favour heat conservation (Section 2.1.2). The areas of the body most prone to heat loss are the limbs or flippers, where a relatively large surface area is exposed to the cold water.

Dolphins have an adaptation to reduce heat loss from their flippers which has similarities with the heat-conservation adaptation found in tuna (Section 6.4.1). Arteries carrying warm blood to the flippers are surrounded by veins within which blood is carried back into the core of the animal. Heat passes from warmer artery to cooler vein, and so is conserved within the dolphin.

8.3.1 Life on the sea-bed in polar regions

The Blue Planet videos do not include any sequences of benthic life in the Arctic or Antarctic, so we will only say a little about it here. Although the spring bloom is short, the organic debris that rains down onto the sea-bed below is sufficient to support as rich a benthic fauna as in other parts of the globe. In very deep water, off the continental shelf, animals are similar to those in other parts of the deep ocean, as conditions are very similar (we will look at the deep-sea benthic environment again in *Discovering the Deep Oceans*). On the continental shelf (e.g. in the Weddell Sea off Antarctica) many of the invertebrates are similar to their temperate counterparts, but because of the cold they have very slow metabolic rates and grow slowly, often attaining great size.

However, the shallow subtidal sea-bed is very different from that at lower latitudes (as shown in Figure 3.5, for example). At the highest latitudes in winter, benthic organisms may be killed by ice forming on the sea-floor, as a result of water being supercooled at the surface, sinking and forming ice crystals around the animals. Also, land-fast ice – i.e. ice attached to the land, also known as fast ice – may have a deep 'foot', and continual motion of this can completely clear the sea-bed. There is little chance for life to establish in summer either, as ice-floes and icebergs gouge and scrape the sea-bed, so that it is simply bare sediment.

8.4 Marine mammals

Marine mammals play a particularly prominent role in the 'Frozen Seas' video, so this seems an appropriate place to say a little more about them. There are three groups of marine mammals:

1 Whales and dolphins, which belong to the Order Cetacea (Figure 1.3).

2 Seals, elephant seals, sealions and walruses which belong to the Order Pinnipedia, and their distant relations, the sea-otters.

3 Manatees, dugongs and sea cows, which belong to the Order Sirenia.

Sea-otters (shown in the 'Seasonal Seas' video) belong to the Mustelidae, the family which includes otters and badgers. The Sirenia live in warm waters and are herbivorous. Sightings of these animals may have been the origin of the old sailors' belief in mermaids (or sirens). We will not say any more about them here.

8.4.1 The wing-footed ones

Seals, elephant seals, sealions and walruses are known as pinnipeds, which means 'wing-footed' (*pinna* = feather or wing).

There are two families of seals, the so-called 'true seals', which have small earholes, and 'eared seals', which have small ear flaps. True seals have a short neck and their overall body shape is sausage-like. They swim by powerful side-to-side movements of their hindquarters (like otters), using their short backward-pointing webbed hind limbs for propulsion in water, rather like a fish's tail. The hind limbs are of no assistance for moving about on land, where true seals are very ungainly. Both hind and front flippers are fur-covered, and the front flippers (which are short and thick, with blunt claw-like nails) are used for steering underwater.

Eared seals have longer necks than true seals, and powerful sloping shoulders. They swim by making long sweeps of their long, leathery foreflippers, either 'flying' through the water like a penguin, or 'rowing' themselves along. Their hind flippers do not seem to be used in sustained swimming, except perhaps as a rudder for steering, but they are webbed and when spread out can be used like paddles, for manoeuvring. The most obvious difference from the hind limbs of true seals is that they can be rotated forward for moving about on land, or for sitting on.

Walruses have a swimming style intermediate between those of eared seals and true seals, but generally have more similarities with eared seals. In terms of evolution, eared seals and walruses are an older group than true seals, having diverged from the stock of dog-like mammalian carnivores about 10 million years earlier – about 25 million years ago, compared with 15 million years ago for true seals.

Question 8.1 Given that sealions were formerly used as performing animals in circuses, would you say they are true seals or eared seals? (There is a sequence showing swimming sealions near the beginning of the introductory video.) ◀

The remainder of the eared seals are species which we generally refer to as fur seals because of their abundant underfur. They are generally smaller than sealions, and have longer flippers and blunter noses.

In size, appearance and behaviour, eared seals are a much more uniform group than true seals. With notable exceptions, they mainly live in cool-water regions, and none of the species breed on ice. They tend to live in highly productive areas, and are mostly generalist feeders, eating a variety of nektonic and benthic organisms, both fish and invertebrates, whichever is most easily available. In all species of eared seals, the male is substantially larger than the female – although elephant seals (which are true seals) also have a great disparity in size between the sexes.

True seals probably originated in warm waters, but are now found mainly in high latitudes. Many breed on ice, and have white pups. They are specialist feeders, so avoiding competition between the different species. For example, in northern polar seas, the ringed seal (which breeds on fast ice or heavy pack-ice) feeds on small fish and planktonic crustaceans, while spotted and ribbon seals (which use slightly thinner pack-ice) feed on shallow-water fish, and on deep-water fish and squid, respectively. Unique amongst the true seals, the bearded seal feeds on benthic molluscs and crustaceans. In southern polar seas, the Weddell seal (which you will see in the video on 'Frozen Seas') feeds on fish below the Antarctic ice-shelf, sometimes diving down to 600 m in pursuit. Another deep-diving seal is the Ross seal, which lives in the pack-ice and feeds on deep-water squid. The 'crabeater' seal (perhaps the most abundant species) eats krill, which it strains through its many-pointed teeth (as does the Antarctic fur seal, an eared seal). Elephant seals feed only on squid, and the magnificent leopard seal is a top predator, taking other seals and penguins.

Pinnipeds generally have large eyes, sometimes very large indeed. They do not have a duct to carry tears away from the eye, so may have tears running down their faces, adding to their apparently doleful expressions. They can see clearly in both air and water and their eyes are adapted to avoid excessive accommodation (adjustment) in moving from one to the other. Their retinas are adapted for low light intensities, which means that there is no colour vision. Like a cat's, the retinas are backed by a shiny surface which reflects the light back through the sensory cells a second time.

8.4.2 Whales

Of all the aquatic mammals, the whale is the one which has most completely severed its links with the land and has become a supreme performer in the sea. Even the pinnipeds need to haul out onto land or ice to breed, and cannot compete with whales when it comes to swimming and diving. Whales and dolphins are known as **cetaceans**, which comes from *ketos*, the Greek for whale. Dolphins, like killer whales, are toothed whales.

How did the whales we know today evolve?

65–50 million years ago, all of the mammals in existence lived on land, so it is clear that aquatic mammals must have evolved from terrestrial mammals. Until recently, all the known fossil remains of early cetaceans indicated an amphibious or wholly aquatic lifestyle, but fossils found in Pakistan (of an animal which has been named *Pakicetus*) now provide a link between recent and present-day whales and the oldest known group of 'even-toed ungulates' – a group of hoofed mammals which today includes hippos, cows, pigs, camels and giraffes. The significant link between *Pakicetus* and early ungulates (e.g. an animal known as *Diacodexis*, Figure 8.2 overleaf) is in the ankle bones, which are of a type suitable for efficient running. Although these ankle bones link *Pakicetus* with animals like modern-day hippos, they indicate that modern whales are *closer* to the early ungulates than they are to modern hippos, cows etc.

Figure 8.2 shows the likely evolutionary route from animals like *Diacodexis* to modern whales. *Ambulocetus* ('walking whale') was amphibious. It may well have moved around like a large sealion, and may perhaps have swum rather like an otter. *Dorudon* was fully aquatic and more streamlined, with greatly reduced pelvis and hind limbs.

There has been much debate about the relationship between the baleen whales (Mysticeti) and the toothed whales (Odontoceti) (cf. Figure 1.3). It used to be thought that these two groups became separate about 40 million years ago, and it was assumed that the specialized carnivore teeth and associated jaw structure of the toothed whales and the dolphins marked them out as evolutionarily distinct from the baleen whales, which live mainly on zooplankton. However, recent work involving DNA sequencing suggests that baleen whales are closely related to sperm whales, which have teeth, whereas the dolphins seem to be a separate group. This suggests that the baleen whales' highly specialized plankton-feeding lifestyle arose relatively recently – perhaps only 25 million years ago.

Modern whales

The bones of modern whales are light and spongy. They do not have to support the weight of the animal, and need only to act as anchor points for the muscles. In the case of the baleen whales, the skulls have been extremely modified in shape, and instead of teeth there are two rows of plates (known as baleen plates) which hang down from the roof of the mouth. The inner edges of these plates are fringed with bristles ('whalebone'), and the whale feeds by using the bristles to sieve zooplankton from huge mouthfuls of water, and then collecting the food from the fringes with its tongue.

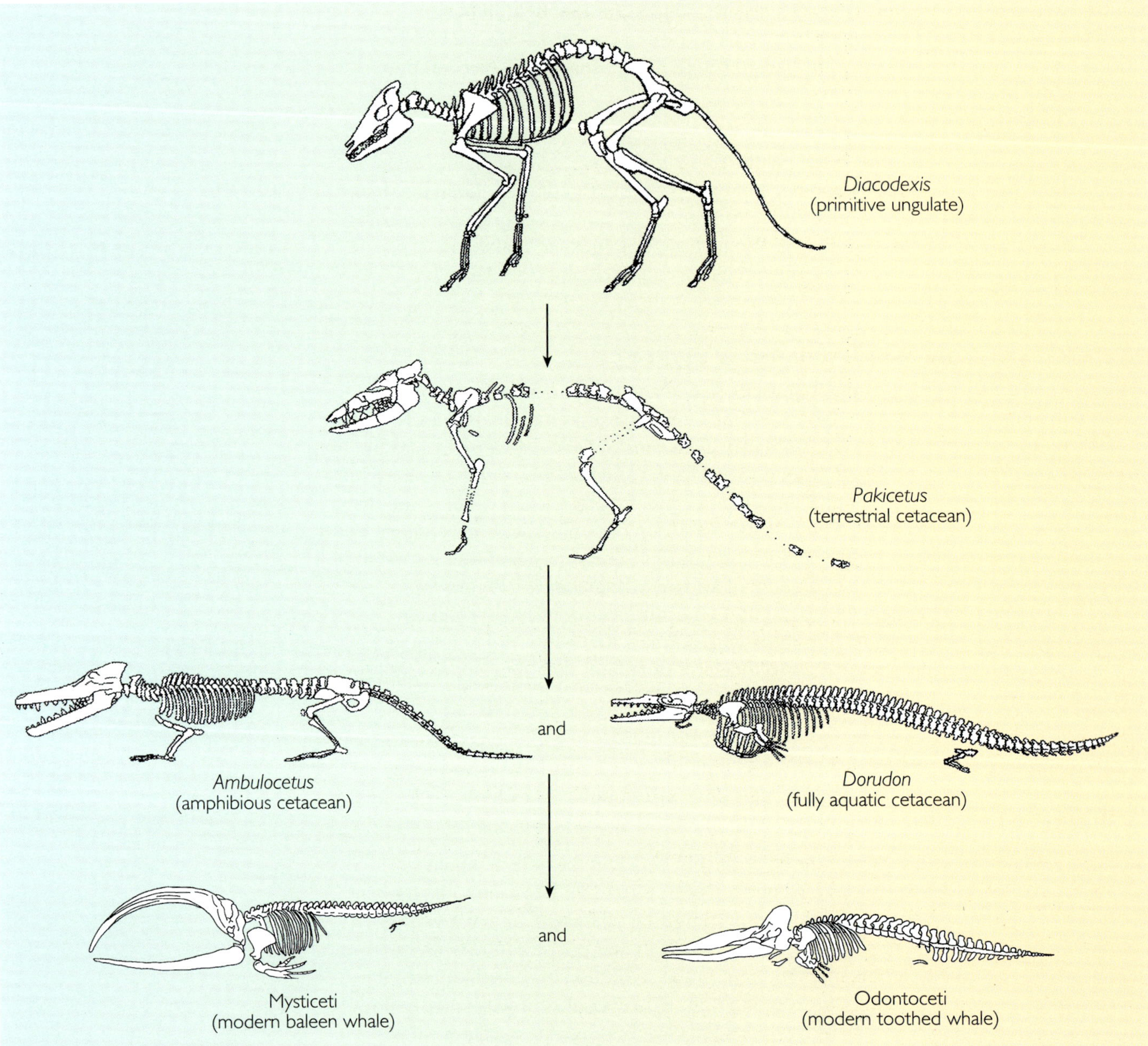

Figure 8.2 The most likely evolutionary route from terrestrial ancestor to modern whales. *Note*: *Ambulocetus* and *Dorudon* are just two representatives of the cetaceans which evolved from *Pakicetus*. (Skeletons not drawn to scale.)

As the relationships between different types of whales can be rather confusing, Table 8.1 summarizes the different families of baleen whales and toothed whales. As mentioned in the notes for the introductory video, the rorquals are those baleen whales that have expandable grooves in their throats, which allow them to engulf huge volumes of water containing large numbers of zooplankton (or occasionally, fish).

Question 8.2

(a) What is the largest member of the Mysticeti?

(b) In what sense is a killer whale a dolphin?

(You may find it useful to consult Table 8.1 and/or look back to Figure 1.3.) ◀

Table 8.1 Families of baleen and toothed whales (including species seen in the Blue Planet videos); see also Figure 1.3.

Baleen whales	
Gray whale: 1 species	
Rorquals: 6 species – blue whale, finback whale, Sei whale, Bryde's whale, minke whale and humpback whale	
Right whales: 3 species – right whale, pygmy right whale and bowhead whale	
Toothed whales	
Dolphins: 32 species, including common dolphins, bottle-nosed dolphins, spinner dolphins, pilot whales, killer whales	
Porpoises: 6 species, including harbour (or common) porpoise	
White whales: 2 species – beluga and narwhal	
Beaked whales: 18 species, including bottle-nosed whale	
Sperm whales: 3 species – sperm whale, pygmy sperm whale and dwarf sperm whale	
River dolphins: 5 species	

Figure 8.3 (overleaf) has been included to show the relative sizes of different groups of whale, as it is not easy to judge the size of animals on video. This diagram was compiled some years ago, and many of the larger whales were drawn on the basis of photographs of corpses of whales killed during whaling.

- You have now seen quite a few video sequences showing whales, either feeding or swimming. Why are the drawings of the rorqual baleen whales in Figure 8.3 somewhat misleading?

- A swimming rorqual is as streamlined as a toothed whale, because the throat grooves are contracted (cf. the blue whale in the introductory video). When a rorqual is feeding, however, the grooves expand and the throat bulges outwards in a more exaggerated way than shown in Figure 8.3 (cf. the rorqual at the very end of the 'Bounty off Natal' video).

It should be said that even photographs and film of large whales do not produce entirely accurate images, because the wide-angle lenses needed to 'capture' the whole animal make them look slimmer than they are in reality.

As Figure 8.3 shows, the only toothed whale which comes near to the size of baleen whales is the sperm whale, with its enlarged head. As you may remember from 'Wild Moves: Water', most of this large volume is occupied by the spermaceti organ, which plays a significant role in enabling the sperm whale to be the champion diver amongst marine mammals. Sperm whales are known to dive to 1000 m or so to catch squid, but from the contents of their stomachs – including stones and tin cans, as well as bottom-living sharks – it is obvious they sometimes actually feed on the bottom. However, the most impressive thing about their diving is not how deep they dive, but how efficiently they do it.

It seems that as the whale dives down out of the warm surface layer, the spermaceti is cooled by an intake of water through the blowhole. This cools the wax so that it

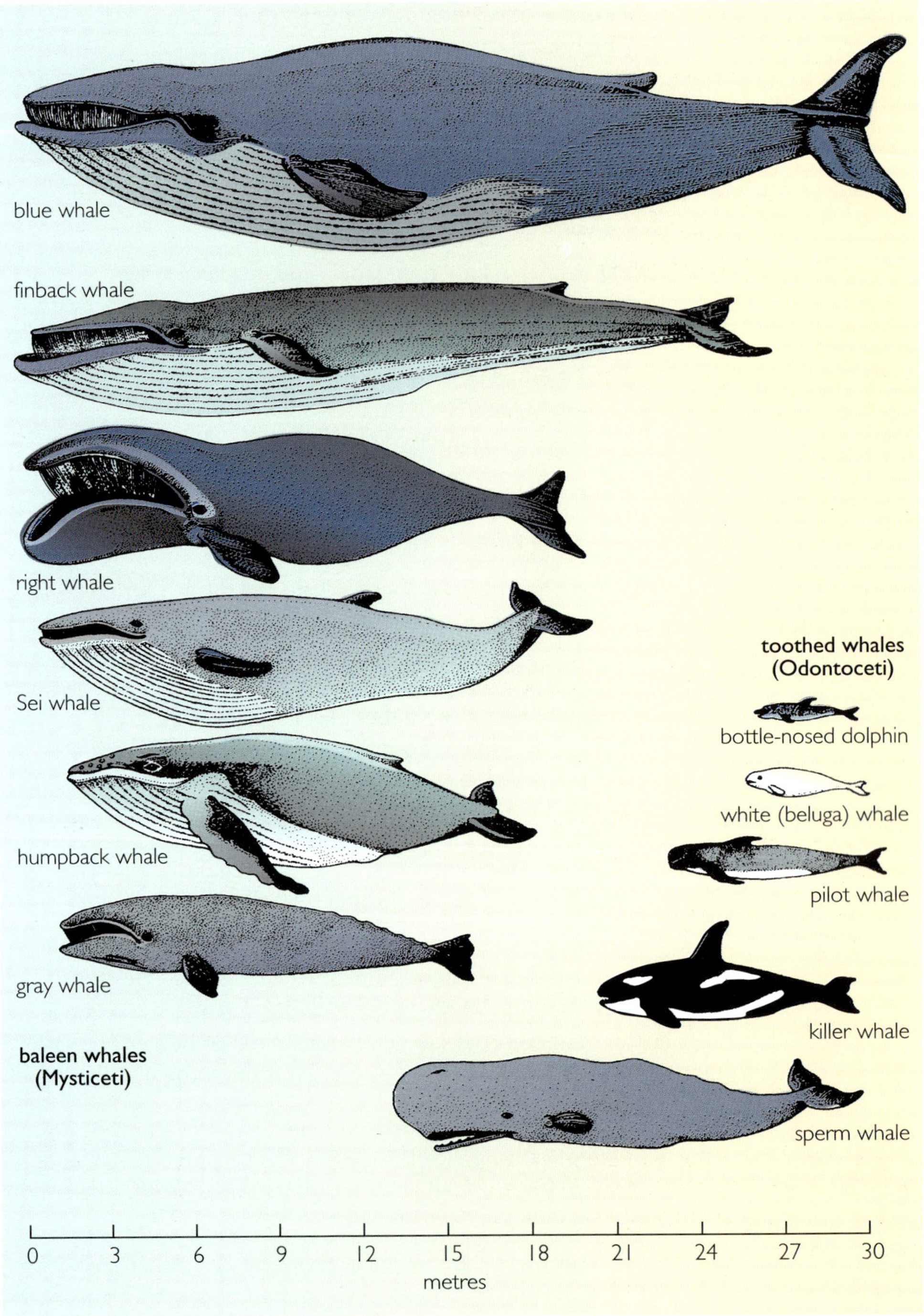

Figure 8.3 Relative sizes of baleen and toothed whales. (Note the caveat in the text.)

solidifies and shrinks, thereby increasing the density of the head and enabling the whale to sink fast. When the whale has finished feeding, it warms the spermaceti by increasing the flow of blood through the capillaries in the front of the head. The wax warms slightly, melts and becomes less dense, and the increased buoyancy allows the whale to rise to the surface with a minimum of effort.

When a whale dives, its lungs compress and the air in them is driven into the windpipe and its branches, and the extensive nasal passages. As the whale rises to the surface, the lungs gradually expand, the blowhole is opened wide and the foul air that has accumulated during the dive is expelled as a cloud of spray. In fact, baleen whales have two nostrils each of which has a blowhole, so what appears to be one blowhole is in fact two parallel slits which are close together when shut. In toothed whales, the two nasal passages join together and there is only one nostril and one blowhole. Sperm whales are unique in that their blowhole is at the front of the head and to one side, so that the spray is ejected forwards at an angle of 45°. This is a result of the fact that the two nasal passages have different functions, the right nasal passage being used to take in water to cool the spermaceti when diving (as described above), the left being used to clear out stale air.

In earlier chapters, it was suggested that while watching the videos you note down characteristics of how whales and dolphins swim, and of whale and dolphin behaviour generally.

- What is the most noticeable difference between how whales and dolphins swim and how fish swim?

- Whales and dolphins swim by moving their tails up and down; when fish swim, they move their tails from side to side.

Whales and dolphins use their flippers for steering, and the dorsal fin (if there is one) may be useful for stabilization (although it could also be used in temperature regulation). The flexibility of the whale's body is enhanced by the fact that the layer of blubber, which helps keep the body temperature at about 38 °C (Section 2.1.2) and may be 20 cm thick, is not tightly fixed to the underlying muscular tissues.

- How would you describe the way that toothed whales hunt for food?

- Toothed whales hunt cooperatively. There are several examples in the videos: bottle-nosed dolphins catching mullet at the end of 'Tidal Seas', dolphins using 'bubble-netting' and driving sardines up to the surface at the beginning of the 'Bounty off Natal', and the killer whales (orca) battering herring with their tails, at the end of 'Seasonal Seas'.

Generally speaking, whales are very social animals, enjoying group interactions and even playing together.

How whales use sound

Another aspect of whale behaviour that you may have noted down is their extensive use of sound, both for communication and (in the case of toothed whales) for echo-location. Toothed whales are sensitive to sounds over a wide range of frequencies, and can distinguish different frequencies with great precision, being progressively better at this with increasing frequency (i.e. higher pitch). They produce a wide range of sounds, some like a continuous whistle (which seem to be for communication) and some as pulses. The pulsed sounds include trains of clicks (which may sound like a buzz) as well as sounds resembling barks, bleats, groans, moans, squawks, squeals and yelps. They also make short sounds when they leap or clap their jaws. Interpreting the significance of these various sounds is not easy because while the sounds made in different situations vary widely, the same sound may be produced in different contexts (e.g. escaping from danger, chasing food, sexual activity or play). This could indicate that the meaning of a sound is determined by its context, or that a particular sound is produced as a result of the same factor (e.g. excitement or stress) operating under different circumstances.

Trains of clicks are also used in echo-location, and toothed whales in general have highly developed echo-location systems. The waxy lens-shaped organ which focuses the sound – known as the 'melon' – is situated in the forehead, and focuses 'clicks' produced in the nasal passages. The returning echoes are channelled to the inner ear along oil-filled sinuses in the lower jaw. The inner ear is insulated from extraneous sounds transmitted along other bones in the skull because it is within a bone that is suspended from the skull by a ligament, and is surrounded with a kind of foam. Toothed whales can identify the direction of the source of an echo or some other sound extremely accurately, to within an angle of a few degrees in both the horizontal and vertical planes.

The use of sound by the Mysticeti has not been as easy to study as that by the toothed whales, although whalers have long known of their acute hearing. The sounds are harder to classify than those of toothed whales, being much more variable. They tend to last longer, and are mostly of much lower frequency. Low-frequency sounds travel through seawater with less loss of energy than high-frequency sounds, and the main use of the sounds produced seems to be communication between individuals which may be very widely scattered. As mentioned in Section 4.6, whales may use the sound channel to communicate over 1000 km or more. Perhaps the most famous whale sounds are the 'songs' of the humpback whale. Different populations have distinctive songs, although they gradually evolve with new motifs being added and others being dropped. Recently, it has been discovered that the song of another nearby population may be adopted, apparently in preference. Within populations, individuals have their own voice characteristics which make their song distinguishable from that of other whales. Humpbacks migrate to warm waters to breed, and on arrival at the breeding grounds, the males begin to sing – the song of a male humpback could be heard in the 'Coral Seas' video [0:35:56].

Hearing and sound production in other marine animals

Seals also have very highly developed hearing, and can hear well in air (as can dolphins in the case of certain types of sound). Communication by sound also seems to be widespread in fish, particularly for distinguishing their own species from other species. Fish often produce sounds in response to stimuli (e.g. when they are alarmed) or during reproductive activity. The sounds that they make (and the sounds they can hear) are low frequency, i.e. of low pitch. Fish with swimbladders, which resonate readily, may use muscles attached to the swimbladder to generate sound. As sound waves are pressure waves, and pressure affects the swimbladder, the presence of a swimbladder, and its position in relation to the inner ear (where sound is received), also affects the sensitivity of a fish to sound – you may recall that many deep-sea fish use their swimbladders to detect sound (Section 6.3). In fish of the herring family, there is also an indirect connection to the surrounding water via the lateral line, which is a pressure-sensitive organ located along the flanks. Finally, we should note that many invertebrates also produce sounds and are able to detect them.

▶▶ *This is a good time to watch the video on 'Frozen Seas' (VC2). During the video you will see (in this order): walruses, harp seals, hooded seals, ringed seals, walruses (again), Weddell seals, fur seals and leopard seals. For each of the seals, try to work out whether they are 'true seals' or 'eared seals'.* ◀◀

Notes on the 'Frozen Seas' video

[0:43:52] Here and later on in this video, note the green colour imparted to the ice by algae living in it.

[0:44:22] The statement about a temperature of −50 °C is, of course, referring to temperature *on land* (on the Antarctic continent).

[0:45:33] As you should now appreciate, the Arctic does *not* freeze from shore to shore each year, as the narration suggests. Most of the ice in the Arctic ice-cap is several years old.

[0:54:50–0:56:55] In this sequence of the polar bear hunting for the ringed seal, you can see the hummocky nature of multi-year ice. In particular, the lair in which the ringed seal pup is hiding seems to be in the downward-extending part of a pressure ridge, i.e. the keel. As it swims away, you can see the keel quite clearly.

[0:58:40] Note the leads, which may later be transformed into pressure ridges if the ice-floes are driven together.

[1:03:43] Walruses use their tusks to stir up the sediment when they are hunting for molluscs, and also for hauling their great bulk up onto the ice.

[1:07:45] The Antarctic ice shelf (the floating seaward extension of glaciers) can be seen in the background.

[1:11:26] Note that inside the krill, you can see the algae they have eaten.

[1:14:26 and 1:23:27] Note the two different ways that chinstrap penguins and emperor penguins leave the water: the former make use of waves, and the latter make use of their own buoyancy.

[1:16:55 and 1:17:23] These fantastically shaped icebergs were once tabular but have tipped over, and have been sculpted by the sea into the shapes you see here.

[1:18:09 and 1:18:47] The minke whale seems to have algal growth on its body, and the humpback carries barnacles and other encrusting organisms. (You will probably have spotted other examples of whales providing living space for smaller organisms, in previous videos.)

[1:23:46] In this sequence, you can see in the background sea-ice that has moved under the influence of wind and cracked, and the separate floes have rafted over one another.

Question 8.3 On the basis of the video sequence showing Antarctic fur seals pursuing krill [1:20:14–1:20:51], explain whether you would classify fur seals as true seals or eared seals. ◀

8.5 The food web in Arctic seas

As the 'Frozen Seas' video shows so dramatically, in both the Arctic and the Antarctic, mammals dominate the upper part of the food web, and are the top predators; while algae – both ice algae and phytoplankton (Section 8.2) – form the base of the food web.

Figure 8.4 *(opposite)* Food web for the polar seas to the north of the North Atlantic (the food web for high latitudes in the North Pacific differs from this in important ways). Note that this food web is simplified, and not all links and species are shown. (Not to scale.)

- What would you say was the key component of the marine ecosystem at high southern latitudes?
- It is, of course, the krill.

The Antarctic krill is the species *Euphausia superba*. Another species of krill, *Meganyctiphanes norvegica*, is found in Arctic waters, but it does not play such a pivotal role in the food web and does not feed on ice algae. Have a look at Figure 8.4, which shows a simplified food web for Arctic waters.

- Can you pick out some of the feeding interactions shown in the 'Frozen Seas' video?
- At the top can be seen a scenario similar to that at the start of the video, with polar bears as top predator (to the left), and carrion-feeding Arctic foxes and birds (to the right). At the bottom left can be seen the walruses feeding on benthic invertebrates (which would include molluscs). Bowhead whales and rorquals (as well as right whales) can be seen feeding on various types of zooplankton.

Question 8.4 On the basis of the feeding interactions shown in Figure 8.4, what would you say is the key organism in the Arctic? ◀

Arctic cod are an important food source for a wide variety of birds and mammals. Their importance in the Arctic food web results partly from the fact that they are adapted to live and feed in a wide range of habitats: at the surface and under the sea-ice; at the edge of fast ice; in shallow coastal waters in summer; and at depths of more than 900 m. They are distributed throughout the Arctic and are extremely abundant. During the long winter they are widely dispersed, but in summer they congregate into enormous schools – all the more convenient for the predatory seals, as well as for the summer-visiting belugas, narwhals and bowheads.

Sadly for the trapped beluga in the 'Frozen Seas' video, the Arctic cod were still dispersed because it was too early in the year. The whales would not have been able to feed well, given that during the relatively brief dives they would have to go on wide-ranging forays, inefficiently collecting individual fish, and then come back to their ice-hole to breathe.

8.6 The 'fragile Arctic'

There is currently much concern about the future of the wildlife in polar regions, particularly that of the Arctic, for two interconnected reasons, both relating to fossil fuels.

As discussed earlier, the low temperatures of the polar regions are a result of the low levels of solar radiation they receive and, in the case of the Antarctic, the fact that it is not warmed by currents flowing from lower latitudes. However, there is also another reason, namely that snow and ice reflect a large proportion of incoming solar radiation back to space – about 80–90% for fresh snow and ice. The high reflectivity of snow and ice is also referred to as a high *albedo*. If the snow and ice cover over an area of the Earth's surface melted completely, this would expose surfaces with a much lower albedo (especially in the case of land, which is dark in colour), and these surfaces would therefore absorb much more solar radiation. This increased absorption

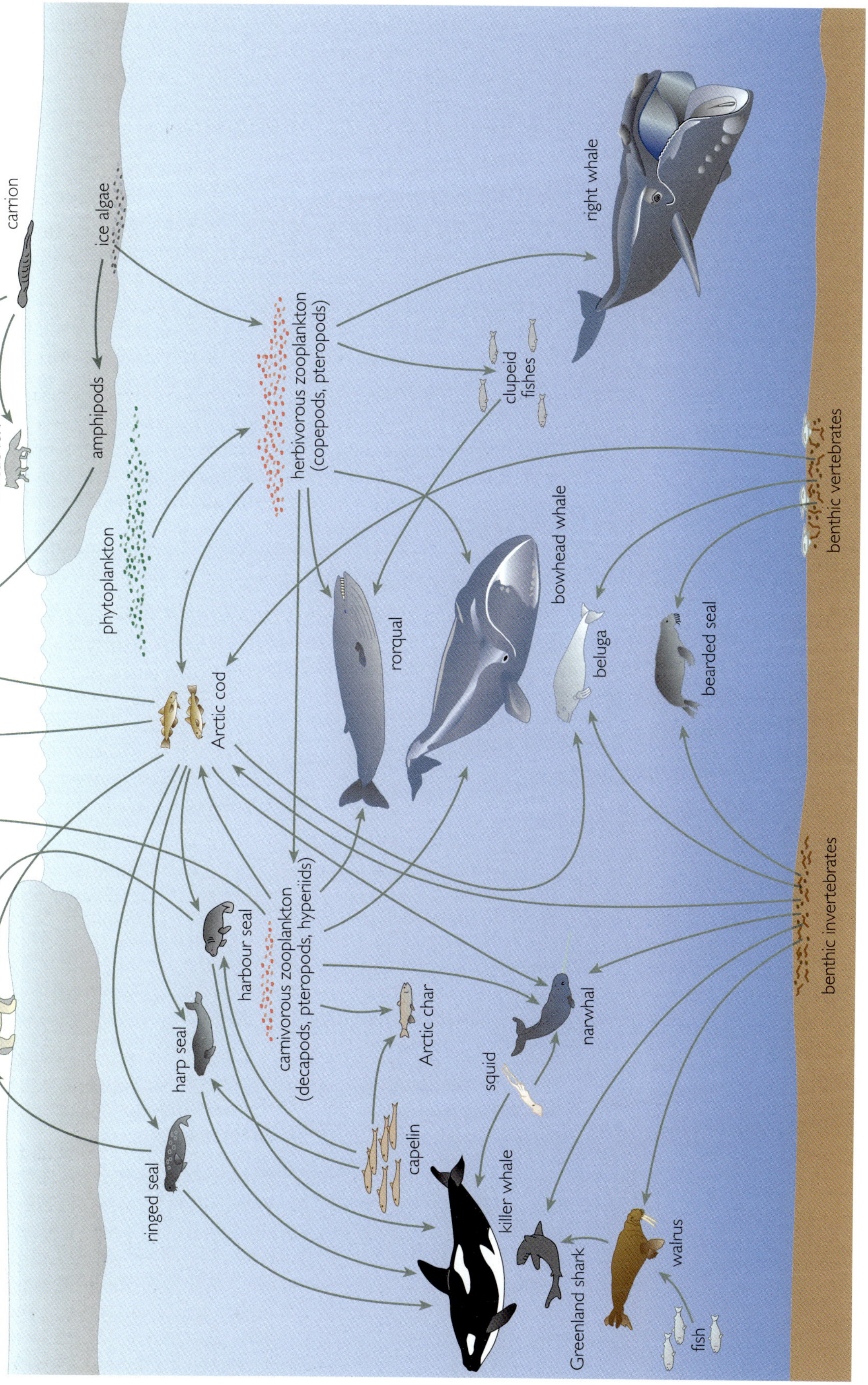
carrion
ice algae
amphipods
Arctic fox
fulmar
ivory gull
kittiwake
guillemot
polar bear
phytoplankton
herbivorous zooplankton (copepods, pteropods)
clupeid fishes
right whale
Arctic cod
rorqual
bowhead whale
beluga
bearded seal
benthic vertebrates
benthic invertebrates
harbour seal
harp seal
carnivorous zooplankton (decapods, pteropods, hyperiids)
Arctic char
narwhal
squid
capelin
ringed seal
killer whale
Greenland shark
walrus
fish

of heat would lead to further melting, and so on – a positive feedback effect. Most scientists now believe that global warming in response to increased concentrations of carbon dioxide in the atmosphere has been underway for some time, and because of the 'albedo-effect', it has been predicted that the Arctic will be the first part of the globe to show clear evidence of global warming.

The extent and thickness of Arctic ice has therefore been closely monitored over recent decades, and the results do indeed show that Arctic sea-ice is thinning and penetrating less far south in winter. In the summer of 2000, there was open water at the North Pole for the first time in living memory. Warming is already causing problems for animals in the Arctic – for example, the sea in Hudson Bay has recently been freezing later and later each year, and the polar bears are having to wait longer before they can go out onto the ice to catch seals. However, it is important to note that on the basis of evidence from a relatively short period of time, it is not possible to be sure that this reduction in ice cover is part of a long-term trend rather than the result of a short-term climatic fluctuation.

The other serious threat to Arctic wildlife now causing concern is more tangible. It seems highly likely that in the near future parts of the Arctic will be at increased risk of pollution associated with oil exploitation. Oil can be particularly damaging under cold conditions, because it does not disperse as quickly as it does at higher temperatures, and may also get trapped beneath and amongst ice-floes. The continental shelves around the Arctic Ocean contain huge reserves of oil and gas, the remains of phytoplankton that were buried by sediments and 'matured' over millions of years in anoxic conditions. At present, oil exploitation is technically impossible over much of the Arctic region. The permanent or seasonal ice cover prevents or hinders exploration and makes drilling extremely difficult and hazardous. In addition, up until the present there have been no suitable routes through Arctic waters for oil tankers which were not also ice-breakers. Melting of parts of the Arctic ice would lead to an opening up of coastal seaways which would make the transportation of oil out of the Arctic much easier, and would facilitate access to the oilfields in Alaska's National Wildlife Refuge, which was protected by law until the end of 2001. (Oil is already extracted from the continental shelf off the north coast of Alaska, the so-called North Slope, but that is carried south in the Alaska oil pipeline.)

Arctic ecosystems are also vulnerable to airborne pollution, particularly from industrial complexes in eastern and western Europe and the United States. Atmospheric conditions over the Arctic favour the condensation of pollutants such as PCBs, which tend to accumulate in body fats, particularly in top predators. Although these pollutants may be tolerated under normal conditions, they may be harmful if the animals are stressed and/or are mobilizing fat reserves.

The term 'fragile Arctic', coined by the media, seems to suggest that Arctic ecosystems are more vulnerable to human interference and natural change than ecosystems in other parts of the globe. But is this true?

The food web shown in Figure 8.4 may look quite complicated, even though it has been simplified for the sake of clarity. However, compared with food webs in other regions, Arctic ecosystems, both marine and terrestrial, are simple, with a low diversity of species and relatively short food webs, i.e. few trophic levels. (This also holds true for Antarctic systems, as you should recall from the 'Ecosystems and Food Webs' module.)

- Why might a simple food web render an ecosystem more vulnerable?

- Because a problem with one link in the web – a temporary reduction in numbers, or an extinction – would have much more serious consequences than would be the case in a more complex system, where the animals have a wider choice of food species.

However, this view is not shared by all ecologists, some of whom argue that simple food webs are more robust than complex ones. Furthermore, although polar ecosystems involve relatively few animals, many of these animals are generalist feeders and do not depend on a single food resource, so this effectively means that there are more routes through the food web.

The way in which (say) pollution or environmental change affects populations of animals depends very much on the time-scale involved. Warm-blooded marine mammals and birds have relatively long lives – 50–100 years in the case of a killer whale, about 40 years in the case of an albatross.

- What implications do such long lives have for the survival of a population threatened by (say) a pollution incident?

- An individual pollution incident is likely to affect a region for (say) two or three years. For long-lived animals, several years with poor breeding success may have little effect on the number of young produced over a lifetime, and therefore little effect on the size of the population.

However, cold-blooded fish and invertebrates tend to have slow growth rates and low reproduction rates and (in comparison to mammals) relatively short lifetimes, so these can be badly affected by relatively short-term environmental changes. A series of relatively minor perturbations could prevent a species from recovering from a bad year, and events that elsewhere would be relatively unimportant could add up to an ecological catastrophe. Nevertheless, in both Arctic and Antarctic ecosystems, although diversity is low, numbers of individuals of a given species may be very large – think of krill and Arctic cod, for example – and this reduces the chance of a 'crash'. Also, Arctic and Antarctic ecosystems are both spread over large areas, so damage to one region might be repaired by immigration of animals from adjacent regions.

Any widespread long-term decrease in numbers of fish or invertebrates would certainly have a serious impact upon the animals that feed on them, especially as the vulnerability of species tends to increase with evolutionary complexity (copepods, for example, are less vulnerable than fish). Most vulnerable of all are the marine mammals and birds, in which pollutants are in any case concentrated because they are at the top of the food web. If populations of top predators were to decline dramatically, the whole ecosystem would alter, both in terms of which species are dominant and in terms of the diversity of species overall.

9 Migrations

The Blue Planet videos contain various sequences that relate to migrations of marine animals. In some ways, the migrations are very different from one another but, as you will see, they also share certain features in common.

9.1 Whale migrations

The Blue Planet introductory video begins with a magnificent blue whale feeding on krill in Arctic waters. Most of the great baleen whales spend part of the year feeding at high latitudes – around the melting Arctic pack-ice and between the Arctic islands, and along the retreating ice-edge in the Southern Ocean (Section 8.2) – and spend the rest of the year in warmer waters where food is more scarce. During the short polar summer, the great baleen whales probably eat about 3–4% of their body weight each day, which in the case of a blue whale amounts to 2–2.5 tonnes of krill. Then, having increased their body weight by perhaps 50–70%, they travel several thousand kilometres to live where there is about a tenth of the food, and they will lose so much weight that by the time they return to their summer feeding grounds their blubber store will be largely used up. Why do they undertake these marathon migrations?

The simple answer is: to breed. But why do they not breed in polar waters in summer, like their smaller toothed relations, beluga and narwhal? Or indeed, like the polar pinnipeds?

One reason could relate to the availability of their respective food supplies.

- Can you suggest what this might be?

- Plankton – the main food of the baleen whales – are only abundant in high-latitude seas for a few months each year, whereas fish – the food of most of the carnivorous toothed whales – are available all year round.

However, this cannot be the whole answer. For one thing, some toothed whales also make quite short summer visits to polar regions. One possibility is that the time spent at lower latitudes is a legacy from the distant past when climatic patterns were different and tropical regions were more biologically productive than they are now. This idea is supported by the fact that fossil remains of the earliest baleen whales have only been found at low latitudes.

It also seems likely that baleen whales do not stay all year at high latitudes because newly born calves do not have sufficient blubber to insulate them from cold polar waters, and so need to be weaned in warmer waters. Also, it is possible that, because the suckling calf has to make such an enormous amount of growth, the food required by the mother cannot be consumed in the short period of high productivity of the polar summer.

- What lower-latitude regions would you expect to be favoured by plankton-feeding whales, including those which have migrated from high latitudes after the polar summer?

- Upwelling areas (cf. Figure 5.10), notably the Equatorial Divergence and eastern coastlines affected by the Trade Winds.

Perhaps the best-known whale migration routes are those of the gray whale, which of all the baleen whales is the one that lives closest to shore, and is often seen within a kilometre of the coast. There are two populations of gray whales, one with winter calving grounds in the shallow lagoons of Baja California and another with winter calving grounds off Korea and around Japan. Each spring, the Californian 'grays' are watched by thousands of people as they travel north along the coast of North America *en route* to the Bering Sea and Chukchi Sea to the north of the Bering Straits, and then again in the autumn as they travel back to Baja California. Meanwhile, similar migrations are taking place along the margin of the western Pacific, to and from the same summer feeding grounds.

Migration patterns are not as simple as we may have suggested, and vary between species and between the same species in the Northern and Southern Hemisphere. For example, not all baleen whales travel to low latitudes to breed. One population of bowhead whales winters in the Bering Sea (between Alaska and Siberia), where the calves are born, and in summer they follow the leads in the pack ice to the Beaufort Sea (off northern Alaska). Another population of bowheads winters and calves in the Labrador Sea, and in summer travels to coastal inlets around Baffin Island.

Some toothed whales also migrate. In the case of sperm whales, females and juveniles usually remain in tropical and subtropical waters, while the males travel from low latitudes to the polar regions. This could be partly because the young have insufficient blubber for polar waters and need protection from their mothers, and partly because the males can avoid competing with their calves for food resources by feeding elsewhere. (Also, some populations of squid, on which sperm whales feed, may themselves be migratory.)

Dolphins and other small whales make seasonal migrations in search of food, either moving onshore and offshore, or visiting particular sites where productivity is high at certain times of year. The dolphins and pilot whales heading off to the Azores at the end of the 'Open Ocean' video are on such a migration.

9.2 Fish migrations

As far as fish are concerned, environments that are good for spawning (i.e. producing eggs) are very often not good for young to grow up in, nor for adults to feed in, and many marine fish species have a migratory cycle which allows each stage to prosper, and so maximizes reproductive success. For example, North Sea plaice (*Pleuronectes platessa*) spawn in the very south-western part of the North Sea, and the young – which are members of the meroplankton (Section 4.4) – are carried in currents to the sheltered waters of the Wadden Sea (off the Netherlands and western Germany). This journey between the spawning ground and the nursery areas is the most hazardous period of their lives. It is timed to coincide with the spring phytoplankton bloom, but if weather conditions result in the bloom being late, the peak in zooplankton numbers, on which the larvae feed, will also be late, and the young plaice will starve to death before they reach the Wadden Sea. If they do not starve, they may well be eaten.

After about five weeks as larvae, the young plaice metamorphose into tiny versions of the adult fish and descend to the sea-bed as they are carried by currents to their nursery areas. After spending a year or more in the Wadden Sea, the young plaice swim to the northern part of the North Sea, where they feed until the time arrives to spawn.

- Thinking back to Section 3.4 (Hitching a ride on the tide), can you recall how demersal fish like plaice save energy during their migrations?

- They swim with the current when the tidal current is flowing in the direction they are travelling in, and rest on the bottom during the other half of the tidal cycle.

Herring (*Clupea harengus*) in the North Sea spawn off eastern Scotland and the larvae drift shorewards. Then, as the young adults grow they move eastwards into deeper water, with the main feeding grounds being off Norway. The herring of the Pacific make similar migrations – you may remember the baby herring in the feeding grounds off Vancouver Island in the 'Seasonal Seas' video.

This type of migratory pattern, with separate spawning grounds, nursery grounds and adult feeding grounds, is adopted by a wide variety of nektonic species – fish, squid and even large crustaceans. Even for strong swimmers – tuna, for example – the migration routes make use of the prevailing currents. The young yellowfin tuna, seen in the 'Open Ocean' video, were carried as larvae to the western Pacific in the westward-flowing currents of the equatorial current system (Figure 5.2).

In the case of animals that live on or near the bottom (like the plaice), whose eggs rise to the surface to become part of the plankton, and develop into planktonic larval animals, the migration has a vertical dimension. Indeed, this is true of all animals that produce meroplankton (as seen in the 'Seasonal Seas' video). There are other animals that migrate into shallower coastal waters to mate, and lay their eggs there – an extreme example of this behaviour is provided by the capelin, seen in the introductory video – and yet others which swim up to the surface to mate, and then return to deeper water to lay their eggs. The spectacular firefly squid, which you will see in the second part of the video on 'The Deep', is one such animal.

As mentioned in Chapter 3, many estuarine invertebrates and fish travel between seawater and freshwater as part of their reproductive cycles.

- Can you give any examples of (1) fish which spend most of their time in the sea, but spawn in freshwater, and (2) fish which spend most of their lives in freshwater, but spawn in the sea?

- The best-known examples are probably (1) salmon, and (2) freshwater eels.

Other sea fish which breed in freshwater – i.e. *anadromous fish* – are the shad and the sea lamprey. Freshwater fish which spawn at sea, including eels of the genus *Anguilla*, are described as *catadromous*. All these fish are relatively primitive, and some biologists believe that their migrations are somehow a hangover from a time when these fish lived in shallow brackish water, in estuaries and along coasts.

However, in the case of eels, the migrations are very long indeed. As far as North Atlantic populations are concerned, there are two species of eel, both of which spawn in the Sargasso Sea, the centre of the North Atlantic subtropical gyre, to the east of the Gulf Stream (Figure 5.9). *Anguilla anguilla* (the European eel) spends most of its adult life in rivers, streams and estuaries in Europe, and *Anguilla rostrata* (the American eel) similarly spends most of its adult life in North American freshwaters.

Question 9.1 Thinking back to Figure 2.2, can you suggest a possible origin for these long migration routes from the mainland (especially the European mainland) to the Sargasso Sea? ◀

The ancient distribution of continents could also help to explain why green turtles that live and feed off the coast of Brazil swim 2000 km to breed on Ascension Island in mid-Atlantic (as shown in the introductory video). However, it does little to explain why leatherback turtles, that are regularly seen feeding on jellyfish and salps (seen in the 'Open Ocean' video) in the north-eastern Atlantic, breed on beaches along the coast of Brazil.

9.3 Vertical migration

Every evening at dusk, over large parts of the oceans, there is a mass migration of marine animals up towards the surface; every morning, around dawn, the animals begin to return to the depths. This amazing phenomenon has been known about for nearly 200 years, but we still do not have an entirely satisfactory explanation for its ecological significance. It is sometimes known as 'diurnal migration', but as diurnal means 'pertaining to the day' (i.e. is the opposite of 'nocturnal'), this behaviour is more properly known as *diel* migration, meaning migration 'once a day' or 'every 24 hours'.

Vertical migration began to be brought to the attention of marine scientists with the widespread use of sonar (i.e. echo-sounding) for bathymetric measurements in the 1950s and 1960s. Sonar traces often show 'deep scattering layers', sound-reflecting layers *within* the water column that look similar to reflections from the sea-bed. Admiralty charts produced in the 1950s therefore included a number of non-existent 'shoals' (i.e. shallow areas), and it was only when it was realized that these layers moved with a 24-hour rhythm that animal behaviour began to be suspected. As many as five different layers can be distinguished on a single echo-sounder record, between depths of about 100 m and 1000 m. These may be caused by gatherings of larger crustaceans (e.g. krill and shrimp), small fish with sound-reflecting swimbladders (e.g. lanternfish), and even large copepods. To some extent, the layers may be artefacts of the fact that for some animals (especially fish with swimbladders) the strength of the echo changes with the pressure the animal is under, so that an echo-sounder can only 'see' the animal over a certain depth range.

At night, the distinct layers are observed to rise to the surface and become diffuse or merge into a broad band extending down to about 150 m. Diel migrations are tuned to the light–dark cycle, and the depth zones occupied by different species are influenced by daylength, as well as factors like cloud cover, or even bright moonlight and eclipses.

The vertical distance travelled over 24 hours varies, with larger species and better swimmers generally travelling further. However, even small copepods will travel several hundred metres twice a day. Copepods and the larvae of barnacles and crabs can swim upwards at 10–170 m per hour, with larger crustaceans, which can swim at 100–200 m per hour, making a twice-daily journey of 800 m or more.

● What possible advantages could there be for zooplankton to migrate in this way? Consider for a while, and try to come up with some suggestions.

Many hypotheses have been advanced to explain vertical migrations. Here are three:

1 Food is more abundant in the sunlit surface layers, but this is also where animals are most vulnerable to predators which hunt by sight. One solution to this might be to hide at depth by day, in darkness or near-darkness, and only rise to the

surface to feed at night. The fact that many migrants are transparent, or very small, suggests that the animals that prey on them do hunt by sight.

2 Another possibility is that zooplankton conserve energy by spending non-feeding time in colder, deeper water. As you know, metabolic rates are lower in colder temperatures (Section 2.1.2), and it has been shown that the amount of energy saved by spending part of the day in a colder environment offsets the energy used in migrating (though both are only a few per cent of metabolic energy).

3 Another hypothesis is that because water at different depths moves at different speeds, and sometimes in different directions, migrating animals can feed in different bodies of water without having to travel horizontally. For example, they could be in plankton-poor waters one night, but when they come to the surface the next evening could well find themselves in a different, more nutrient-rich body of surface water, with more phytoplankton. This could also prevent them overgrazing a particular patch of productive water.

The most likely explanation is the first one, but it is possible that all of these hypotheses are correct, with different factors being more or less important depending on the circumstances. It seems that the migration of zooplankton is the incentive for the vertical migration of other larger animals, including fish and squid. Some of these may migrate from a depth of 1000 m – the record is held by a lanternfish (*Ceratoscopelus warmingeri*) living off the Azores, which migrates through about 1600 m, taking three hours to make the journey each way.

Whatever the underlying reason, the phenomenon itself, filmed so that small organisms can be seen clearly, is spectacularly beautiful (as you will see in the next part of 'The Deep' video).

The deep ocean

10

For this chapter, you will be using the *Discovering the Deep Oceans* book (*DDO* for short) and watching the remainder of the Blue Planet video on 'The Deep'. First, though, we should look again at topics we introduced in Chapters 4 and 6, in the context of life in the deep ocean.

10.1 Another look at buoyancy, fish muscle and bioluminescence

Buoyancy

As you will see in 'The Deep' video, many deep-sea fish manage to conserve energy *and* catch their prey by hanging motionless in the darkness waiting for a meal! To maintain their position in the water column, they need to be neutrally buoyant, with an average density similar to that of seawater – they cannot use dynamic lift if they are motionless (Section 6.3).

- Thinking back to the 'Living in the Oceans' module, can you remember how deep-sea angler fish manage to be neutrally buoyant without the aid of a gas-filled swimbladder?

- Angler fish have light bones, and they also store oils and fats.

This technique of having most components of their bodies greatly reduced in weight is adopted by many deep-sea fish – often, the only part of the skeleton that is well calcified is the jaws. The muscles often have a high water content, and their bodies contain large pockets of a watery fluid which is less dense than seawater – the angler fish and the gulper eel (in the next part of 'The Deep' video) are both about 95% water. By contrast, hatchetfish and lanternfish which live higher up in the water column (i.e. above 1000 m, in the twilight zone) both have swimbladders and so can afford to have heavier bodies: they are much less watery and their skeletons are fully calcified.

- Do you recall how the swimbladders of many mid-water and deep-sea fish differ from those of fish living nearer the sea-surface? What particular use do swimbladders have in very deep water?

- The swimbladders of many mid-water and deep-sea fish contain lipids rather than gas. In very deep water, swimbladders are used to detect low-frequency sound, rather than for buoyancy.

Fish muscle

As indicated at the start of Section 6.2, red muscle (used for sustained swimming) is characteristic of fish living in the well-lit surface layers of the ocean; most fish species living below about 500 m have *no* red muscle.

- By considering the lifestyle of the angler fish, can you suggest why such fish do not need any red muscle?

- Fish with the lifestyle of angler fish do not need to swim for long periods because: (1) they do not hunt down prey (instead, they wait for the prey to come to them); and (2) they do not need to escape from fast-swimming predators which hunt by sight (e.g. tuna).

Bioluminescence

In Chapter 4, and the first part of 'The Deep' video, we looked at how animals in the 'twilight zone' of the ocean (specifically the hatchetfish) use bioluminescence to protect them from predators.

Question 10.1 Can you remember just how the hatchetfish uses bioluminescence? ◀

In the second part of 'The Deep' video, you will see some more spectacular examples of bioluminescence in the oceans. There are various types of light organs (i.e. photophores) and some animals have three or four different types at different sites on or in their bodies. For example, the firefly squid which appears in 'The Deep' has hundreds of one type of light organ covering its body (probably to provide 'countershading' when viewed from below, like the hatchetfish), and another type of light organ at the ends of its tentacles (perhaps for attracting mates or dazzling predators). The optical structures associated with light organs are as complex as those found in eyes, and include lenses and filters, and light guides and light pipes (i.e. biological optical fibres) to allow the light to be emitted some distance from the light organ.

How did bioluminescence evolve in the ocean? This is a question which has perplexed scientists for a long time – indeed, Charles Darwin singled it out as something that his theory of natural selection could not account for. Very few terrestrial organisms produce bioluminescence (these include fireflies and glow-worms, plus some bacteria and fungi), but in the sea it is extremely widespread, being found at all depths and in a wide variety of organisms, including bacteria and dinoflagellates, jellyfish and comb jellies, sea-pens, squid and fish. In total, organisms from 16 different phyla have been found to produce bioluminescence.

- What might this suggest about the evolution of bioluminescence? Is it more likely to have evolved at one point in time and then been carried forward in different groups of organisms, or to have evolved separately in different groups?

- It is more likely to have evolved separately in the different groups. It is hard to see how a feature found in (say) bacteria, dinoflagellates and squid could *not* have evolved independently in each case.

Bioluminescence is produced as a result of molecules of substances known as luciferins reacting with oxygen, and effectively 'burning up' (there are many types of luciferin – the word just means 'light-bearer'). This reaction would not produce light energy were it not for the presence of an enzyme (biological catalyst) called a *luciferase* (of which there are various types). The luciferase slows down the reaction and also allows some of the energy to be released as light, rather than heat. In addition, it coordinates the reactions in the different molecules of luciferin so that they all 'fire off' at once, producing one bright flash instead of lots of small ones.

Most organisms make their own luciferin, while others acquire it in their diet, as we acquire many vitamins. Yet others – including some squid, tunicates and fish – play host to (i.e. have symbiotic relationships with) colonies of luminescent bacteria. However, the key to producing 'useful' light is luciferase, and many marine biologists believe that before bioluminescence evolved, enzymes of this type could already have been present in cells, but performing another function. As luciferase reacts with oxygen, it is possible that it developed from enzymes known as oxygenases, and was originally involved in making oxygen available for respiration, or perhaps in metabolizing toxic substances.

A more recent theory about the evolution of bioluminescence concentrates on the luciferin. The most abundant type of luciferin is a very simple one which was first isolated from a jellyfish (*Aequoria victoria*). Because jellyfish are sometimes classified as coelenterates, this luciferin is called coelenterazine. Coelenterazine is also found in comb jellies, sea-pens, and some fish and squid, all of which acquire it in their diets – no-one knows from what. Experiments with coelenterazine have shown that it reacts vigorously with, and destroys, oxygen-carrying molecules known as free radicals, which are themselves highly reactive and can destroy DNA and cell membranes, and generally cause cells to age and die prematurely. The ocean has a high concentration of free radicals because they are produced in surface layers by the action of ultraviolet light on water, and are also a by-product of metabolic processes. The new theory is that coelenterazine initially evolved as a defence against free radicals, a defence particularly needed in near-surface waters. Over time (so the theory goes), animals moved deeper into the ocean, into the regions of permanent darkness. Coelenterazine's defence role was no longer so necessary, but there *was* an evolutionary pressure for the development of means of communication. Gradually, over time, and in numerous different organisms, coelenterazine changed its role to producing bioluminescence.

▶▶ *If you have not already done so, you should now look at the video on 'The Deep' from [1:32:11] to [2:02:30] (you might find it helpful to rewind to the beginning and watch the first part again). We recommend that you save the last part until you have read Section 10.4 and* DDO *Chapter 4.*

While you watch the video, you might like to note down the various different uses to which bioluminescence may be put. As usual, you may find it helpful to first read through the notes below. You can look at them again after viewing, if you wish. ◀◀

Notes on the 'The Deep' video (part 2)

General note: Whereas the first part of the 'The Deep' was about the 'twilight zone', for much of the second part we are seeing animals that normally live in complete darkness, except when they are illuminated by bioluminescence (or the lamps of a submersible). However, at [1:43:41] there is an excursion up to shallower depths with the mating firefly squid, and this is followed by a sequence about the large-scale vertical migration that occurs at dusk and dawn, as described in Chapter 9. After that, the story line takes us back down into the depths, along the continental shelf, down the continental slope and out onto the abyssal plain. You might like to look back at Figure 2.4 to remind yourself about these features (note that the depths and distances mentioned in the narration vary from location to location and are not as hard and fast as might be suggested).

[1:38:40] Despite our discussion of red muscle earlier in the chapter, free-living male angler fish *do* have red muscle, because they need to chase down a female!

[1:40:55 and 1:41:50] You may remember that both copepods and ostracods are to be found amongst the Arthropoda branches of the 'Biological Diversity' tree, because they are both crustaceans.

[1:47:13] You can see some spectacular orange sponges here.

[1:47:13–1:47:45] We will be discussing the significance of marine snow for deep-sea life in *DDO*, Section 3.3.1.

[1:48:02] Note the relatively coarse sediment, derived from the land, at the top of the continental slope.

[1:48:50–1:49:20] The tracks on the sea-bed show where the echinoderms have consumed the marine snow (cf. *DDO*, Plate 3.3). Note the 'tube feet' of the marching echinoderms.

[1:51:01] The corals shown here are the colonial cold-water corals, mentioned in Chapter 7.

[1:52:02] As mentioned in Chapter 1, surprising as it may seem, tunicates belong to the same phylum as human beings – the Chordata.

[1:54:20–1:55:10] This sequence clearly shows the fine-grained nature of deep-sea sediment, very different from the sediment of the continental shelf and slope.

[1:55:50] Having no jaws, hagfish are very primitive indeed, and belong to the Class Agnatha of the Phylum Chordata (Sub-phylum Craniata). Despite having a cartilaginous skeleton, they are not elasmobranchs.

[1:59:58] The Marianas Trench is a subduction zone trench in the western Pacific. It lies seaward of an arc of small islands, and is the subduction zone to the east of the 'Mariana back-arc basin' labelled on *DDO*, Figure 4.14 (cf. the left-hand side of Figure 2.3). Ocean trenches are large-scale features – what you see in the video are small-scale fractures in ocean-floor rocks, they are *not* views of the trench as a whole.

[2:02:15] Have a close look at this octopus.

Question 10.2 Make a list of the different uses to which bioluminescence is put. (You should be able to come up with three or four uses.) ◀

Question 10.3 To what phylum of animals do the 'sea-lilies' seen in the video [1:50:26] belong? ◀

Question 10.4 Why do you think the cold-water corals [1:51:19] need to be able to capture much larger prey than shallow-water reef-building corals? ◀

Question 10.5 Is 'Dumbo' a 'sea-bat' (as described in Section 7.3.2) or the more common type of octopus? How can you tell? ◀

▶▶ *You should now begin reading* DDO. *You should have been well prepared for much of the material here through your study of Chapters 1 to 9 of this book. However, depending on your background you may find some parts rather challenging, so where necessary we have provided supplementary notes for activities and questions. We suggest that you keep this book to hand while you read* DDO *and refer to the relevant parts of Sections 10.2 to 10.4 as you go along.*

Important: *Do not worry if you get stuck, and make use of the chapter summaries in* DDO *to ensure that you have grasped the main points.* ◀◀

10.2 Guide for *DDO* 'Clear, still and heavier than molten gold'

In this chapter, we try to answer the question: why did the view that the deep ocean waters were devoid of life persist for so long, in spite of evidence to the contrary?

Section 2.1 The azoic theory

Question 2.1 You should be able to answer the first part of this question with little difficulty, and, by referring back to Section 1.3 or Chapter 4 of this book, you should also be able to write down an equation.

Figure 2.5 (a) You may remember that in Figure 3.4 of this book, several of the large patches of white in the waters around the British Isles are being caused by millions of highly reflective platelets from coccolithophores. (b) Remember that these are the remains of the chambered shells of tiny single-celled animals.

Box 2.2 Some basic ocean physics (pp. 14–15)

Hydrostatic pressure Do not worry if you cannot follow the mathematics in this box. The main thing to take in is that the pressure bearing down on an area of sea-bed (for convenience, a 'unit area', e.g. one square metre) is the weight of the overlying water.

In-text question at the bottom of the left-hand column on p.14: To calculate the mass of overlying water, we multiply the volume of water by its density. To convert this mass into weight, we multiply by g, the acceleration due to the Earth's gravity. This distinction between an object's mass (i.e. the amount of material in the object) and its weight (the downwards force due to gravity) is needed because while the mass of an object is constant, its weight depends on where it is. Objects (including people!) weigh much less on the Moon than on Earth, although their mass is the same; objects in space are weightless, but are not 'mass-less'!

Stability and convection in the ocean You have already met this topic in Section 4.3, in the context of winter mixing which 'restocks' the surface ocean with nutrients.

Activity 2.1 If you feel sufficiently confident, by all means work straight through this activity. If not, for each part in turn, read the question, think about it, and then read the answer. This will be fine in the context of the topics we are concentrating on in S180.

Section 2.2 The 4-degree fallacy

Activities 2.2 and 2.3 You should be able to have a go at tackling these. Don't forget to read through the answers carefully.

Figures 2.13 and 2.16 If you need a reminder about how to read graphs, see the first in-text question in Section 4.2.1 of this book.

Box 2.3 The salinity of seawater (p.19)

This expands on the discussion given near the start of the course, in Section 2.1 of this book. The symbol for 'parts per thousand' (‰, analogous to % for 'per cent' or 'parts per hundred') is rarely used today. At the end of the box are listed the 11 most abundant ions in seawater (given in order of decreasing abundance), expressed using chemical symbols. In words, these are:

chloride (the ion formed from the chlorine atom), which carries one negative charge (Cl^-);

sodium, which carries one positive charge (Na^+);

sulphate, which is a single ion formed from one sulphur atom (S) and four oxygen atoms (O), and carries two negative charges (SO_4^{2-});

magnesium, which carries two positive charges (Mg^{2+});

calcium, which carries two positive charges (Ca^{2+});

potassium, which carries one positive charge (K^+);

bicarbonate (now often called hydrogen carbonate), which is a single ion formed from one hydrogen atom (H), one carbon atom (C) and three oxygen atoms (O), and carries one negative charge (HCO_3^-);

bromide (the ion formed from the bromine atom), which carries one negative charge (Br^-);

hydrogen borate, which is a single ion formed from two hydrogen atoms (H), one boron atom (B) and three oxygen atoms (O), and carries one negative charge ($H_2BO_3^-$);

strontium, which carries two positive charges (Sr^{2+});

fluoride (the ion formed from the fluorine atom), which carries one negative charge (F^-).

As stated at the end of the box, you are **not** expected to remember this list.

Section 2.3 The launch of the *Challenger* Expedition

You should have no particular problems with the rest of the chapter, although if you are not comfortable with graphs and powers of ten, you may prefer to just read the answer to Question 2.3. In the context of this course, it does not matter if you cannot follow all of the answer. When you have finished reading Chapter 2 of *DDO*, try Question 10.6 below.

Question 10.6 Look carefully at Figure 2.1 of *DDO*.

(a) Why does this illustration indicate that the *Cyclothone signata* live above 1000 m depth? (*Note:* this was *not* the same species of *Cyclothone* as used to compile Figure 6.8 of this book.)

(b) Why do you think their flesh is soft and flabby? ◀

10.3 Guide for *DDO* 'From lifeless abyss to cradle of creation'

The initial part of this chapter revisits material you were introduced to in Chapter 2, so you should have no trouble with the in-text question at the bottom of p.26.

Section 3.1 The continuity of the chalk

You should have no difficulty with any of this material.

Section 3.2 The strange story of *Bathybius*

Box 3.1 and Question 3.1 You should be able to have a go at tackling these, whatever your background.

Section 3.3 'Bathysnap' and beyond

This section revisits topics introduced in Sections 3.3 (Feeding strategies and techniques) and 4.3 (Heat, light, mixing and nutrients), in this book.

Question 3.2 If you have trouble with this question, remember the discussion at the start of Chapter 8 (Polar seas) in this book.

Activity 3.1 You should be able to have a stab at part of this on the basis of what you learnt in Chapter 4 of this book (Life, light and nutrients), as well as on the basis of the preceding text in *DDO*.

Activity 3.2 This is one of the hardest activities in *DDO*. Do not attempt it unless you feel confident about working with equations like Equation 3.1, and particularly want to try the activity for yourself. The points being brought out by Activity 3.2 are as follows:

(a) If we use the theoretical equation to calculate how long it takes for a dead planktonic organism to sink through the water column to the deep sea-bed, we get an unrealistically long time.

(b) As organic debris sinks down through the ocean, it is also carried laterally.

(c) In any case, planktonic remains are rarely completely spherical as the theoretical formula assumes, and are also (initially at least) quite buoyant. They are also quite likely to be consumed, and would sink to the bottom much faster if incorporated into a faecal pellet, which would be about a hundred times larger than an individual planktonic organism.

10.4 Guide for *DDO* 'An alternative way of life'

This chapter builds on material covered in Section 2.2 of this book (The shape of the ocean basins).

Section 4.1 A FAMOUS adventure

Figure 4.3 and Activity 4.1 In interpreting these contours, remember that the contour numbers give depths *below sea-level*. To help you, deeper areas are shaded darker blue. (Note that here you are seeing 'close-up' features that hardly show up at all in the plate-tectonic map in Figure 2.2 of this book.)

Section 4.2 Getting warmer ...

Activity 4.2 If you are not confident about handling chemical equations, just read through the question and then study the answer.

Figures 4.9 and 4.11 and related discussion If you find this hard, don't spend a lot of time puzzling over it. The main point to note is encapsulated in Figure 4.10: if you plot on a graph the concentrations of two constituents that are mixing together, one against the other, you will get a straight line. Plots like this are often used in oceanography, and similar ones are used in geochemistry.

Activity 4.3 This activity makes use of the 'mixing-line' principle just discussed. It is fairly demanding, so we suggest that unless you are very keen to work through it, you simply look at the answer. All you need to know is given in the summary.

Section 4.3 Whales as stepping-stones

Plate 4.3b In 'The Deep' video, you will see film of a whale carcase that had similarly been colonized by bacteria (suggesting that such colonization of whale skeletons is not unusual).

There is an error in *DDO*, p. 58: In the answer to the in-text question, and at the start of the following paragraph, 'sulphide-oxidizing' should say 'sulphate-reducing'.

Section 4.4 Postscript

By now, you may well have your own views about where life originated. Certainly, this debate is one that will run and run!

Activities 4.4 and 4.5 Neither of these have 'right' answers – we hope you will have a go at both of them.

▶▶ *If you have not already done so, you should now look at the remainder of the video on 'The Deep' from [2:02:30] to the end, as you will be able to see many of the things described in Chapter 4 of* DDO. *As usual, you may find it helpful to first read through the notes below. You can look at them again after viewing, if you wish.* ◀◀

Notes on the 'The Deep' video (part 3)

[2:02:41] In case you were wondering, this is not a real panorama over the Mid-Atlantic Ridge! (If you are not convinced, think about the scale of the Mid-Atlantic Ridge, and about how far light travels underwater.)

[2:03:13] These rocks are pillow lavas, similar to those shown in *DDO*, Figure 4.5.

[2:04:13–2:07:50] From time to time during this sequence about the hydrothermal vents, you can see small particles rising upwards. These are bits of organic debris (fragments of bacterial mats etc.) being carried up in the warmed water, which is rising because it is less dense than the surrounding water (cf. *DDO*, Figures 4.12 and 4.13).

[2:08:14–2:11:20] Other locations with 'cold seeps' are shown on *DDO*, Figure 4.14. You might be interested to know that this brine lake was formed as a result of circulation of water trapped in sediments and forced by pressure to migrate through a layer of *evaporites* – salt layers deposited about 200 million years ago, early in the opening of the Atlantic when the Gulf of Mexico was a very shallow sea. The methane is coming from organic-rich sediments that accumulated over the continental margin of the young ocean.

▶▶ *Before moving on to the final part of the course, about the global fishing crisis, you might like to watch again the videos you have already seen. You will probably find that you get much more out of them the second time around.* ◀◀

Questions: answers and comments

Question 1.1

(a) Corals belong to the Phylum Cnidaria.

(b) (1) Sea-anemones are very close relations, and belong to the same class, the Anthozoa; (2) of the three, sponges are the least closely related as they belong to a different phylum, the Porifera.

Question 1.2

Clicking on the Arthropoda branch (number 6) reveals that peracarids are more closely related to lobsters than to barnacles. Lobsters belong to the Class Malacostraca, as do the peracarids; barnacles belong to a different class, the Cirripedia.

Question 1.3

(a) Convergent evolution results from the animals concerned having adapted to very similar lifestyles.

(b) Each of these animals belongs in a different class of the Phylum Chordata: sharks belong to the Chondrichthyes (cartilaginous fish); tunas belong to the Osteichthyes (bony fish), ichthyosaurs were reptiles (Reptilia), and dolphins are mammals (Mammalia). You may have noticed that these four classes of animals belong to the Modern Fauna shown in Figure 1.2.

Question 2.1

The cross-section in Figure 2.4 does not correspond to any real ocean. An east–west section across the Pacific would have trenches on both sides (and a ridge more to the east than central); one across the Atlantic would have no trench, and relatively wide continental shelves on both eastern and western sides; one across the Indian Ocean would have a central spreading ridge and a trench–island arc system on the east.

Question 2.2

The following are good examples of (1) low-energy coastlines, and (2) high-energy coastlines:

(1) Morecambe Bay, Weston-super-Mare, the coastline around the Wash, and many other estuarine areas.

(2) The coasts of Pembrokeshire and Cornwall, and north-west Scotland; and Chesil Beach near Portland – the ultimate pebble beach!

You may well have thought of other good examples.

Question 3.1

(a) According to Figure 3.2, there are two high tides ('peaks' in water level) and two low tides each day in the Tay estuary. This means that the twice-daily lunar tide predominates over the daily solar tide, as it does around most coastlines. (The more dominant the solar tide is, the more there tends to be one main high tide and one main low tide per day.)

(b) (1) At the peak of spring tides, the tidal range in the Tay estuary is about 5.5 m (about 3 m below the 0-line plus about 2.5 m above the zero line). (2) During the smallest neap tides, the tidal range is about 2 m.

Question 3.2

(a) The statement is true. When the Moon is full, there are spring tides; during the following week it moves towards third quarter (Figure 3.2), and neap tides, so the tidal range is decreasing.

(b) When it is New Moon and spring tides for us in Britain, it is also New Moon and spring tides for Australians. The phase of the Moon is the same the world over – for example, a New Moon is observed the world over whenever the Moon is between the Earth and the Sun. Similarly, spring and neap tides occur at the same time wherever you are (although there will be small variations in exact timing, caused by local sea-bed topography and the shape of the coastline).

Question 3.3

Important factors would be:

- the type of substrate (rocky, sandy, muddy);
- temperature (and temperature range);
- salinity (and salinity range);
- how exposed or sheltered the site is;
- how long the site gets exposed to the air during the course of the tidal cycle;
- what predators live nearby;
- whether there is a good food supply for the species in question;
- what competing species there are.

If you thought of all of these factors, you were doing very well.

Question 3.4

(a) The baby crabs return exactly one month after the eggs were laid. This will again be a time of neap tides, as the spring–neap cycle is about a month (actually 29.5 days). The Moon will again be a Half Moon. (The narration says that the eggs are laid during 'the smallest tides of the month', but of course there are actually two periods of neap tides every month.)

(b) There is no obvious answer to this question. One possibility is that if the baby crabs arrive on the beach during a *rising* tide in a neap period, they have the least chance of being carried out to sea again when they are trying to get onto land.

Question 3.5

(a) The surf-riding snails are best described as scavengers.

(b) You may have spotted the following suspension-feeders: the clam [0:25:58], mussels [0:36:29], barnacles [0:36:29] and [0:39:25], and brine shrimps [0:58:29]. All of these are active feeders.

Humpback whales could also be described as suspension- or filter-feeders, as they strain plankton from the water column. Jellyfish could be described as suspension-feeders (though not filter-feeders).

Question 4.1

If the tilt of the Earth's axis increased to 30°, the Tropics of Cancer and Capricorn would be at 30° N and 30° S, and the Arctic and Antarctic Circles would be at 60° N and 60° S respectively.

Question 4.2

Sunlight would penetrate further down through the water column in the open ocean because coastal waters are more turbid, containing larger concentrations of sediment from the land *and* larger concentrations of phytoplankton (cf. Figure 4.1). Coastal waters also contain greater concentrations of dissolved organic compounds, brought in by rivers (cf. the yellowish Baltic water off the coast of Norway in Figure 3.4) and produced by coastal plankton.

Question 4.3

(a) Dark upper surfaces mean that predators above the fishes find it hard to see them, and silvery undersides mean that predators below find it hard to see the fishes against the light coming down from the surface.

(b) Red animals are red because they reflect *only* red light. As Figure 4.6a shows, within a very short distance of the sea-surface there is no red light, so a red animal will look dark or black, along with those that really *are* black, and will be inconspicuous in the gloom. All pelagic shrimp that live below 500–700 m by day are bright red, while those living at shallower depths are transparent or semi-transparent.

Question 4.4

Temperature decreases with depth in the thermocline (by definition). As this has a greater effect on the speed of sound than the increasing pressure, the speed of sound must decrease with depth in the thermocline. Below 1000 m depth, the temperature profile is vertical, or nearly so. A vertical temperature profile means no change of temperature with depth. Therefore, below 1000 m depth (as in the mixed layer), the speed of sound is determined only by pressure. As pressure increases with increasing depth, the speed of sound must also increase with depth below 1000 m (as it does also in the mixed layer). There is therefore a *minimum* in the speed of sound at the bottom of the thermocline/top of the cold deep layer.

Question 5.1

(1) The poleward-flowing warm current in the North Atlantic is the Gulf Stream, and its counterpart in the North Pacific is the Kuroshio; (2) the poleward-flowing warm current in the South Atlantic is the Brazil Current, and (3) that in the southern Indian Ocean is the Agulhas Current. (In the South Pacific, where the western boundary of the ocean is rather broken up, the most comparable current is the East Australian Current.)

Question 5.2

Figure 5.7 shows that Cape Douglas is one of the sites where nutrient-rich Cromwell Current water upwells to the surface, and Figure 5.8 shows that – not surprisingly – this is a site where large algae (seaweeds) flourish. As you saw in the introductory video, marine iguanas feed on such algae, so this is a good place for them to live.

Question 5.3

The amount of *new* plant material produced each year on land is roughly the same as that produced in the oceans but, as discussed in Activity 1 of the 'Ecosystems and Food Webs' module, much of the large biomass of land plants is *non-growing* woody material which persists from year to year. The average lifetime of terrestrial vegetation is very long compared with that of marine plants (on average, about 18 years compared with 10–20 days for phytoplankton before they are eaten or die). So, compared with terrestrial vegetation, the 'turnover time' of marine vegetation is very short – a lot is produced each year, but none of it lasts long and so at any one time the total amount present is relatively small.

Question 5.4

(a) Yes. Figure 5.10 suggests that less productive regions such as the open oceans have longer food chains (or more complex food webs), while more productive regions (upwelling areas) have shorter food chains.

(b) As explained in Activity 3 of the 'Ecosystems and Food Webs' module, short food chains are more efficient than long ones, as less is lost (mainly to respiration) in conversion between trophic levels. In upwelling areas, the chain from primary producer to whale involves only two 'conversion' stages at which losses will occur.

Question 6.1

Visible features that are characteristic of sharks include:

- an asymmetrical tail, with the upper part more prominent than the lower part (we will be discussing this later);
- visible gill slits (there is a particularly clear view of the gill slits of a nurse shark in the 'Tidal Seas' video [0:49:47]);
- tough, flexible skin, rather than scales;
- the jaw hinge is below the body, with the result that the mouth is underneath the snout (in most fish, the jaw hinge is aligned with the 'mid-line').

Question 6.2

The fins in question are as follows: sea-horse – pectoral fin and dorsal fin; stickleback – dorsal and pectoral fins; bowfin – dorsal fin; knifefish – anal fin; John Dory – dorsal and anal fins; sunfish – dorsal and anal fins.

Question 6.3

(1) If the 'gas container' is rigid, its volume stays the same when the animal changes depth, and the lift generated by the gas within it hardly varies. This is an advantage, in that there is no possibility of the animal finding itself rising or sinking in the water column as a result of a positive feedback effect, and there is no need to expend energy in continually adjusting the volume of the container.

(2) A serious disadvantage is that because pressure increases with depth, the depth range of the animal is greatly constrained by the strength of the 'box'. For example, cuttlefish cannot go deeper than about 200 m without their buoyancy organ (the many-chambered cuttlebone, covered by a membrane) imploding.

Question 6.4

Tuna have torpedo-shaped bodies which reduce drag, and have small fins along the rear end of the body that may delay the onset of turbulence. Their streamlined shape is enhanced because they have grooves into which they can flatten their fins. Their swimming style is efficient because it involves minimal body movement, with forward thrust provided by powerful tail strokes. The tail itself is of high aspect ratio.

Question 6.5

Both statements are false. The first is false because as a fish's swimming speed increases, so more white muscle is progressively brought into play ('Swimming in Fish' [0:11:08–0:11:47]). The second must be false because white muscle is used particularly for *bursts* of fast swimming. After it has been used – by, for example, a salmon leaping a salmon run – the fish needs time to recover (to excrete the waste products produced by anaerobic respiration, or allow them to be oxidized), as discussed in Section 6.4, and in 'Swimming in Fish' [0:20:49–0:20:56]. (This point comes up again in 'Wild Moves: Water'.)

Question 6.6

Both mackerel (seen in 'Swimming in Fish') and sharks (seen in 'Wild Moves: Water') have bodies which are more dense than water. To avoid sinking, both need to swim continually in order to generate dynamic lift. The techniques they use to generate dynamic lift have much in common. Mackerel use their pectoral fins and their tails to produce extra dynamic lift (which only comes into play when the fish is moving relative to the water: 'Swimming in Fish' [0:16:55–0:17:24]). As mentioned in Section 6.2, mackerel also generate lift by swimming at an angle (which is why, when they tire and are swimming slowly, they swim noticeably 'tail down in the water' [0:20:37] – cf. the in-text question about mackerel in Section 6.3). Recent research, described in 'Wild Moves: Water' suggests that sharks get lift from their asymmetric tail, and swim at an angle to balance this force.

Question 6.7

Marine mammals have not evolved special buoyancy aids because they have air in their lungs (which therefore act as if they *are* buoyancy aids). (The blubber of marine mammals will also help to reduce their overall density.)

Question 6.8

Possible reasons for dolphins' spectacular swimming performance include:

- ridges on the skin stabilize the flowing water and reduce turbulence (turbulence greatly increases drag);

- the 'three-hinge' motion of the body during swimming, and the flick of the tail at the end of every stroke, together create a lot of power;
- there may be extra storage of energy in the skin and blubber layer, which when released provides extra 'spring' (analogous to the release of elastic energy employed by kangaroos);
- the habit of 'porpoising' (i.e. leaping out of the water while travelling) is useful for reducing frictional drag with the surface layer of water.

Question 7.1

Temperatures on the western sides of the Atlantic and Pacific are generally higher than they are on the eastern sides at the same latitude. This is because western boundary currents (like the Gulf Stream) carry warm water polewards, while eastern boundary currents (like the California Current) carry cold or cool water equatorwards (Figure 5.2). Water temperatures are further lowered along the eastern sides of the tropical Atlantic and Pacific by the upwelling that occurs there, in response to the Trade Winds (Section 5.2.1). As a result, temperatures conducive to coral-reef growth are found over a much wider latitude range on the western sides of the Atlantic and Pacific than on the eastern sides.

Question 7.2

Butterflyfish are flat, with a rounded outline, corresponding to the fish-shape at the apex of the 'fish triangle' (Figure 6.3). This is the shape best suited to good manoeuvrability, as is the rounded tail. Manoeuvrability is very useful for swimming amongst the intricate coral 'landscape' and, especially, for evading predators (butterflyfish are not particularly fast).

Question 7.3

According to Figure 6.6, the parrotfish in the 'Coral Seas' video have truncate tails (which are for slightly faster swimming than rounded tails, and provide slightly less help in manoeuvring). The parrotfish that can be seen most clearly seems to be swimming by using its pectoral fins like oars.

Question 7.4

The jacks have lunate tails for fast swimming (cf. Figure 6.6). In side profile, they resemble tuna, but when they turn it can be seen that they are almost flat-sided. These attributes mean they can swim relatively fast, but are sufficiently manoeuvrable to pursue their prey amongst the coral.

Question 7.5

Mass spawning probably has the same advantage as the mass egg laying and hatching of the olive Ridley turtles, seen in the introductory video, i.e. that the predators are overwhelmed by so much food and cannot possibly eat it all (and in this case, the simultaneous spawning is of a number of species, not just one species). Spawning at night would also reduce the chances of a large proportion of the eggs being eaten. In addition, mass spawning of corals of the same species increases the chances of eggs becoming fertilized.

About a week after Full Moon is a time of neap tides (Figure 3.2) and weak tidal currents. This could be an advantage because it means that the eggs and sperm are not spread out or carried away before there is time for fertilization to occur. (In fact spawning also occurs in calm weather, when wave action is least.)

Question 7.6

- Colours and patterns can be used for display, both for mating (as in the case of the cuttlefish) and for aggression.
- Colours and patterns can be used to aid recognition of animals of the same species, for mating, and to avoid competition.
- They may be used as camouflage, to avoid predation.
- They may be used as camouflage by ambush predators, like the lionfish (which seems to have two 'fake' angelfish in amongst its other camouflage).
- They may also be used to deter or confuse predators – a lot of coral reef fish seem to have large fake 'eyes' on parts of their body other than their heads, while the real eyes are hard to see because of a stripe on the body.

Question 7.7

Corals have adapted to thrive in low-nutrient environments. High concentrations of nutrients favour phytoplankton growth, and nutrient-rich coastal waters are turbid because of large populations of phytoplankton, and this would cut down the light available to the zooxanthellae. More seriously, high nutrient levels would favour benthic algae, and as discussed shortly in connection with El Niño events, these too could harm reefs by smothering them.

Question 8.1

Sealions are eared seals. Perhaps the most obvious clue is that they can turn their hind limbs forward to sit on, and can be remarkably agile on land – which is why they were formerly used in circuses. Their overall shape is that of an eared seal, with a long neck and powerful sloping shoulders.

Question 8.2

(a) The blue whale is the largest animal on Earth and is a baleen whale (Figure 1.3 and Table 8.1), and so it is certainly the largest member of the Mysticeti.

(b) The killer whale – *Orcinus orca* – is a member of the Delphinidae, the dolphins (Table 8.1, Figure 1.3). (Incidentally, porpoises – which are often confused with dolphins – are a separate family altogether: the Phocoenidae.)

Question 8.3

In this sequence, you can see the front flippers being used extensively for swimming and manouevring, rather than lying along the sides (i.e. swimming is *not* by means of moving the hindquarters from side to side). These observations indicate that fur seals are eared seals, but the most conclusive evidence is that ear flaps can actually be seen near the start ofthe sequence! (In fact, these have to be eared seals because, as mentioned in the text, all fur seals are: eared seals = fur seals plus sealions.)

Question 8.4

The food web shows that although some of the animals (including the largest) are feeding on various planktonic organisms, the rest depend directly or indirectly on the Arctic cod, which therefore plays a pivotal role in the functioning of the marine Arctic ecosystem.

Question 9.1

The Atlantic only began to open about 200 million years ago. Eel populations that lived in the bodies of water along the new coastlines may have bred out in the more saline waters and spent the rest of their life cycle in freshwater. As the Atlantic opened, the distance between their preferred breeding area and the coast gradually increased, but the migratory pattern remained. As you can see from Figure 5.2, the North Atlantic subtropical gyre is asymmetrical, which could explain why the preferred breeding area is now nearer the western coastline than the eastern one. (However, as the Atlantic had been opening for some tens of million of years when the first eels evolved, it seems as if they must always have made quite long migrations, which in itself is rather puzzling.)

Question 10.1

The hatchetfish has downward-pointing photophores which break up its silhouette as viewed from below. By means of adjustable filters, and eyes that point both up and down, it fine-tunes the light so that the blue–green shade exactly matches that coming down from the sea-surface.

Question 10.2

Uses of bioluminescence that appear in 'The Deep' include:

- Camouflage to avoid predators (like the hatchetfish).
- Camouflage to confuse or startle predators (like the copepod).
- As 'headlights' to help search for prey (like the fish with photophores below its eyes); also for illuminating red prey with red light (the fish with the 'sniper-scope').
- As a lure to attract prey (like the angler fish).
- Attracting a mate (like the female angler fish, and perhaps the firefly squid).
- Communicating in general (like copepods).

Question 10.3

'Sea-lilies' are crinoids, primitive echinoderms (see also *DDO*, Figure 2.8), i.e. they belong to the Phylum Echinodermata.

Question 10.4

Cold-water corals do not have any symbiotic bacteria and so need to obtain *all* their food by capturing it. In other words, in contrast to reef-building corals, they live entirely as predators.

Question 10.5

'Dumbo' is a sea-bat. It is drifting over the sea-bed with its tentacles spread so that the membranes between them form a parachute. The 'ears' are, of course, fins. (Also, it is a reddish-orange, the correct colour for a sea-bat.)

Question 10.6

(a) The *Cyclothone signata* appear to have rows of photophores along their sides, which could be designed to break up their outlines. This suggests that they live in the 'twilight zone', i.e. in very dim light, between the bottom of the photic zone and about 1000 m depth. There would be no point in having this type of camouflage below 1000 m depth. (Beebe went down 2200 ft, or about 700 m.)

(b) The *Cyclothone* have soft and flabby flesh because they have a very high water content to help keep their density low (Section 10.1), although as they feed by pursuing copepods, their muscles cannot be all *that* flabby.

Acknowledgements

Every effort has been made to trace all copyright owners, but if any has been inadvertently overlooked, we will be pleased to make the necessary arrangements at the first opportunity. Grateful acknowledgement is made to the following sources for permission to reproduce material in this book:

Cover image Alfred Pasieka/Science Photo Library; *Frontispiece* Peter Parks/ imagequest3d.com; *Figure 1.2* J.J. Sepkoski Jr (1990) 'Evolutionary faunas', in Briggs, D.E.G. and Crowther P.R. (eds) *Palaeobiology: A Synthesis*, Blackwell Science, adapted from J.J. Sepkoski Jr (1984) 'A kinetic model of Phanerozoic taxonomic diversity', *Palaeobiology,* **10**, pp.246–267; *Figure 2.1* NASA; *Figure 3.4* SeaWiFS images processed by NERC Remote Sensing Data Analysis Service, Plymouth, using data received at NERC Satellite Receiving Station, University of Dundee: courtesy NASA, SeaWiFS Project and Orbimage Inc.; *Figure 3.5* R.L. Smith (1966) *Ecology and Field Biology*, 2nd edn, copyright © 1966, 1974 Robert Leo Smith, by permission of Pearson Education; *Figure 4.1* NSF/NASA-sponsored US Global Flux Study Office, Woods Hole Oceanographic Institution, with Goddard Space Flight Center, University of Miami, University of Rhode Island; *Figure 4.6* J.M. McCormick and J.V. Thiruvathukal (1981) 'Physical nature of sea water', *Elements of Oceanography*, 2nd edn, p.135, W.B. Saunders & Co.; *Figure 4.9* InterNetwork Inc, NASA/JPL and GSFC; *Figure 5.1* A.H. Perry and J.M. Walker (1977) *The Ocean–Atmosphere System*, Pearson Education; *Figures 5.4, 5.9* NASA-sponsored CZCS Project and Goddard Earth Sciences Data and Information Services Center; *Figure 5.7* G.T. Houvenaghel (1978) 'Oceanographic conditions in the Galapagos Archipelago and their relationship with life on the Islands', in Boje, R. and Tomizak, R. (eds), *Upwelling Ecosystems*, Springer-Verlag GmbH; *Figure 5.8* P.W. Glynn and G.M. Wellington (1983) *Corals and Coral Reefs of the Galapagos Islands,* © University of California Press; *Figures 5.10, 8.3* C.M. Lalli and T.R. Parsons (1993) *Biological Oceanography*, Butterworth-Heinemann; *Figure 6.1* C.C. Lindsey (1978) 'Form, function and locomotory habits in fish', in Hoar, W.S. and Randall, D.J. (eds) *Fish Physiology*, Vol. VII, © 1978 Academic Press; *Figure 6.2b* J.J. Videler (1993) *Fish Swimming*, Chapman & Hall; *Figure 6.8* Q. Bone and N.B. Marshall (1982) *Biology of Fishes,* Chapman & Hall; *Figure 6.9* L.C. Rome and A.A. Sosnicki (1991) 'Myofilament overlap in swimming carp', *American Journal of Physiology,* **260**, C289–296, American Physiological Society; *Figure 6.10* H. Dewar, J.B. Graham and J.W. Brill (1994) 'Studies of tropical tuna swimming performance in a large water tunnel', *Journal of Experimental Biology,* **192**, pp.33–44, Company of Biologists Ltd; *Figure 8.1* NASA (1992) *Arctic and Antarctic Sea Ice, 1978–1987: Satellite Passive–Microwave Observations and Analysis* (NASA SP-511); *Figure 8.3* R. Payne in Lalli and Parsons *op cit.*